Benjamin S. Bloom

J.P. Keeves

C. Arnold Anderson

International Educational Research

PAPERS IN HONOR OF TORSTEN HUSÉN

Other Titles of Interest

International Educational Research

PAPERS IN HONOR OF TORSTEN HUSÉN

Edited by

T. NEVILLE POSTLETHWAITE

University of Hamburg, FRG

Phillips Memorial
Library
Providence College

PERGAMON PRESS

OXFORD · NEW YORK · TORONTO · SYDNEY · FRANKFURT

U.K.	Pergamon Press Ltd., Headington Hill Hall, Oxford OX3 0BW, England
U.S.A.	Pergamon Press Inc., Maxwell House, Fairview Park, Elmsford, New York 10523, U.S.A.
CANADA	Pergamon Press Canada Ltd., Suite 104, 150 Consumers Road, Willowdale, Ontario M2J 1P9, Canada
AUSTRALIA	Pergamon Press (Aust.) Pty. Ltd., P.O. Box 544, Potts Point, N.S.W. 2011, Australia
FEDERAL REPUBLIC OF GERMANY	Pergamon Press GmbH, Hammerweg 6, D-6242 Kronberg, Federal Republic of Germany
JAPAN	Pergamon Press Ltd., 8th Floor, Matsuoka Central Building, 1-7-1 Nishishinjuku, Shinjuku-ku, Tokyo 160, Japan
BRAZIL	Pergamon Editora Ltda., Rua Eça de Queiros, 346, CEP 04011, São Paulo, Brazil
PEOPLE'S REPUBLIC OF CHINA	Pergamon Press, Qianmen Hotel, Beijing, People's Republic of China

Copyright © 1986 Pergamon Press Ltd.

First edition 1986

Library of Congress Cataloging in Publication Data

International educational research.
1. International education—Research—Addresses, essays, lectures.   2. Education—Research—Addresses, essays, lectures.   3. Education and state—Addresses, essays, lectures.   4. Comparative education—Addresses, essays, lectures.   5. Husén, Torsten, 1916– —Addresses, essays, lectures.   I. Husén, Torsten, 1916– .   II. Postlethwaite, T. Neville.
LC1090.I566   1985   370′.7′8   85–16943

British Library Cataloguing in Publication Data

International educational research
1. Education
I. Postlethwaite, T. Neville   II. Husén, Torsten
370   LA132

ISBN 0–08–031812–6

Printed in Great Britain by A. Wheaton & Co., Ltd., Exeter

Preface

The Book

This book is dedicated to Torsten Husén, who will be 70 years old on 1 March 1986. Torsten Husén began his career with the study of history, philosophy and psychology in the 1930s in Lund and continued in military psychology in the 1940s. He then began research on education, class and mobility, as well as school differentiation problems in the 1950s. The 1960s saw him take up problems of the school curriculum and cross national studies of educational achievement. In recent years, he has concentrated more on studies in higher education and public policy. Throughout his career, however, he has always been interested in the use of research for policymaking.

This book does not cover all facets of Torsten Husén's career but is centered on cross national studies of educational achievement—their organization, results and utility, the training of research workers through international seminars and graduate schools of comparative and international education, educational reform and learning from other nations, and finally, reform and policy analyses.

Cross National Studies and Educational Achievement

The first cluster of articles concerns *cross national studies of educational achievement*. The first article is by Mats Hultin, a Swede, who retired in 1984 after 20 years of service with the World Bank where the bulk of his time was spent in the education sector. His account of what sort of cross national research can be used under what conditions by an international agency such as the World Bank is fascinating. Torsten Husén has for many years been a consultant to the World Bank both officially and unofficially through his many meetings and discussions with senior educational officials of that agency.

The next five articles are all written about various aspects of the work of the International Association for the Evaluation of Educational Achievement (IEA) of which Torsten Husén was one of the founding fathers and was its Chairman from 1962 to 1978. The first article "Science Education: The Contribution of IEA Research to a World Perspective" is written by John P. Keeves who is the chairperson of the IEA Second Science Study which is currently under way. He was also the co-author of the international report on the first IEA Science Study.

John Keeves took his doctorate under Torsten Husén in the early 1970s. He retired from the Directorship of the Australian Council for Educational Research at the end of 1984 and is now a Visiting Professor at the Centre for the Study of Higher Education at the University of Melbourne. The second article "The IEA Literature and Composition Studies and their Elucidation of the Nature and Formation of Interpretative and Rhetorical Communities" is by Alan C. Purves who was the author of the international report of the IEA study of literature education, and who is now the chairperson of the IEA Study of Written Composition. Alan Purves first met Torsten Husén in 1964 and has worked with Torsten on several ventures over the years. Alan Purves wrote this article while he was at the University of Illinois. The third article "Cross National Research in Mathematics Education" is by Roy W. Phillipps of the New Zealand Department of Education. Roy Phillipps was the chairperson of the IEA Second Mathematics Study which has recently been completed. He served as Executive Director of IEA from 1972 to 1975 and was also the National Research Coordinator for New Zealand's participation in the IEA six subject study 1967–72. The fourth article "International Comparisons of Cognitive Achievement" is by an eminent scholar, James S. Coleman, who has always helped IEA with his advice, although he has never worked directly for the association. As he points out in his article, with a well conceived example, he feels that it is possible to exploit the international nature of IEA data more than has been done in the past. Jim Coleman and Torsten Husén have been friends for two decades and they, too, have worked together on several ventures. Jim Coleman, whose major writings are known throughout the world, is Professor of Sociology at the University of Chicago. The final article in this cluster is written by me. It is entitled "Organizing Cross National Research Projects" and attempts to draw lessons from experience for the good coordination of cross national research projects. I was the coordinator of IEA from 1962 to 1972. I studied for my doctorate under Torsten Husén and completed it 1966. In 1972 I went to work at the International Institute for Educational Planning (IIEP) in Paris. Torsten was the Chairman of the Governing Board of that Institution. Shortly after I took up my current position at the University of Hamburg, I was asked to succeed Torsten Husén as Chairman of IEA. In short, we have been involved in many ventures together and this continues to be the case. At the time of writing, we have just finished being co-editors-in-chief of a 10 volume International Encyclopedia of Education.

It is fitting that articles associated with IEA should form one cluster in this book. Torsten led IEA in its pioneering and most productive era. The Ministry of Education personnel in many of the countries participating in IEA have reason to appreciate the many services he has rendered them.

Training and Cooperation

The second cluster of articles focus on the *training of competence in education internationally and the development of cooperative projects*. Both of these are areas to which Torsten Husén has been committed over a period of three decades.

The first article in this cluster is entitled "The International Seminar for Advanced Training in Curriculum Development and Innovation" and is by Benjamin S. Bloom of the University of Chicago. Ben Bloom was one of the founding fathers of IEA together with Torsten Husén (Sweden), C. Arnold Anderson, A. W. Foshay (USA), and W. D. Wall (UK). As with so many prime movers in pioneering ventures, bonds of close friendship were forged which will never be broken. Many of the results of IEA's work pointed to the prime role of curriculum in determining differences in achievement between pupils and between nations. Throughout the 1960s, Ben Bloom had been heavily involved with curriculum problems and with ways of undertaking *systematic* curriculum development within nations. In his article, Ben Bloom traces the development, execution, and impact of another pioneering effort — a training seminar for curriculum teams from twenty-three countries — which he organized, with Torsten Husén's active support — under the aegis of IEA. It is worth mentioning that the African Curriculum Organization (ACO) which embraces more than twenty African nations is one outcome of the Gränna seminar which Ben Bloom does not mention in his article.

The second, third and fourth articles in this cluster describe the training of graduate students and their doctoral theses. One describes the development and activities of the Graduate Programs of Comparative Education at the University of Chicago and is by C. Arnold Anderson, the first Director of the Center for Comparative Education at that University. Arnold Anderson was a Fulbright professor in Sweden in 1954–55 and 1955–56, the latter year in Uppsala and Stockholm. It was then, he reports, that he learned what a pleasant colleague Torsten Husén could be. In 1957, Arnold Anderson joined the University of Chicago faculty and presented a case for an IEA type study to the departmental faculty. Together with Benjamin Bloom he applied for funding from the US Office of Education for an IEA study.

A second article is by Ingemar Fägerlind who succeeded Torsten Husén in the Chair of Education and head of the Institute for International Education at the University of Stockholm. Torsten Husén initiated the creation of this Institute in Stockholm in 1969 by negotiating with the Swedish authorities the move of the IEA headquarters to

Stockholm. Both articles present a short description of the types of research work undertaken and the concomitant training of various competencies. A third article is by Michel Debeauvais of the University of Paris in which he reflects on the criteria to judge doctoral theses in France. When Michel Debeauvais was the Director of the International Institute for Educational Planning (IIEP), Torsten Husén was the Chairman of the Governing Board. Michel Debeauvais is the President of L'Association Francophone d'Education Comparée.

In the final article in this cluster James Perkins presents his experiences and ideas on development for cooperation. Jim Perkins, who was President of Cornell University in the 1960s and who was chairman of several US presidential committees, has been Chairman of the International Council for Educational Development (ICED) since 1970. The ICED is composed of scholars and practitioners from many countries — men and women who are interested in the comparative study of the development of education and education for development particularly in higher education. Torsten Husén and Jim Perkins met when they were both at the International Conference on the World Crisis in Education in 1967. President Lyndon B. Johnson had asked Jim Perkins to serve as co-chairman of that conference. Torsten Husén has been on the Board of ICED since 1971.

Educational Reform and Learning from Other Nations

The third cluster of articles concerns *educational reform and learning from other nations*. The first "Learning from Other Nations for Educational Reform in School and Adult Education: The Case of Germany" is by Hellmut Becker, Director-Emeritus of the Max Planck Institute for Educational Research in the Federal Republic of Germany. As can be seen from his article he has also held many leading positions in Germany in terms of educational policymaking. Torsten Husén was a member of the Governing Board of the Max Planck Institute for Educational Research from 1964 to 1980.

The second article "Learning from Other Nations for Educational Reform: The Case of Higher Education in the Federal Republic of Germany" is by Dietrich Goldschmidt, a sociologist and Emeritus Director of the sociology of education department at the institute of which Hellmut Becker was director. Dietrich Goldschmidt has been a member of a joint German-Swedish governmental commission on co-determination in education. Torsten Husén and Dietrich Goldschmidt have also met each other over a period of two decades not only in connection with the Max Planck Institute for Educational Research but also in connection with international seminars on higher education held in Aspen, Colorado.

The third article "Learning from Other Nations for Educational Reform: The Case of Poland" is by Jan Szczepański. Jan Szczepański was a member of the State Council of Poland and the chairman of the reform committee the work of which he describes in his article. Jan Szczepański and Torsten Husén met in Aspen in 1973 and have been friendly ever since. They are both foreign members of the US National Academy of Education and of the US National Academy of Arts and Sciences. Both were fellows at the Wissenschaftskolleg zu Berlin in the fall of 1984.

Reform and Policy Analysis

The last two articles include one by Alain Bienaymé, an economist from the University of Paris (Dauphine) on "Efficiency and Quality of Higher Education" where he presents the case of France but many ideas are drawn from outside France. Alain Bienaymé and Torsten Husén met through the Aspen seminars and ICED. Alain Bienaymé has pointed out that Torsten's great talents have been recognized in France especially when, following *les événements* of 1968, France began to consider its reform of higher education. Torsten was a member of the OECD committee on the review of the French educational system. As has been mentioned before, he was the chairman of the Governing Board of IIEP in Paris and many of his colleagues remember him as a vivid example of how to escape parochialism and take on multi-disciplinary and international perspectives.

The final article is by Martin Trow, a sociologist at the University of California at Berkeley, on "Researchers, Policy Analysts, and Policy Intellectuals". Martin Trow and Torsten Husén first met when they were both fellows at the Center for Advanced Study in the Behavioral Sciences in 1965–66. They have also met at the international seminars on higher education at Aspen and in the 1980s in seminars on research and policy making. Several of Torsten Husén's interests across the years have been mentioned. As Martin Trow has pointed out to me Torsten Husén has never allowed any achievement or expertise to constrain his next set of intellectual interests. This is clear in the volume on *Educational Research & Policy* that he co-edited with Maurice Kogan in 1984, and from which the essay by Martin Trow is drawn. That essay develops an interest of Husén's in the question of whether and how social research influences public decisionmaking and public policy. The essay develops Husén's hypothesis that research rarely influences policy directly, but does so (if at all) through a variety of indirect mechanisms. One such mechanism has recently been formalized in the United States through the emergence of "policy analysis" as a new profession, rooted in postgraduate professional schools in ten or twelve leading American research universities and graduate programs in many others. These schools focus their energies on a 2-year professional degree, the "Master of Public Policy", whose recipients then take up posts in governmental agencies, local, state and national, in "think tanks", and in private industry. But while in those positions they may have a large amount of responsibility in the framing of public policy through their analyses of policy issues, their teachers in the graduate schools and programs, the "policy intellectuals", continue to do basic research on those same public issues. The paper argues that it is through the influence of the work of those policy intellectuals on the policy analysts "out in the field" that basic research has its largest influence on public decisionmaking and policy.

The Man

Torsten Husén was born on 1 March 1916, in Lund, Sweden. He grew up in a little town in Southern Sweden where his father, a farmer's boy, ran a small timber agency. From the local primary school in this rural area Torsten proceeded to Gymnasium in a nearby small town, Växjö, and from there to the University of Lund where he took his doctorate and from there to a Professorship in Stockholm in 1953 and from there on to the international educational scene.

Torsten has described his life in his autobiography *An Incurable Academic* (Oxford: Pergamon Press, 1983) and I shall, therefore, not enter into any details here. This Festschrift is dedicated to Torsten not only from the authors of the various chapters in the book but also from his many friends in all continents.

However, this is also an opportunity for me to write, on a personal note, some of the things which modesty prevented Torsten from writing in his autobiography. I first met Torsten Husén on 7 December 1962 at breakfast in the Statler Hilton Hotel in New York City. I was a young researcher just having joined the International Association for the Evaluation of Educational Achievement (IEA) and was about to meet the leading IEA people, including the Chairman, Torsten Husén. It was also my first visit to the United States and I had arrived from Europe late the evening before. I remember being very nervous indeed but being put at ease immediately when I was introduced to the avuncular figure of Torsten. His "caring to help" during that week in New York much impressed me and it was the beginning of a long friendship.

Torsten has been involved and influential in different spheres of education. I have known him in only three of them — IEA, the International Institute of Educational Planning, a UNESCO institute, and as a Professor of Education at the University of Stockholm. Torsten was the Chairman of IEA from 1962 to 1978, the Chairman of the Governing Board of IIEP from 1970 to 1980 and a Professor of the

University of Stockholm from 1953 to 1982 when he became a Professor Emeritus.

Torsten became the second Chairman of IEA in June, 1962 shortly after IEA was established as an association of a dozen leading educational research institutes. Given the pioneering venture of IEA at that time working meetings were typically of one week duration involving conceptual, technical, diplomatic, and administrative tasks. These meetings involved a great deal of tension and the chairing of them was critical. Torsten's quick mind, wisdom, impassive face, slow deliberative speech, and kindness constituted a rare but fully appropriate combination. During the 1960s, in particular, there were several occasions when Torsten had to exercise all his abilities in order to ensure that IEA was kept on an even keel. IEA was a daring innovation and over time proved to be of great benefit to many systems of education and educational research at large. Major research centers decide whether or not to join IEA and the fact that centers from over forty countries joined is witness to the utility of such research work. It is doubtful if the founding fathers in 1959 — and Torsten was one of them — ever realised that 25 years later the organization would not only be well but still growing. Had it, however, not been for Torsten's foresight, wisdom, and diplomacy in the 1960s this might never have occurred. I am the current Chairman of IEA and I am very thankful that I can still count on Torsten's help when I need it.

A quote from Alan Purves sums up what all people involved in IEA feel: "I first came to know Torsten Husén well at the IEA meeting in Hamburg in 1966, when the literature study came before the group. As I have remarked in my chapter, Torsten was one of the advocates of the study, but what impressed me then and has always impressed me is his ability to organize a research effort. Torsten operates in such a fashion that a group of disparate people can come together to work hard for a period of time and finish the working session with a feeling of true collegiality. Everyone becomes equally important when he chairs a meeting, and people from different disciplines are scrupulously heeded. His closing "Dear friends . . ." is always heartfelt and welcome. It is thanks in great measure to Torsten Husén that IEA has survived into the second and third generation of researchers.

Torsten was the Chairman of the IIEP Governing Board when I was a staff member at IIEP. At that time, there was a problem concerning IIEP's world role in educational planning and its role *vis-à-vis* UNESCO. The problem concerned the amount of "intellectual autonomy" that IIEP should have — particularly in terms of determining its own program of work and in the selection of staff members. The Governing Board of IIEP and its staff perceived such autonomy as being highly desirable. Officials in UNESCO, on the other hand, perceived that they should determine IIEP's program. Admittedly, this black and white statement of the position exaggerates the two positions. Rather, it was a matter of where the balance lay. The frustration of having to think in terms of power and bureaucracy rather than in terms of the needs of educational planning and the substance of useful programs must have been enormous.

One of Torsten's abilities which has never failed to impress me is that of picking doctoral students. He always selected doctoral students who required minimal supervision. He has also supervised more doctoral students than any other professor of education in Sweden. As a doctoral student, and I have heard the same from other doctoral students, the big problem was getting to see Torsten when he was not constantly interrupted by the telephone or visitors. However, once this formidable barrier was overcome, his wisdom and experience were always worth having. His encouragement of younger colleagues from all parts of the world to further their studies has always been great. There are many doctoral students throughout the world who owe Torsten a great deal. There are many colleagues, too.

From the above it can be seen that many parts of education and educational institutions have benefited from Torsten Husén having come into contact with them. We thank him for his friendship, his collegiality, his wisdom and his hard work.

T. Neville Postlethwaite

February, 1986

Contents

xiv   *Contents*

Cross National Studies and Educational Achievement

The Role of Cross National Research in World Bank Education Operations

MATS HULTIN

The World Bank is now the largest agency of education financing in the developing world. Such financing can only be efficient and relevant if it reflects the state of the art and recent research in education. The findings of cross national educational research are of specific importance in the Bank context, as the Bank is supporting education projects in some ninety countries which vary in several respects. Nevertheless they share many features which are common to the development process including education and thus make international comparisons meaningful. The Bank serves in this way not only as a financier of education but also as a middleman between the global educational research community and the education authorities in the developing countries, as a disseminator of educational research findings and as a conveyor of educational experiences among the developing countries. The work is done in cooperation with Unesco but it can perhaps be claimed that the Bank part of it is more concrete and practical because of its close tie with financial operations.

The major aim of this paper is to describe the role of cross national educational research in the development of the World Bank education financing policy, projects and procedures over the two past decades with 300 education projects at a total project cost of some US$ 12 billion. It will also deal with specific issues related to educational opportunities, internal efficiency, external productivity, school management and education costs. On some issues the findings of cross national research have been most useful to the World Bank in its education operation, while on other issues the role of cross national research has been more limited because of a lack of research of relevance to the developing countries (LDCs).

Relevance to LDCs is an important qualification in the Bank context. The Bank staff tries to keep itself up to date in its knowledge about educational research wherever it originates but must always bear in mind its relevance to the Bank customers — the poor developing

1

countries. This screening process is important as long as some 90–95 per cent of all educational research is conducted in the developed countries, by the researchers from developed countries and to a large extent about topics specific to developed societies. It is true that the situation is changing and an increasing number of research institutes in developing societies participate in various types of comparative educational research. The International Institute for Education Planning in Paris (IIEP), the International Development Research Center in Ottawa (IDRC), the International Association for the Assessment of Educational Achievement (IEA) and national agencies such as Swedish SAREC and many universities play an important role in a process of widening the international research community. Caution about the transferability of research findings from developed to developing countries is nevertheless still called for. World Bank staff and other research disseminators are forced to stay abreast of educational research, understand what is relevant or irrelevant in the LDC context and show a good judgement in research application. This is a tall order and not always easy to meet, as everyone knows who has worked with education in the LDCs.

World Bank Policies, Programs and Procedures

The Five Principles

In its current assistance to education in LDCs the World Bank seeks to promote education development on the basis of five broad principles which were laid out in the Bank's education policy paper of 1980. The five principles are:

(i) basic education should be provided for all children and adults in the developing countries as soon as the available resources and conditions permit. In the long term, a comprehensive system of formal and nonformal education should be developed at all levels;

(ii) to increase productivity and promote social equity in the developing countries efforts should be made to provide education opportunities, without distinction of sex, ethnic background or social and economic status;

(iii) education systems should try to achieve maximum internal efficiency through the management, allocation and use of resources available for increasing the quantity and improving the quality of education;

(iv) education should be related to work and environment in order to improve quantitatively and qualitatively the knowledge and skills necessary for performing economic, social and other development functions;

(v) to satisfy the above objectives developing countries will need to build and maintain their own institutional capacities to design, analyze, manage and evaluate programs for education and training.

Policy Development

It took the Bank roughly 15 years to develop a policy, program and procedures which reflect the above comprehensive five principles. Cooperation with the research community in this development work was far from accepted in the beginning. I remember vividly my reaction to the secrecy in the Bank education work when I joined the Bank in the mid-1960s. I came from an open bureaucracy with intense open cooperation with research and clients and joined an organization where, at that time, not only banking operations (which is understandable) but also policy development were supposed to take place completely inside the organization with almost no consultation with researchers or with those the policy most concerned — the borrowers. Bank education staff members were supposed to keep abreast on the state of the art more or less in their spare time and without outside input and live on whatever knowledge capital they might have accumulated prior to their Bank assignments. Bank staff participation in educational research meetings was very limited and seen as a kind of luxury which was unduly infringing on the regular lending work. I even remember difficulties in obtaining permission to visit major international education exhibits although up-to-date knowledge of school equipment and books must have been seen as a fairly obvious asset for someone involved in the provision of such items to LDCs.

Fortunately, the Bank attitude improved as time passed and management changed. The improvement was much accelerated by the arrival of Robert McNamara as Bank president. He soon clarified for Bank management and staff the desirability and necessity of a more open and better communication with clients, the research community and other interested parts. Furthermore, he required a very forward-looking planning and policy development in each lending sector including education. This would have been impossible to execute without consultation with outside researchers, the use of cross national research and the development of a considerable indigenous Bank research capacity. McNamara explicitly supported research and his seriousness in this respect was manifested in his designation of a vice presidency for research. The World Bank education policy papers produced in 1971, 1974 and most recently in 1980 reflect an increased use of researchers and research findings as well as of consultation with the clients. This is particularly true for the 1980 paper. It was preceded by a considerable review of educational research by Bank staff and consultants. UNESCO's statistical bureau produced statistics, particularly on education efficiency, for the paper (1979). Recent developments of education in the Third World were of particular relevance for the paper but education in OECD countries was also reviewed. The draft of the paper was not only discussed by Bank staff but also commented on by some twenty internationally well-known researchers, including Torsten Husén. The draft was, furthermore, discussed with some 200 government administrators and educators in ten seminars in Latin America, Asia and Africa. A substantive "selected" bibliography shows clearly that cross national research played an important role in the formulation of the policy presented in the paper.

The 1980 Bank education policy paper was not only based on research but also discusses educational research and research needs in the developing countries. It makes a concrete plea for the improvement of the research capacity of the developing countries in education and suggests expanded programs, staff training, and the like. The paper makes an explicit reference to the value for the developing countries of actual participation in cross national research and in international research networks, such as IEA. As a consequence of its endorsement of research the Bank is financing research out of its own administrative budget and a large number of studies through its loans. This research is to a large extent cross national in purpose and nature and covers topics listed among the "five principles": access and equity, internal and external efficiency, capacity building and costs. By 1985 there were several hundred Bank supported research projects and a good hundred papers produced. The Bank seeks in this way not only to use findings of cross national research but also to produce and contribute to such research itself.

The Bank's research staff has continuously been increased to support this policy. An educational research division conducts research itself, reviews research components in the Bank financed education projects and guides operational colleagues in their identification, appraisal and evaluation of those components. Their role as producers of cross national research and disseminators of its findings to Bank staff and clients has become substantial. A large number of educational papers written during the last decade by Bank staff like Aklilu, Cochrane, Haddad, Heyneman, Hicks, Jallade, Jamison, Lee, Loxley, Moock, Noor, Psacharopoulos, Selovsky, Simmons, Tan, Woodhall and Zymelman demonstrate this well.

Educational Programs

In the beginning of the World Bank's financing of education in the early 1960s the Bank's justification for the lending was rather unsophisticated and the approach narrow. The lending was primarily justified on manpower grounds. Programs in industry, agriculture, and transportation, in developing countries could not be executed as planned because of shortages of skilled manpower. Consequently, the Bank financed a large amount of industrial and agricultural schools, technical universities and so on. It also supported the vocationalization of secondary schools in an expectation that this would increase the supply of middle level technicians. The policy reflected research by Harbison, Myers, Svennilsson and other manpower economists as well as recommendations by various OECD bodies. With the exception of some Ford foundation work by Tobias and others the manpower research of that time referred almost solely to the industrialized countries and their conditions but was nevertheless applied by the Bank and other agencies to education projects in developing countries where conditions were in many ways different. In hindsight, it may be said that this application was made in too unrestricted a way and there is some basis for Foster's statement of a "vocational school fallacy" in the LDCs. We shall return to this issue later in the paper.

In the 1970s the Bank began to see education in a wider perspective and beyond simple skill training. The policy became comprehensive. Macro-economic reasons for support of human resources development became accepted. In the 50s and 60s it was believed that there was an established positive correlation between secondary school enrollment and GNP increase. In the 70s support of education in general and at all levels was seen as an important part of the work for economic development. Cross national research evidence proved this relationship. Social rates of return to investments in education at all levels appeared high compared with many investments in physical assets in developing countries. For instance, figures of 20 percent or even higher were mentioned as the rate of return for investments in primary education in cross national research studies from LDCs. Non-oil exporting countries whose economy grew faster during the postwar decades had schooling and literacy rates which were higher than those of the countries with a slower economic growth in the same income per capita brackets. Cross national research indicated, furthermore [and still does], that educated workers, including farmers, produced more than uneducated workers, other factors being equal. (Chinese researchers have later gone even further and claimed that farmers with secondary education do better than farmers with primary education only.) Although it is difficult to prove categorically, circumstantial evidence shows that the cause and effect relationship was in the direction from education and literacy to growth and not in the other direction. Life expectancy is an important economic and social indicator and the correlation between life expectancy and literacy is positive and high. It is higher than the correlation between life expectancy and any other of nine basic needs indicators, such as calory intake, access to clean water, health care, and so on.

Thus, cross national research going far beyond the concept of the

school as a supplier of narrow skills developed in the late 60s and the 70s
and came to have a profound impact on the World Bank's thinking and
policy in education financing. The research showed clearly that each
level of good education — formal and nonformal — contributes to the
economic growth of a nation. A narrow focus on skill development was
not appropriate. It could in fact be claimed that the provision of
universal basic education was a first imperative in some nations. Some
research seemed to indicate that there was a minimum threshold level of
literacy needed for an economic "take off". I remember figures of 70
percent being mentioned. Be this as it may be, the cross national
research that was available during that period indicated that education
was a necessary means for a nation's economic growth. These arguments
may seem like common sense to educators but ministries and other
agencies of finance everywhere — and that includes the World Bank —
liked and likes quantified evidence. Hence, when some quantified
evidence was produced about the profitability of investments in
education, the World Bank reacted accordingly and the lending for
education projects increased considerably in size and content.

The Bank was well aware that education might be a necessary means
for economic growth but it was equally aware that it was not a sufficient
means. Other sectors of the society had to be developed simultaneously
and in parallel. Some recipient nations did not fully appreciate the
second condition and over-invested in education at the expense of other
sectors of the economy and society. When later economic growth (for
this and for many other very complicated reasons) did not occur, there
was a tendency to blame education for not delivering as promised.
There are several such cases in Africa.

If Western type vocational education was somewhat uncritically
introduced in the LDCs in the 1960s as an outcome of cross national
research of those days, the World Bank education debate in the 1970s
was focussed on the applicability in the LDCs of Jenck's analysis of
Coleman's research on US education. Some Bank staff accepted Jenck's
interpretation that schooling did not really matter much in the US and
that factors external to the school were more important for student
learning. They furthermore claimed without having much research
evidence that the same was true for the LDCs. A confusing Bank debate
was further confused by the very political interpretation by researchers
such as Bowles and Carnoy of what the school systems produced in a
Western society. The extreme consequence for the World Bank of
Jenck's and others' thesis as understood by some Bank staff was that
Bank lending for education was poor investment and that it increased
inequities. The lending, it was argued, should be redirected to straightforward skill training the way it had started a decade earlier.

It took time and much debate to get a general Bank staff agreement that there was not sufficient evidence that Jenck's thesis was applicable in the LDC context. As time passed, a hypothesis which I first heard presented by Foster obtained credibility in the Bank. The hypothesis which later has been proved, for instance through Heyneman's research in Uganda (1980), implied basically that the importance of formal schooling for student achievement stood in inverse relationship to the GNP per capita; the poorer a country is, the more important for student learning is the school and the less important are the external school factors as they exist in a developing society. This makes good sense for those who know socio-economic conditions and the role of schools in poor countries where books, radios, TV sets and the like are few and all types of communication difficult and literacy level of parents low. It implies that schools are good investments in LDCs, even if that would be less true for the USA. The "Jenck's discussion" in the World Bank represents a good although somewhat negative example of the role of cross national research in World Bank educational operations. The most important lesson was that for cross national research to be of full value to the Bank it must be really cross national, that is, cover developed as well as developing nations.

The widened development perspectives in the 1970s thus led to a comprehensive World Bank education aid policy. Reduction of poverty and promotion of equity became important concerns in addition to pure economic growth. At the operational level unequal access to schools and low education quality became reasons for lending in addition to manpower shortages. The lending came to cover all types of formal and nonformal education. It covered a spectrum from the construction of simple classrooms in primary schools to complicated administrative buildings in universities, from primary school textbook provision to the provision of research equipment in university laboratories, from the training of special teachers to research on school leavers, from curriculum development to evaluation of examination systems. This broadening of World Bank educational lending reflects, to a great extent, a Bank response to cross national research. It shows a perception of the state of the art in education.

Various issues related to World Bank educational lending will be discussed in the following but the most important aspects of the lending as it developed in the 1970s and as it remains in the 1980s are: (i) the switch of emphasis from quantity to quality in education, and (ii) the necessity of providing quality education at lower costs. This is in much contrast to the situation in the 1960s when the main objective of the lending was to provide more student places, particularly in vocational/ technical schools. It does not require much research to know how to provide more student places. To improve quality and cost effectiveness are very different matters. The role of cross national research in the

Bank work has therefore become more important as years have passed. A more detailed presentation of the current lending portfolio proves the point.

In response to this broader policy, lending to primary and nonformal education increased after 1970 and now comprises some 40 percent of the total. Bank lending for curriculum development, learning materials production, educational planning and management has also increased. These components generally require considerable technical assistance which, contrary to the beliefs a decade ago, has increased and now amounts to 20 percent of the lending. The technical experts may be nationals or foreigners but generally come from universities and, almost automatically, bring cross national research experience to the projects. A successful execution of most technical assistance components, in fact, requires such experience. This is also demonstrated by the impressive list of policy changes which have been associated with Bank financed education projects over the years. There have been some 200 cases of curriculum reforms, 150 cases of changes in school structure (including class sizes, multigrade teaching, double shifting), 70 cases of changes in teacher qualification, and 10 cases of changes in the language of instruction. Discussions on curriculum reforms as well as more pedestrian discussions on class size, double shifting and the like have been much helped by IEA type research.

Cross national research findings have also been important in the Bank's financing of new modes of deliveries in education. The Bank has financed some 60 projects with audio-visual materials production, 30 with textbook production, another 30 with educational radio, 25 with mobile training units and some 10 with educational television. The Bank's financing of new modes of deliveries includes program preparation, testing, staff training, program execution, evaluation, etc. Some textbook projects have been very large and included over 100 million textbooks. It would have been irresponsible for the Bank to enter into such big enterprises without a good perception of the role of textbooks in learning and of their cost effectiveness. A textbook project in the Philippines included a large research component which measured the learning difference among Filipino students with and without textbooks. In some cases findings from comparative educational research have been used by Bank staff to dissuade clients from educational innovations. This has been particularly true in educational TV when the Bank has shown that educational TV has, so far, not proven to be the highly cost-effective means of learning that was anticipated some decades ago. (China is the only LDC I know of where I, with good conscience, can say that educational TV functions as well as its potential.)

Educational Procedures

The findings from cross national research have been useful for the

Bank not only in the development of an educational financing policy and in the formulation of project components; the methods used in such research have also been employed in project work by Bank staff for education sector analysis and for project evaluation. A Bank management requirement of 5 years Bank lending programs necessitated studies which covered a country's whole education sector and discussed a range of operational options for years to come. The management's increased interest in project outcomes and impact also necessitated increased attention to project evaluation. The first detailed Bank guidelines for education sector work were written in 1969 and guidelines for project evaluation shortly thereafter.

The sector study teams were requested to assess the objectives, structure, content, size, assets, technology (management, staffing, learning and teaching methods), performance, cost and financing of the educational system of the country being studied. The assessments should be undertaken in the light of claimed and desirable development objectives and current and future resources. They should also refer to prospective future developments. The work might include various teacher and student surveys, manpower research and other similar studies. It was expected that the study team would have access to a considerable amount of cross national research data and use them for comparative purposes in their work to facilitate the identification of educational priorities on fundable projects. In this context the Bank also developed a system of education indicators which includes national expenditures on education, enrollment ratios, students per teacher, and so on. Educational sector studies produced in the 70s and 80s have adhered to the guidelines and used the indicators. The first sector study was conducted by a national team in Ethiopia and a most recent major study concerns China. The systematic use of comparative educational data, including those from various cross national research in the sector work on China, has been much welcomed by the Chinese who after a long period of relative isolation are interested in knowing where they stand in education, particularly in comparison with OECD countries. Chinese education authorities have also used such data in their internal educational debate. Other LDCs have reacted in a similar way to the sector studies.

Research knowledge and skills are as important in educational project evaluation as in educational sector work. Evaluation of Bank-financed educational projects was originally seen as an internal Bank matter and it dealt primarily with implementation problems and financial audits, reviews of buildings constructed and student counts. A change gradually took place. It was felt that performance audits were needed and that evaluation must assess project outcome and impact. It should be more thorough, quantified, scientific and less impressionistic. It should be

formative as well as summative. In addition to ex post evaluation
monitoring and evaluation systems should be built into the projects.
IIEP — with Postlethwaite in charge of the work — was requested in the
mid 70s to study a number of Bank-financed educational projects to
suggest appropriate evaluation machineries, particularly to assess the
qualitative improvements (and student achievements) the projects were
supposed to produce. The assignment of Postlethwaite to this job reflected an intentional attempt by the Bank to arrive at evaluation methods
which would capitalize on IEA experiences and be closely related to
international comparative educational research. One of Postlethwaite's
findings — not surprisingly — was that the qualitative achievements of
many Bank-financed projects would be difficult to measure, since the
qualitative objectives of the projects were often too vaguely defined. In
other words, one recommendation was that the Bank should be much
more precise in its formulation of qualitative objectives.

The IIEP study and subsequent discussions in the Bank led to several
improvements in project evaluation. It has been accepted that proper
evaluation requires baseline data often to be collected already at the
sector study stage, that evaluation is a continuous process during the
project implementation, that it must, in some way, be institutionalized
and that, of course, project objectives must be defined in such a way that
their achievement can be measured. Some evaluation of Bank financed
education projects has used good educational research methods and has
used IEA instruments for some student achievement measurements.
More could nevertheless be done; it must be remembered that Bank
educational operators are often pressed in their work to produce more
new projects rather than to assess the old ones. Cooperation in
evaluation work with some borrowers has, however, been quite successful. China is again a point in case. China's current participation in the
IEA research could be seen both as a part of educational sector work to
identify education priorities (and possible Bank financed projects) in
China's secondary education and as an evaluation of already ongoing
teacher training programs. China's participation in IEA which was
already urged by the Bank in a 1981 Bank educational sector paper on
China also reflects a Bank belief that the global LDC community would
benefit much from Chinese education data and experiences.

The World Bank's strategy has been to see evaluation not primarily as
an assessment of past activities but rather as a management tool and a
means of identifying current and future needs and priorities. It should
in this way become part of sector work. Student achievement measurements, school resource surveys and tracer studies should be conducted
and seen as future oriented operations. Even more, much of what has so
far been seen as national parts of cross national research could and
should rather become institutionalized work by scholars in regular

school planning and management. I would even like to avoid using the word "research" in this context, as research denotes a specific non-routine task while I would like to see the above activities undertaken as routine work. UNESCO regularly reports student enrollments, teaching staff, school budgets and similar quantitative information in its year book. Is it unrealistic to expect at some future date that quality information about students achievements and other qualitative outcomes will also be provided internationally and regularly? Must information of the number of students per population age group as already provided remain less politically sensitive than the achievement of those same students?

Five Current Issues

In this paper we have so far discussed the role of cross national research in the development of World Bank educational financing policies and in the identification and formulation of the Bank financed educational projects. We have concluded by describing how some approaches and methods borrowed from cross national research are being used in World Bank lending procedures. We shall now discuss some current issues in Bank educational financing and the potential role of cross national research in helping to resolve these issues.

Educational Opportunities

The first issue relates to expanding and equalizing educational opportunities. Enrollment in education has increased enormously during the years since the second World War and the median primary education enrollment ratio is now around 80 percent in the LDCs. But population growth continues and the absolute number of illiterates is increasing. There also continues to be an uneven use of educational opportunities. Some population groups are, for social or economic reasons, apathetic toward the educational opportunities provided or do not consider education for their children worth the opportunity costs involved. We know, for instance, that the current rural economic policies in China have increased peasants' income but also increased the economic incentives for farmers to keep all family members at work on the farm. As a consequence, enrollment in rural China, particularly among boys, has decreased. There is a similar situation in some states in India and elsewhere. Educational opportunities exist but are not fully used and it has proven difficult to enroll the last 20 percent of the age group. This is an area for more research in the LDCs by educational sociologists. Research findings in this area would be useful across all developing nations. The remedies probably lie outside the education sector.

Internal Efficiency

A second issue is the low internal efficiency of education in many LDCs as measured by retention rates or by achievement. It is know from UNESCO studies that survival rates in education in low income countries are about half of those in many OECD countries (1979). We know, furthermore, from achievement studies by IEA and other institutions that the mean score, for example in science education, of students in LDCs is below the mean score of students in OECD countries and in some Far East nations. This information is a basic necessity but it must be supplemented by cross national research helping educational authorities and aid agencies to identify the remedies. It can with some simplification be said that educational projects in LDCs aiming at qualitative improvements of their educational systems have so far comprised a smorgasbord of every possible remedy, including curriculum changes, textbooks, teacher training, new equipment, school meals, classrooms etc., without much knowledge about which remedy would work best and be most cost effective. This approach has not only led to high investment costs but has also caused recurrent costs which some countries have eventually been unable to meet. I am not so naive that I believe that cross national research will be able to provide clear-cut recipes to various investment alternatives but I see it as a worthwhile task to research the cost effectiveness of various inputs to education more systematically than has so far been the case. The education authorities, particularly in Africa, will increasingly have to ask themselves if scarce money should go to books, to teachers or to other inputs — money is not and will not for a long time to come be available for everything. Cost effectiveness studies have not been a strong side of existing cross national research and even economists of education like Bowman and Blaug have, to my knowledge, not yet undertaken the type of cost effectiveness studies I ask for in this context.

External Productivity

A third major issue in LDC education is the external productivity of education systems; the relation between education and work. Many LDCs face the paradoxical situation of a surplus of school graduates and a shortage of skilled labor. As already mentioned, the World Bank and other agencies have invested from the beginning and still continue to invest heavily in technical and vocational education and in diversified secondary schools to meet the skill shortage. But the experiences as a result of these investments have been mixed and it is not only in Foster's Ghana that one could speak of a vocational school fallacy. I have myself visited vocational and technical schools in 22 LDCs but have, with the exception of the countries in the Far East, seen few school workshops and laboratories being operated in a way that I, as a former engineering college principal, would like to see them. Training run by enterprises has generally been better but has also had serious shortcomings, particularly in terms of the narrow approach that has been adopted.

It has proven difficult to find the right types of vocational and technical education and training in the LDCs. Many problems lie outside the education systems and relate to salary levels of skilled workers and technicians, the overall value system of the society with a lack of appreciation of manual labor and so on. Jobs may exist and also the schools for providing training for those jobs but the effective demand for the jobs and the training is just not there. These external issues exist in almost all LDCs. Not even a country like Cuba, which for decades has emphasized equality, the honor of physical work and has a good vocational school system, has been able to solve them. But there are many internal issues in addition to the external ones which need research.

It is striking how uninterested in general the cross national research community has been in the problems of vocational education in the LDCs despite the many unanswered questions. Which are the appropriate entrance requirements and levels for various types of technical/vocational education in the LDCs? What is the appropriate degree of specialization? Who should be responsible for technical/vocational education? Ministries of Education? Enterprises? Specialized agencies? At what level of development should a diversified education system, such as in OECD countries, be introduced in the LDCs? If ever? What about on the job training? Apprenticeships? What type of training in rural areas and for what? Urban life? Rural life? What kind of education facilities? What type of teachers? What type of manpower forecasting? The list can easily be extended. It creates an impression of little learnt during 20 years of support of vocational/technical education in the LDCs by the Bank and other agencies. Some of my World Bank colleagues may feel that they know the answers while I, to my embarrassment, must admit much less certainty today than 10 or 20 years ago. I should, however, hasten to state that the experience of 4 years of work during the 1980s on education in China has proved to me that vocational and technical education and training can function well under specific circumstances, although even there agricultural training is listed at the bottom of the students' application lists. Vocational schools and training centers apparently also do quite well in Korea and Singapore. An increased interest in the problems of vocational and technical education and training by the cross national research community would be welcome. Research topics are legion and a study of success stories in the Far East could be useful reading for other LDCs.

School Administration

Inefficient administration and management comprise a fourth issue which troubles education in many LDCs and also affects the World Bank financed educational projects. Bank staff members have spent a considerable amount of time and effort in educational projects to discuss ways of improving management. But the efforts have generally ended up in simple proposals of more management training without always defining the objectives or content of such training. Consultants and management experts are used but refer to or apply Western — North American management training more often than is appropriate. Organizational and decision-making models also coming from the West have also too often been proposed. Efficient school administration in a developing society is more than the timely salary payment and the reduction in teacher and student absenteeism and the keeping of books and student accounts. It is a question of the whole bureaucracy and value system. It may even be a question of unpleasantries such as corruption and nepotism. Any administrative reform work must acknowledge that there are societies where tribal and family loyalties have far higher priority than any civil service codes and where political patronage goes all the way through the hierarchy down to the hiring of night watchmen. Cases exist where expatriate university professors have been forced to retire when they have refused to play the indigenous examination game. It may not be the job of cross national research to eradicate nepotism or corruption (management may, in fact, despite Myrdal's opinions as expressed in *Asian Drama* — occasionally benefit from some of the ills mentioned — we don't really know). That is a job for the country's politicians and administrators and not for the researchers. The cross national researchers may however, follow the example of Myrdal and study how education administration really works in the LDCs. How can it become more institutionalized and less dependent on the skills of specific individuals? If institutionalization — a popular fashion during the last few years among development experts — is still a distant goal, what type of individuals should meanwhile manage the schools and the education offices to improve school management? This is not unimportant, as IIEP and IEA studies show that good student performance appears more positively correlated to the quality of the local school manager than might be anticipated.

Research on school management and administration is difficult. What is available primarily from American institutions has so far not been of much use for World Bank staff in their work to help improve LDC educational administration through Bank financed projects. Their recommendations have dealt with technical, fairly superficial actions but have left the major underlying sociological, anthropological and cultural factors uninvestigated. There is room for more research by educational sociologists — perhaps assisted by IDRC which previously has expressed interest in the sociology of education.

Educational Costs

The fifth and final issue related to World Bank educational financing is educational costs. Educational costs, both in absolute figures and as a percentage of GNP and as a percentage of the National budget, have steadily increased year after year in most LDCs with some slight slowing down after the oil crisis of the 1970s. The median figures are now 4 per cent of GNP and 16 per cent of the National budget respectively. The range is, however, wide and some countries in Africa devote about 10 per cent of GNP and 40 per cent of the National budget to education without having yet achieved universal primary education or a reasonable supply of secondary school places. In the long run no country can possibly allocate so much of its resources to education without sacrificing other urgent national needs. It was predicted in a Bank study a decade ago (1975) that some African countries would face serious escalation of educational costs if less expensive production methods in education were not found. These methods have not been found or at least not been applied.

Bank educational economists have been assigned to work with African colleagues to help them find ways of cutting costs without too much sacrifice of educational quality. This requirement leads us back to the second issue discussed above about the quality and internal efficiency of the educational systems. Which inputs are most cost effective and should therefore continue to be well financed, which inputs are less cost effective and therefore liable to budget cuts? An experienced former secretary of education in an OECD country remarked some time ago that those things which really matter in the education budget and influence educational costs have a tendency to be overlooked both in research and in budget discussions. His point was that changes in curricula, improvement of teacher training, and the introduction of comprehensive schools may all be costly reforms, but changes in the number of periods per week a teacher is required to teach, in the weekly schedule of the students, in the duration of the academic year and, of course, in class size influence educational costs much more. A comparison among countries shows a surprising difference in these latter respects. Teaching duties for teachers in secondary schools vary from ten to twenty-five periods per week or more; student schedules may vary from 20 to 40 classes per week; the academic year may vary from 150 to 200 days, and class sizes from ten to ninety. There are few, if any, pedagogical explanations for these differences which more often than not have historical explanations.

The per student cost differences become, of course, very large and there is little evidence that the high cost systems perform better than the low cost systems. Some cross national research evidence exists about the influence of class size allocated time and time on task on student performance but more research could be done both on these and others. Systematic cross national research could provide findings of large economic value. It could provide educational authorities with important tools in their cost saving attempts and protect them from indiscriminate across the board budget cuts enforced by the financial authorities of the country.

Conclusions

I have shown in this paper that cross national research has played an important role during the history of World Bank educational financing. The research of Torsten Husén's "own" association IEA has been important, particularly in the Bank's discussion about project components for better quality in education. The studies of the IIEP over which Board Torsten Husén presided for a number of years, have helped Bank staff in educational planning, management and cost considerations. Torsten Husén's and other researchers' direct input to Bank work through papers and lectures at World Bank seminars has been an important dissemination of cross national research findings to Bank staff and clients and much appreciated. The role of cross national research in Bank education work could nevertheless be further enhanced. An increased attention in future cross national research on the cost effectiveness of various inputs into the educational systems of the LDCs is of particularly high priority. The findings could provide LDC decision-makers with improved tools in their efforts to provide better education at affordable costs.

Let us finally again recall that only 5 to 10 percent of all educational research takes place in developing countries. A global cross national education research network must have a much larger percentage of educational research conducted in the LDCs to become representative. The majority of the world's children attend schools in the LDCs and they badly need improved learning based on relevant research in their own schools as conducted by their compatriots.

References

Aklilu *et al.* 1983 *Education and Development: Views from the World Bank.* The World Bank, Washington, D.C.

Aklilu *et al.* 1983 *Education and National Development.* The World Bank, Washington, D.C.

Bowles S. 1980 "Education, Class Conflict, and Uneven Development". In J. Simmons (ed.) *The Education Dilemma.* Pergamon, New York.

Carnoy M. (ed.) 1972 *Schooling in a Corporate Society. The Political Economy of Education in America.* David McKay Company, New York.

Cochrane S. 1979 *Fertility and Education. What do we really know.* Johns Hopkins University Press, Baltimore.

Coleman J. *et al.* 1966 *Equality of Educational Opportunity.* US Government Printing Office, Washington, D.C.

Foster P. 1965 "The Vocational School Fallacy in Development Planning". In C. A. Anderson & M. J. Bowman (eds) *Education and Economic Development.* Aldine Publ. Co., Chicago.

Haddad W. 1978 *Educational Effects of Class Size.* World Bank, Washington, D.C.

Haddad W. 1979 *Educational and Economic Effects of Promotion and Repetition Practices.* World Bank, Washington, D.C.

Haddad W. and Avalos B. 1979 *A Review of Teacher Effectiveness Research in Africa, India, Latin America, Middle East, Malaysia, Philippines, and Thailand: Synthesis of Results.* IDRC, Ottawa.

Harbison S. H. and Myers C. A. 1964 *Education, Manpower and Economic Growth.* McGraw Hill, New York.

Heyneman S. *et al.* 1978 *Textbooks and Achievement. What we know.* World Bank, Washington, D. C.

Heyneman S. and Jamison Q. T. 1980 "Student Learning in Uganda: Textbook Availability and Other Factors" in *Comparative Education Review,* No. 24, pp. 206–20.

Heyneman S. 1982 "Resources Availability, Equality and Educational Opportunity Among Nations". In L. Anderson & D. Windham (Eds) *Education and Development.* Lexington Books.

Heyneman S. and Loxley W. 1983 "The Impact of Primary School Quality of Academic Achievement Across Twenty Nine High and Low Income Countries". In *American Journal of Sociology,* No. 88.

Heyneman S. *et al.* 1984 "Textbooks in the Philippines: Evaluation of The Pedagogical Impact of a Nationwide Investment". *Educational Evaluation Policy Analysis,* Vol. **6,** No. 2.

Heyneman S. 1984 "Research on Education in Developing Countries" in *International Journal of Educational Development,* Vol. **4,** No. 4.

Hicks N. 1980 "Economic Growth and Human Resources". World Bank, Washington, D.C.

Hultin M. *et al.* 1975 *Costing and Financing Education in LDCs.* World Bank, Washington, D.C.

Jallade J. P. 1973 *The Financing of Education.* World Bank, Washington, D. C.

Jamison D. *et al.* 1978 *Radio for Education and Development.* Sage Publ., Beverly Hills & London.

Jamison D. *et al.* 1982 *Farmer Education and Farm Efficiency.* Johns Hopkins, Baltimore.

Jencks C. *et al.* 1972 *Inequality; Reassessment of the Effect of Family and Schooling in America.* Basic Books, New York.

King T. *et al.* 1980 *Education and Income.* World Bank, Washington, D.C.

Lee, K. H. 1981 "Equity and Alternative Education Methods: A Korean Case Study". *Comparative Education Review,* February 1981.

Lee, K. H. 1983 *Human Resources Planning in the Republic of Korea.* World Bank, Washington, D.C.

Lee K. H. 1984 *Universal Primary Education — An African Dilemma.* World Bank, Washington, D.C.

Loxley W. 1983 *A Comparison of Achievement Outcomes in Selected OECD Countries. An Analysis of IEA Data.* World Bank, Washington, D. C.

Metcalf D. 1984 *The Economics of Vocational Training. Past Evidence and Future Evolutions.* World Bank, Washington, D.C.

Moock P. 1983 "Overview of the World Bank's Research on Education" in *Canadian and International Education,* Vol. **12,** No. 1., Ottawa.

Noor A. 1981 *Education and Basic Human Needs.* World Bank, Washington, D.C.

Noor A. 1982 "Managing Adult Literacy Training", *Prospects,* Vol. **12,** No. 2, UNESCO, Paris.

Mingat A. 1984 *On Equity in Education Again.* World Bank, Washington, D.C.

Psacharopoulos G. 1980 *Higher Education in Developing Countries.* World Bank, Washington, D.C.

Psacharopoulos G. 1982 "Education as an Investment". *Finance and Development,* September 1982.

Psacharopoulos G. 1983 *Education Research at the World Bank.* World Bank, Washington, D.C.

Psacharopoulos G. 1984 *The Contribution of Education to Economic Growth.* American Enterprise Institute, Washington, D.C.

Psacharopoulos G. 1984 "The Assessment of Training Priorities in Developing Countries". *International Labor Review,* Vol. Sept./Oct., Geneva.

Psacharopoulos G. 1984 *Education for Development. Analysis of Investment Choices.* World Bank, Washington, D.C.

Psacharopoulos G. 1984 *Diversified Secondary Education and Development*. World Bank, Washington, D.C.

Selowsky M. 1981 "Nutrition, Health and Education. The Economic Significance" in *Journal of Development Economics*, Vol. **9,** and World Bank, Washington, D.C.: Reprint Series No. 218.

Svennilson I. 1963 "The Concepts of Economic Growth". Proceedings of the 11th Int. Conference of Agr. Economics, Oxford University Press, London

Simmons J. 1974 *Education Poverty and Development*. World Bank, Washington, D.C.

Simmons J. *et al.* 1978 "The Determinants of School Achievement in Developing Countries: A Review of Research" in *Economic Development and Cultural Change*, January 1978.

Tan J. P. *et al.* 1984 *User Charges for Education. The Ability and Willingness to Pay*. World Bank, Washington, D.C.

Tan J. P. 1984 *The International Flow of Third Level LDC Students to DCs* World Bank, Washington, D.C.

Tobias C. *et al.* 1968 *India's Manpower Strategy Revisited 1947–67*. N. M. Tripathi Limited, Bombay.

UNESCO 1979 *Wastage in Primary Education*. UNESCO, Paris.

Woodhall M. 1983 *Student Loans as a Means to Finance Higher Education*. World Bank, Washington, D.C.

World Bank 1971 *Education Sector Study*. World Bank, Washington, D.C.

World Bank 1974 *Education Sector Working Paper*. World Bank, Washington, D.C.

World Bank 1980 *Education Sector Policy Paper*. World Bank, Washington, D.C.

World Bank 1981 *China: Education*. Chinese Economics Report. World Bank, Washington, D.C.

World Bank 1985 *China: Long Term Issues and Options. Annex A. Issues and Prospects in Education*. Johns Hopkins University Press, Baltimore.

Zymelman M. 1976 *The Economic Evaluation of Vocational Training Programs*. Johns Hopkins Univ. Press, Boston.

Zymelman M. 1976 *Patterns of Educational Expenditure*. World Bank, Washington, D.C.

Zymelman M. 1978 *The 'Burden' of Educational Expenditures and its Forecast*. World Bank, Washington, D.C.

Zymelman M. 1980 *Occupational Structures of Industries*. World Bank, Washington, D.C.

Science Education:
The Contribution of IEA
Research to a World Perspective

JOHN P. KEEVES

During the past 100 years the findings of scientific research and the products of scientific and technological development have transformed the world in which we live. As a consequence schools throughout the world have assumed the responsibility of passing on knowledge about science to succeeding generations, as well as developing a population that has an understanding of science to ensure the use of scientific knowledge for constructive ends and the betterment of life.

The Origins of Science Education

The teaching of science in schools would appear to have first become widespread in Western Europe during the middle of the nineteenth century, and the system of science teaching by lectures and demonstration experiments was traditionally a characteristic of German science education. It was not until the 1870s when Matthew Arnold, an inspector of schools, and T. H. Huxley, a great protagonist of scientific truth and the theory of evolution and a brilliant lecturer and teacher, argued for the inclusion of science in the school curriculum that the teaching of science became widespread in British schools (Ingle and Jennings, 1981). Huxley also emphasized the importance of training students to use their hands, eyes and senses, and thus laid the foundations for the teaching of science through laboratory work that has been traditional in Britain. Around the turn of the century another distinguished scientist, H. E. Armstrong, exerted a strong influence on science teaching through his advocacy of the heuristic method or discovery approach and the teaching of scientific method (Armstrong, 1903). The acceptance of these principles of science education, if not wholly in practice, involved a substantial time commitment to the learning of science and led to specialization by some students in science as distinct from the humanities in English secondary schools. The British traditions of science education spread to other countries, such as Australia and New Zealand, where the British influence was strong and

19

a similar approach to science teaching developed in these countries. The characteristics of this approach were an early specialization in science, the use of concyclic methods for the presentation of content, a separation of the scientific disciplines of physics, chemistry and biology, with physics and to a lesser extent chemistry, dominating the science curriculum, and an emphasis on laboratory training.

Science, largely with a practical emphasis was taught in many American schools during the early part of the nineteenth century. However, in the 1870s, in response to the claims for a place for science in the school curriculum by such men as Herbert Spencer and T. H. Huxley, Harvard College began accepting science courses for college entrance and the teaching of science at the high school level became widely accepted (Atkin and Burnett, 1969). The recommendations of the National Educational Association's Committee of Ten in 1893 were to set the pattern of science education in the United States that has largely continued unchanged to the present day. In the elementary school, a course in nature study based on botany and zoology was proposed, and at the secondary school level year long courses in geography, including geology and meteorology, biology, chemistry and physics were advocated. Following the huge increase in enrollments at the high school level in the years immediately prior to 1920, the United States Bureau of Education issued a bulletin on *Reorganization of Science in Secondary Schools* which emphasized the specific values to be derived from the teaching of science and gave strong support for laboratory work and the use of the project method (Fowler, 1964). This report which had a highly significant influence on high school science teaching listed the principal courses in high school science as general science, biology, chemistry and physics and thus consolidated the established pattern for the high school science curriculum. During the 1930s, the writings of John Dewey on the concept of scientific method as a series of steps: (1) defining the problem, (2) collecting of data, (3) stating a hypothesis, (4) testing the hypothesis, (5) drawing a conclusion, and (6) applying the findings emphasized the role of problem solving in laboratory work in science education. Furthermore, the Progressive Education Association's report on the *Function of Science in General Education* in 1938 emphasized the need for the science curriculum to be based on factors of scientific utility with a commitment to the scientific method and problem-solving (Atkin and Burnett, 1969).

In Eastern Europe and the Soviet countries the continental European approaches to science teaching were accepted and widespread use was made of the lecture-demonstration technique with extensive use of text and notebooks. Similar methods of science teaching were adopted in Japan during the Meiji Era and after World War II with the redevelopment and rapid growth of Japanese education. Moreover, in the developing countries, many of which had strong affiliations with England, the British approach to science teaching was acknowledged but the practical situation demanded reliance on lecture methods of teaching, rote learning and memorization. This was partly because most students were being taught in a language that was not their mother tongue, and partly because a lack of facilities and large class sizes prevented other approaches to science teaching being used.

The dominant theme that gradually emerged during this period in all countries of the world was that science was a necessary experience in the education of all children, at all stages of schooling. The extent to which this was achieved of course varied greatly. However, the precept "Science for all" was widely proclaimed.

The Wave of Science Curriculum Reform

The mid 1950s marked the beginnings of a period of 20 years of reform in science education. The origins of reform would appear to lie in the changing views of the nature of the scientific method which were greatly influenced by J. B. Conant's book *On Understanding Science* that was published in 1947 (Conant, 1947.) Conant questioned the accepted "methods of science" and identified the "tactics" and "strategies" of science, involving an interplay between societal forces, technological development and the emergence of new ideas. The subsequent writings of Popper and Kuhn on the philosophy of science have revealed that the methods that scientists actually use are similar to the ways in which children think. Thus the reform that took place in science education from the late 1950s to the late 1970s not only sought to introduce new ideas into the science curriculum but also sought to explain the ways in which scientists worked and to provide similar types of experiences to promote student learning through the skillful use of film, demonstration experiments and laboratory exercises. There was also widespread recognition of Piagetian theories with an emphasis on the role of autonomy in learning, the need for action-oriented approaches to learning, and the use of a spiral curriculum that presented the concepts of science in appropriate ways at successive stages of schooling (Bruner, 1960).

In Britain the reform movement in science education had its origins in debate within the committees of the Association for Science Education (formerly, the Science Masters' Association and the Association of Women Science Teachers), the funding of improved facilities for the teaching of science, and the need to develop new curricula to meet the needs of the increasing numbers of students being retained at the secondary school level. The period from 1960 to 1980 saw a veritable explosion of activity in curriculum development which was financed initially by the Nuffield Foundation and subsequently by the Schools

Council and other agencies. The beginnings of this work in Britain cannot be traced, as is sometimes assumed to the launching of Sputnik in 1957 by Russian scientists. Approximately 30 curriculum development projects were established and hundreds of books were prepared. The majority of these projects emphasized the doing of science rather than the passive learning of science. There is little doubt that this burst of activity had a widespread influence on science education in Britain, but the new books and materials were very demanding of both teachers and resources and were not universally adopted, leading many to question the value of the effort and the directions that it followed. One shortcoming is clear: too little was done to show the relevance of science in the world outside the laboratory and the importance of science and technology in today's world.

In the United States, the National Science Foundation was established in 1950 to support basic scientific research, science education programs at all levels and programs to strengthen scientific research potential. Initial programs in the area of science education were in the fields of inservice teacher education, in 1954, and the design of a new physics course, in 1956. The launching of Sputnik by the USSR in 1957 indicated the advances achieved by Soviet science and technology, and led in the United States to a greatly increased allocation of resources for education not only in science but also in other areas of the curriculum, particularly mathematics. The Tenth Report of the International Clearinghouse in 1977 listed over 500 curriculum projects which had been set up in the United States, mainly in science and mathematics (Lockard, 1977). The major characteristics of these curriculum materials were: (1) the modernization of content, (2) greater attention to the development of favourable attitudes, (3) emphasis on the nature of scientific inquiry, (4) flexibility of use, and (5) orientation around major conceptual themes. While it must be acknowledged that the educational system is highly resistant to change and thus extremely stable, there can be little doubt that the overall effects of the widespread programs of curriculum development had a very significant impact on teaching in schools not only in the United States but also in many other countries of the world. The many evaluation studies that were carried out, together indicate small but recognizable gains, but probably rather less than had been expected. The low level of adoption of the products of many of the projects is no indication of their effects, since the workers on the curriculum projects became, in the main, the authors or teachers of the new courses. Perhaps the most disappointing feature of the 20 years of innovation and development of new curricula, and more especially inservice teacher education, was that it all came to an abrupt halt approximately 20 years after it started in a climate filled with strong criticism of the schools, the teachers and some of the products of curriculum development. In particular, there was marked controversy associated with the teaching of certain ideas concerned with the evolution of man and the MACOS (Man a Course of Study) project materials (See Welch, 1979).

Programs of curriculum development, innovation, and inservice education were not limited to Britain and the United States. The reform movement was world-wide and the efforts of UNESCO, the charitable foundations, and national governments have had a highly stimulating influence on science education (Baez, 1976). For example, the Danube Seminars organized by the Roland Eötvös University and the Roland Eötvös Physical Society of Hungary contributed significantly to generate and spread programs of reform in Eastern European countries (Marx, 1979).

This is the setting across the world in which the International Association for the Evaluation of Educational Achievement (IEA) has sought to conduct studies into science education. The first investigation was undertaken in 1970 at the height of the wave of curriculum reform. The second study was planned for the early 1980s with little realization that it would be commenced in a climate that was so strongly inimical to science education and the teaching of science. Nevertheless, the evidence derived from the First IEA Science Study has made a clearly identifiable contribution to the debate on issues associated with curriculum reform in science and it is about that contribution that this article is primarily concerned.

The First and Second IEA Science Studies

The First Science Study was undertaken in 19 countries. The countries included the United States, the British group, (Australia, England, New Zealand, and Scotland) the Western European group (Belgium (Flemish), Belgium (French), The Federal Republic of Germany, Finland, France, Italy, The Netherlands, Sweden), Eastern Europe (Hungary), the Asian-Pacific region (Japan), and four developing countries (Chile, India, Iran and Thailand). Students were tested in most but not all countries at three age levels, as follows:

Population I All students aged 10.0–10.11 years. This was the last period in most school systems in which the students were under the supervision of a general class teacher, rather than a science specialist teacher.

Population II All students aged 14.0–14.11 years. This was the last point in most of the school systems where 100 per cent of an age group were still in compulsory schooling.

Population IV All students who were in the terminal year of full-time secondary education programs which were either pre-university programs or programs of the same length.

In the Second IEA Science Study it is expected that 26 countries will take part, including 10 of the 19 countries that participated in the first study. In the second study there is a greater number of countries from North America (Canada, United States), the Asian-Pacific Region (Hong Kong, Japan, Singapore, South Korea) and the developing countries (including China, Ghana, Nigeria, Papua New Guinea, The Philippines, Zimbabwe, Tanzania) and additional countries from the Eastern European group (Hungary and Poland), as well as an adequate range of countries from the British and Western European groups. However, greater flexibility has been permitted in the choice of target populations. While three population levels have again been identified, some countries have chosen grade samples in preference to age samples, and not all countries have been able to test at all levels.

The two investigations are not primarily studies to assess a country's average level of achievement in science. While level of achievement is an important consideration, the "achieved" curriculum as measured by achievement tests is viewed in relation to the "planned" curriculum in science, as prescribed by central or individual school syllabuses, and the "translated" curriculum as taught by each classroom science teacher whose students were tested. This idea was developed tentatively in a paper from the First IEA Science Study which showed the marked differences between the three levels of the curriculum for Population IV students in three countries, the Federal Republic of Germany, Australia and the United States (Keeves, 1974*b*). It also showed the high level of correspondence between these three aspects of the curriculum and raised clearly the need to provide an account of the different factors that influenced curriculum planning in each country and the opportunity that students had to learn the content and processes being tested. The aims of the IEA Science studies are to examine the differences in curricula which occur and their relation to the outcomes of science education programs assessed in terms of achievement, attitudes and yield, as well as to identify factors that contribute to differences in outcomes, at the system, school and student levels. The findings of the first study have been reported by Comber and Keeves (1973) and numerous other publications. All that can be accomplished in this article is the highlighting of factors that have a clearly identified influence on curriculum development and science education programs in the different countries of the world.

Cross national studies have two unique contributions to make to an understanding of educational phenomena. On the one hand, such studies provide parallel analyses for each country. In each case the countries serve as replications of an experiment and afford opportunities to examine in a broader context relationships that have been observed previously only in a single national system. On the other hand, these studies make possible comparisons across countries, by examining in what respects countries differ in their curriculum emphasis and level of performance, and by attempting to understand those differences in terms of the characteristics of the countries involved.

Opportunity to Learn Science

The science achievement tests were constructed with great care to ensure that they would be suitable for use across the full range of countries taking part in the inquiry. Nevertheless, it was recognized that the level of performance of the students in each country would depend on the nature and emphasis of the science courses being taught in each country. It has been shown in the introductory section of this article that the countries of the world could be grouped together according to their traditions and the stage of reform in their science education programs. In order to assess the type of science courses being taught, in practice, in each country, the science teachers in each school were asked to come together at about the time that testing took place to consider whether the students in their school who were answering the tests had had the opportunity to learn the content of the items. In this way by combining together the responses from the teachers within a school and across schools within a country it was possible with some accuracy to assess the opportunity that the students within a country had to learn the content contained within the tests that were employed. Opportunity to learn was thus a measure of the translated curriculum.

At the Population I (the 10-year-old) level no recognizable relationship existed in 1970 between the performance of the students in a country on the science tests and the opportunity to learn the content tested as assessed by the teachers in the schools. These results suggest that at this age level the knowledge and understanding of science that is acquired by the students in most parts of the world is gained, in part, by what is taught within the schools but also, in part, in an informal manner from general reading and the mass media. Consequently, the teachers' perceptions of the suitability of the items, or perhaps the expectations of the teachers with regard to student performance within a country, do not correspond closely with actual level of performance.

At the Population II (the 14-year-old) level in the developed countries a general relationship was found to exist between level of performance on the tests and opportunity to learn the items tested. Of considerable interest was the very high level of both opportunity to learn and achievement on the science tests of the Japanese students at this age level, although level of achievement was also high at the 10-year-old level. Science education in Japan differs significantly in kind from that which occurs in other parts of the world. Indeed, the evidence available shows that 10-year-old students in Japan perform at nearly the same level as 14-year-old students in the United States, and 14-year-old students in Japan exceed, in general terms, the average level of performance of students in their final year of schooling (Year 12) in the United States. The Japanese students were not tested at the Year 12 level, so that no estimates could be made of their relative level of achievement at the terminal stage of schooling. However, the opportunity to learn science that had been provided by age 14 years, almost inevitably guaranteed a very high level of both opportunity to learn and achievement at the terminal stage of schooling. The apparently high level of achievement of Hungarian students at the 14-year-old level was also of interest. However, by this age level in Hungary, a significant proportion of the less able students, particularly in rural areas, had been permitted to leave school, thus inflating the apparent level of performance of those who remained.

At the terminal secondary school level, Population IV, the results recorded showed a surprising pattern when average level of performance was plotted against the opportunity to learn provided to the students in a country. At this level there was not one "line of best fit" required to display the relationships but two. On one line lay the four countries with a common tradition in science education that was identified above as British: Australia, England, New Zealand and Scotland. These four countries had average science scores several points above those of the other developed countries, when allowance had been made for the students' assessed opportunity to learn. On a second line lay the majority of countries of Western Europe, with a noticeably higher level of performance recorded in the Federal Republic of Germany and the Netherlands. Again these countries would appear to have very similar traditions in science education at the pre-university stage of schooling. Amongst this group of countries lay the United States with its own, quite unique (at least among the countries under survey) science education policies and practices.

Included in this investigation were four developing countries: Chile, India, Iran and Thailand. Their lower level of economic development and their lack of a tradition of universal compulsory education for at least 9 years of schooling showed up very dramatically in their performance on the science tests. The level of achievement of the students was, in general, a full student standard deviation below the performance of the students in the developed countries taking part in the study. However, the differences between the two groups, the developed and developing countries, in assessed opportunity to learn did not reflect in full the magnitude of the observed differences in achievement. Work undertaken in other IEA studies has revealed that the major difference that characterizes the learning of students in developed and developing countries is that, in general, students in the latter group are not learning at school in their mother tongue (Thorndike, 1973). Thus, a lack of facility in language must be considered to be a major determinant of their lower level of achievement. It would seem probable that there were substantial numbers of students in the developing countries, who took the tests in 1970, who were significantly disadvantaged by the relatively high readability level required by the testing program, and who had not achieved an adequate level of performance in their national language to read satisfactorily the testing material given to them.

More recently, Heyneman and Loxley have extended the range of these studies using the science tests that were employed in 1970 through evaluation programs in a very wide range of developing countries. Their analyses indicate the importance of access to a textbook for the effective learning of science in a developing country. In addition, the findings from several studies suggest that access to a textbook is more influential for children of low socio-economic status than for those of high status. (Heyneman and Loxley, 1983; Heyneman, Farrell and Sepulveda-Stuardo, 1981).

Holding Power and Science Education

Of considerable importance in the development of effective programs of science education particularly at the terminal secondary school stage is the proportion of the age group remaining at school to this level. This proportion is commonly referred to as the "holding power" or the "retentivity" of the school system. While all the developed countries have almost the complete population at school at the 10-year-old level, this is not so for the developing countries. Similarly at the 14-year-old level, most of the developed countries have a very high proportion of the age group at school. However, at the terminal secondary school stage countries have widely different holding powers. In 1970, the retentivity estimates ranged from a high figure of 75 per cent of the age group still at school in the United States to a low figure of 9 per cent still at school at the pre-university level in the Federal Republic of Germany. However, the estimates recorded depended, in part, on how the target population was defined at the Year 12 level in each country.

Comber and Keeves (1973) showed that although there was a general relationship between mean performance at the Population IV level and the holding power of the school system for a country, a stronger relationship (-0.77) emerged when holding power was related to a country's growth in level of achievement from Population II to Population IV. The amount of growth in science achievement was also found to be related to the nature and extent of social selectivity operating.

Indicators of social selectivity, based on classifications of the occupation of the student's father and on the level of education attained by the father and mother of the student were used. The indices employed in the study were the differences between the average number of years of the father's (or mother's) education for the Population IV group and that of the father's (or mother's) education for the Population II group. For the index of father's occupation the ratio of the percentages at Populations II and IV in the professional and managerial occupational group to the percentages in the unskilled and semi-skilled worker group were used. Correlations between growth in achievement scores and the occupation index (0.74), the father's education index (0.54) and the mother's education index (0.46) were recorded across the 13 developed countries for which data were available. The data indicate that the mean level of gain in performance from Population II to Population IV increases with greater educational selectivity and that this is accompanied by greater social bias.

In developing curricula at the terminal secondary school stage, the extent to which the school population at this level has experienced this educational and social selectivity must be taken into consideration. However, in the planning of science education programs the educational and social composition of the student group is rarely taken into account. Consequently, it is necessary to ask whether in such countries as the United States and Sweden, where a relatively high proportion of the 17-year-old age group remain at school to the terminal secondary school stage, the lower average level of performance of the students is accompanied by a lower level of achievement of the more able students. It is clearly the more able groups of students who specialize in science and mathematics on whom each country will depend for its highly trained scientific and technological personnel.

Degrees of Excellence

To estimate the relative performance of the more able students Comber and Keeves (1973) calculated mean scores for the top 9 per cent, 5 per cent and 1 per cent of the age group, based on the scores of those students who remained at school to the terminal secondary school stage. When the data collected in 1970 from the developed countries were examined in this way, the countries appeared to fall into three distinct groups, within which the differences in level of performance of the top 1 per cent and the top 5 per cent were relatively small. These groups were: the four countries with a British science education tradition, Australia, England, New Zealand and Scotland; the Northern European countries, together with the United States of America and the Romance language countries including the Belgiums, France and Italy. Among these groupings of countries there are common traditions in science education which influence the level of performance in science of the more able students, whether or not, large or small proportions of an age group remain at school at the terminal secondary school stage.

During the past 20 years the reform movement in science education in the United States has had a significant impact on science programs in other countries. However, it is necessary to recognize that science education in the United States serves students of much greater ranges of ability, with rather different educational and occupational expectations than are to be found in other countries. Thus it is important that each country should be fully aware of the composition of its student group and its science education traditions before it undertakes a program of reform in science education.

Sex Differences in Participation and Achievement in Science

In some countries the educational opportunities for male and female students differ markedly, and these differences are not only more evident in the areas of science and mathematics but the consequences of differences between the sexes in achievement in science and mathematics are greater than for other subjects with respect to occupational and career opportunities. It is to be expected that sex differences in participation and achievement in science across countries will give rise to differences between countries in the way in which science is taught and science curricula are developed, as well as to differences between the sexes in attitudes towards science and in aspirations for entry into a scientifically based occupation.

At all stages of education beyond the years of compulsory schooling Comber and Keeves (1973) showed that there were striking differences between countries in the relative participation of male and female students in education and in different types of science courses. In most countries, however, physics and chemistry were subjects taken largely by male students, and biology courses were taken, in the main, by female students. In spite of differences between the sexes in participation in the different branches of science, it was clear that not only did boys perform consistently better than girls in the sciences, but the gap between the sexes in achievement widened as students grew older from the 10-year-old to the 14-year-old to the 17- and 18-year-old age levels. Furthermore the sex differences in achievement were much more pronounced in the physical sciences than in the biological sciences. In addition, it was not only in the cognitive area that sex differences were apparent, but also in the area of attitudes since boys showed consistently more favorable attitudes towards science than did girls and responded more favorably to a science interests and activities scale.

However, some countries provided exceptions to these general patterns. For example, in England at both the Population I and Population II levels, the girls performed better than the boys in biology. In Flemish-speaking Belgium, though not in French-speaking Belgium, at both Population II and Population IV, the girls outscored the boys in the area of chemistry. While this result might have arisen from bias in the samples, it might well have reflected the low level of emphasis given to the study of chemistry in this school system. The low scores in this aspect of science suggested that little chemistry was taught at either level. An interesting general finding was that there were not marked differences between the sexes on items that assessed knowledge of science but there were substantial differences on those items that assessed an understanding of science.

It is interesting to speculate on the origins of the sex differences in attitudes, aspirations, participation and achievement in science, as the existing circumstances require that some action should be taken if possible, to rectify this undesirable and potentially wasteful situation. It had been hoped that further evidence would have emerged from a comparison of the sizes of the sex differences in achievement and attitudes when boys and girls were taught together in coeducational schools. However, the initial evidence obtained from analyses of the data relating to this issue proved very confused. Kelly (1978) undertook further detailed analyses and in summarizing her findings drew attention to the fact that at each age level tested the standardized sex differences in achievement in science were surprisingly uniform across countries. Thus although there have been traditionally marked differences between countries in attitudes towards the role of women in society, and although in many countries these attitudes are undergoing rapid change, no one developed country had excessively large or excessively small sex differences. The size of the sex differences in achievement was more related, as discussed above, to the nature of the subject area than to the country involved.

Kelly sought to test a range of critical hypotheses, namely:
1. Girls achieve less well than boys in science because society does not encourage or expect girls to achieve as well as boys.
2. Science is presented in schools in a way more suited to boys than girls.
3. Girls achieve better with teachers who emphasize the textbook and verbal methods of learning than with teachers who emphasize laboratory and discovery methods.
4. Girls achieve better in science in girls-only schools than in coeducational schools.
5. Girls achieve better in science with women science teachers.

However, these five hypotheses were all clearly rejected after detailed analyses.

There was, nevertheless some support from the available evidence for the following propositions.

1. Sex differences are reduced when girls have taken as many science courses as boys.
2. The lower performance of girls compared with boys in science is associated with their holding less favorable attitudes towards science than boys.

It is clear that this problem both needs and warrants a very thorough investigation, since the pattern of findings is different to that obtained from a study of sex differences in achievement in mathematics, when it might have been expected that sex differences in performance in these two subject areas would be strongly related. The similarity across countries in the sex differences in attitudes, participation and achievement may arise from the largely common origins of the science curricula which have been introduced across countries during the past 100 years. It would appear that the development of mathematics courses has taken place over a much longer period of time, that arithmetic and mathematics have maintained a central place in the curriculum of the grammar schools for several centuries, and that there are stronger differences between countries in their traditions of mathematics teaching. Consequently a thorough investigation into the nature and origins of the differences between the sexes in attitudes, participation and achievement in science, should consider the establishment and development of the present science curricula across countries and seek to explain how the manner in which the curricula were derived has influenced differences between the sexes in societal expectations for the study of science in schools. Only when such an understanding has been achieved, would it be possible to make the necessary changes in the science curriculum and the manner in which science is presented in schools in order to rectify the lack of equity that would appear to exist.

The Effects of Schooling

Over the past 20 years there has been a growing concern about the level of resources allocated to schools and the effects of increasing these resources on the quality of education. In the field of science education in Australia, for example, very considerable resources have been made available in order to improve the quality of science teaching through the provision of significantly better conditions for learning science by the building of new science laboratories in schools throughout the country. However, an evaluation of the effects of these improved facilities has resulted in equivocal findings (Ainley, 1978). The results of the Survey of Equality of Educational Opportunity undertaken by James Coleman and his colleagues (Coleman *et al.*, 1966) were widely publicized and their gloomy view, that schools brought little influence to bear on a child's achievement that was independent of home background and general social context has been supported by subsequent reanalyses of the same body of data (Jencks, *et al.* 1972). Clearly the issues are of immense importance to policymakers, administrators and to teachers in classrooms, and further examination is warranted into the effects of both the conditions of learning provided in schools and the time spent at school in learning science on the outcomes of education, and in particular, on educational achievement. Both topics, the conditions of learning and time spent on science will be considered in the sections that follow.

The Conditions of Learning Science

An investigation of the effects of the conditions of learning science on the outcomes of achievement and attitudes cannot be undertaken without the development of a causal model concerned with the interrelationships between social context, home background, educational provision and outcomes. The model is necessarily complex and involves a network of interrelated variables. Simple bivariate techniques are both inappropriate and inadequate for the examination of these issues. Contrary to the criticisms advanced by Pedhazur (1982) extensive debate was undertaken by all concerned in the IEA Six Subject Study on the development of a theoretical model in which home and student background influenced the type of school and type of program within the school, that influenced the learning conditions provided by the school, and that in turn influenced the kindred variables of student habits, motivations and expectations, and finally the outcome of science achievement. This model and its development was argued fully in the report of the first science study and is presented in Fig. 1 in diagrammatic form.

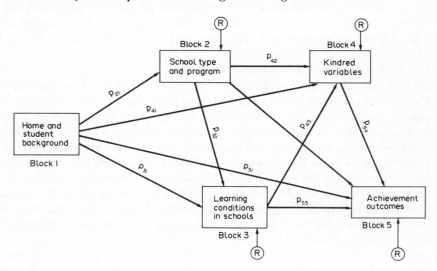

FIG. 1. Causal Model for School Achievement

Platt (1975) in his discussion of the model was correct in his suggestion that home and student background, type of school and type of program involved "earlier learning conditions", while the third block of variables involved "recent learning conditions". Coleman (1975) and Platt (1975) in discussing models used in the IEA studies were critical of the analyses carried out and the presentation of results in terms of the proportion of variance accounted for. The researchers engaged in the study would not, I believe, accept that the model was in error, but that the procedures of analysis were not sufficiently far advanced in 1972 to permit the use, with confidence, of alternative analytical techniques. The subsequent development of these analytical techniques has endorsed the usefulness of the forming of composites or rosettes of variables instead of blocks of variables, and indicating the magnitudes of the effects of the composites with respect to the criterion measure of science achievement, by regression coefficients, instead of using the variance contributed by the entry of each block in a stagewise regression analysis of the model with science achievement as the outcome. There is little doubt that the results would be substantially the same, namely, that in the study of science the learning conditions which are operating in the schools do not merely have a trivial effect on science achievement, but have a significant influence. However, a substantial problem arises in the generalization of these findings and in the statement of their policy implications, in so far as within each country the pattern of variables included within the block concerned with the learning conditions in schools is very different. At the different levels of schooling, and in the different countries, and at the two different levels of analysis, betwen schools and between students, different variables entered the regression analyses and different factors would appear to be operating.

In Table 1, information is recorded on the proportion of variance accounted for by the third block of variables, the learning conditions in schools, which were entered into the regression analyses. These analyses were carried out at three population levels, across the two levels of analysis and in the 19 different countries. It should be noted that, in general, substantially less variance is accounted for by the learning conditions in the schools in the between students analyses than in the between schools analyses, although the between students analyses at Population IV are an exception to this statement. In most countries the factors associated with the learning conditions in schools are making a strong contribution to accounting for the differences between schools and between students in levels of achievement. It must be noted that this contribution is made after such factors as type of school and type of program within school, where appropriate, have been allowed for. The two countries where relatively small proportions of variance have been explained are England and Japan at the 10-year-old (Population I) and the 14-year-old (Population II) levels. These data would, in general, appear to establish beyond question that factors associated with the provision in school for science programs cannot be dismissed as trivial as would appear to be the case in the field of reading (see Thorndike, 1973).

TABLE 1

Summary Table of Proportion of Variance Accounted for by the Learning Conditions in Schools in Regression Analyses with Science Achievement as the Criterion

Table records % of Variance	Between Schools			Between Students		
	Pop I	Pop II	Pop IV	Pop I	Pop II	Pop IV
Australia	−a	15	12	−a	11	20
Belgium (Flemish)	−b	−b	−a	8	12	−a
Belgium (French)	−b	−b	−a	21	−b	−a
Chile	36	15	12	9	6	8
England	2	4	17	3	7	41
Federal Republic of Germany	34	26	10	10	14	8
Finland	11	12	17	4	10	7
France	−a	−a	6	−a	−a	5
Hungary	26	7	13	7	5	10
India	28	21	45	20	8	17
Iran	13	−b	8	6	9	4
Italy	12	5	22	4	6	16
Japan	2	10	−a	1	4	−a
The Netherlands	8	12	19	7	10	31
New Zealand	−a	20	25	−a	8	31
Scotland	5	3	21	5	9	34
Sweden	11	44	30	5	7	20
Thailand	−a	−b	−a	−a	23	−a
United States	8	11	13	9	7	8
Mean	15	15	18	8	9	17
Range	34	41	39	20	19	37

Note: a. Did not test at this level
      b. Data inadequate for detailed analyses

Among the factors reoccurring in the analyses at each level, and for each population and in each country, were those associated with participation, years spent in the study of science, time spent on the study of science in the current year, and time spent on science homework, as well as the time spent on all homework. The effects of such variables warrant a more detailed examination which will be undertaken in the next section.

Learning Time and Science Achievement

J. B. Carroll (1963) has proposed a model of school learning. The five factors included in the model were grouped under two headings: (1) determinants of time needed for learning; and (2) determinants of time spent on learning. The second group of factors proved in the First IEA Science Study to be strongly related to achievement in science. In order to provide a full account of the nature and range of the factors associated with determinants of time spent on learning the results which will be presented in the following section are restricted to the findings obtained in one country, where the opportunity to replicate the analyses across six state systems of education, provided confirmation of the strength of the observed relationships.

These analyses were carried out at three distinct levels, namely: between systems, between schools within systems, and between students within systems. The first named analyses sought relationships between variables to explain the differences that existed between systems. The second and third sets of analyses sought replications and similarities in effects that would support the stating of generalizations which applied to schools and students within these systems. The advantages of undertaking analyses within a set of generally parallel systems are that the confounding effects of variables that might intrude and distort relationships between time and science achievement are eliminated. Experimental studies that would control for these confounding effects by randomization are impossible to contrive with sufficiently large numbers for clear findings to be established. Consequently, two different procedures are available to exercise some control. First, control is introduced by restricting the range of factors, which is appropriate provided sufficient variation exists with respect to the factors under examination. Secondly, the use of aggregated data with an adequate number of students included within the aggregates provides control over the random fluctuations in the practices of individual teachers as well as the random behavior of individual students. Under these circumstances, it might be expected that, if relationships existed, they would be observed more clearly. Furthermore, since time is a variable with a recognized metric, the unstandardized regression coefficients have a meaning across different levels of analysis.

In Table 2 data are presented (from Keeves, 1974a) for the six Australian state systems of education at the Population II (14-year-old) and Population IV (terminal secondary school) levels, with respect to the mean science achievement test scores and the mean time spent on the

John P. Keeves

TABLE 2

Achievement in Science and Time Spent in Learning — Australian Data

Date of Testing 1970	Population II			Population IV				
State	Number of Students	Mean Science Score	Time on Science Hours/Week	Number of Students	Mean Science Score	Time on Science Hours/Week	Science Homework Hours/Week	Total Time Hours/Week
New South Wales	701	23.48	3.28	554	24.21	4.52	2.98	7.50
Victoria	699	20.81	2.58	462	23.55	4.37	3.58	7.95
Queensland	668	25.24	3.96	466	25.43	4.85	3.91	8.76
South Australia	786	26.49	3.95	502	29.34	5.26	4.73	9.99
Western Australia	669	26.46	3.67	411	25.65	5.00	3.80	8.80
Tasmania	631	21.64	3.31	176	25.72	6.30	3.34	9.64
Relation with Criterion								
Correlation r (product-moment coefficient)			0.88			0.45	0.84	0.85
Regression a (intercept on axis)			9.79			19.10	15.10	9.94
b (slope of regression line)			4.12			1.29	2.83	1.79

study of science. The data presented were collected in the First IEA Science Study in 1970. Unfortunately, in this study data were not available to estimate time spent on the study of science during earlier years, largely because in most of the school systems, time for the study of science was not tightly prescribed. Simple regression analyses were undertaken to investigate the existence of relationships between the measures of time and science achievement.

The strength of these relationships is clear, and it is estimated that, for each additional hour spent on the average in the learning of science during the current year at the lower secondary school level, there would be an expected gain on average in science achievement, as indicated by the slope of the regression line, of approximately four score points (b = 4.12) and that, for each hour per week spent at the terminal secondary school level, there would be an expected gain on average in science achievement of approximately two score points (b = 1.79). At the terminal secondary school level, time spent at home on science homework made a far greater contribution to learning than time spent in the classroom at school. The expected gain on average in score on the science achievement test was approximately three score points (b = 2.83) for each additional hour per week spent on homework. At the 14-year-old (Population II) level time spent on homework did not contribute significantly to science achievement and the results have been omitted from Table 2.

The existence of such relationships between time spent in school on learning science and achievement test scores is strong evidence that schools have a clearly identifiable influence on the learning of science. It is evident that in the planning of courses of instruction in schools the consequences of curricular time cannot wisely be ignored.

It is also of interest to examine whether the existence of relationships at the aggregated level of the school system is supported by corresponding relationships at the levels of both between schools and between students. In Table 3 results are presented from the between students and the between schools regression analyses with achievement in science as the criterion for the different time related variables which were entered into the regression analyses in a stagewise analysis of the data after the Learning Condition variables (in block 3) had been entered. Variables were defined differently at the different levels of analysis (between schools and between students) and at the two different population levels in order to form appropriate composite variables for entry into the regression equations. Nevertheless, the evidence is unequivocal. Variables associated with the study of science and time spent in the study of science as well as on science homework are strongly related to achievement outcomes. The replication of effects across the six state samples and for Australia as a whole strongly supports this claim.

TABLE 3
*Time Related Regression Coefficients***

Population II (14-Year-Old level)	Taking Science	Hours Study Science	Hours Homework	Science Homework
Between Students				
Australia	2.34 (0.06)	0.41 (0.05)	2.11 (0.17)	0.44 (0.03)
New South Wales	*	*	1.69 (0.13)	
Victoria	*	*	1.35 (0.11)	
Queensland	4.81 (0.15)	0.58 (0.11)	1.78 (0.14)	
South Australia	4.74 (0.10)	0.80 (0.08)	1.87 (0.13)	
Western Australia	4.60 (0.11)	0.45 (0.06)	2.37 (0.19)	
Tasmania	*	0.72 (0.08)	2.43 (0.19)	
Between Schools				
Australia				2.01 (0.26)

Population IV (terminal secondary school level)	Years Study of Science	Science Study and Homework	Total Science Homework
Between Students			
Australia	*	1.70 (0.45)	
New South Wales	*	1.33 (0.34)	
Victoria	0.94 (0.18)	1.63 (0.45)	
Queensland	0.42 (0.10)	2.09 (0.52)	
South Australia	0.73 (0.13)	0.99 (0.24)	
Western Australia	1.33 (0.23)	0.80 (0.17)	
Tasmania	1.57 (0.30)	1.02 (0.31)	
Between Schools			
Australia			1.00 (0.16)

* Variable deleted by regression in the stagewise regression analysis.
** Metric coefficients recorded with standardized coefficients in parenthesis.

It is clear for those responsible for the planning of the science curriculum within the schools, if it is considered desirable to increase the level of performance that is expected from students with respect to identified achievement outcomes in the subject area of science, then it is necessary to provide adequate time for these outcomes to be achieved.

It is evident that if more time is given to science teaching in the curriculum and to homework in science, then, on average, increased learning will take place. However, such time can only be obtained at the expense of other subjects in the curriculum. It is, nevertheless, necessary to recognize that the model advanced by Carroll has much more to say about learning within schools than is contained in these simple dictums.

Keeves (1972) carried out a longitudinal study of science and mathematics learning in Canberra schools, at the same time as the First IEA Science Study was being undertaken as a cross-sectional investigation in 19 countries. He showed that the attentiveness of the student to the learning tasks prescribed by the teacher was a significant factor influencing achievement over a school year. While prior achievement in science had an influence on attentiveness as did the motivation of the student, such factors as: the press for work habits and order, the affiliation of the teacher with the class, the interaction between the teacher and the individual student, the emphasis on language and oral work and the extent of guidance provided in academic work were also found to influence the attentiveness of the student in science classes. Thus it is not only the amount of time prescribed for the study of science in the school curriculum that is related to learning outcomes. The use made by teachers and students of this time is also important. Prescribed time is specified in the curriculum of the school. The effective use of the time prescribed, is related to the skill of the teacher and the conditions operating in schools.

Malleable Variables Influencing Achievement

Rosier (1974) has shown that the variables included in the regression equation for students in Australian schools after the Block 3 stage, at which the learning conditions in schools were included, were: whether or not the student was studying science, hours spent on the study of science, hours spent on homework — all variables associated with time spent. There were two other important variables: emphasis on practical work and investigation, and the hours spent by the teacher in preparation. Likewise at the terminal secondary school level the important variables included: years spent studying science, time spent in the study of science and on science homework, the emphasis on practical experience in the study of science, an emphasis on the acquisition of information as well as teaching to think scientifically, and the availability of laboratory assistants and ancillary staff. In summarizing the analyses

that had been carried out, Rosier suggested that in addition to the time-
related factors there seemed to be a cluster of interrelated factors which
influenced achievement in science. While each factor by itself might
make only a small contribution to effective learning, the significant
factors when taken together were interconnected and contributed to the
view:

> the effective learning of science takes place in a consistent school environ-
> ment where students receive competent systematic instruction in carefully
> structured science courses (Rosier, 1974: 187).

There would appear to be clear evidence from these analyses that the
learning conditions provided in Australian schools contribute to the
students' level of achievement in science. Moreover, the evidence is
supportive of the key factors in the model of school learning advanced
by Carroll. The findings of the Equality of Educational Opportunity
survey (Coleman, 1966) that schools contribute little to learning
outcomes must be challenged, and the policymakers encouraged to act
on the evidence that the availability of laboratory assistants and ancillary
staff are factors related to gains in achievement. Moreover, teachers
should recognize in the conditions for the effective learning of science
stated above encouragement to plan carefully their programs to
maximize student learning.

Towards the Future

Empirical research into the teaching of science for some would seem
to assume a static situation. However, over the past 100 years science
education has not remained static, and will continue to evolve. The signs
are that science teaching around the world is entering another period of
rapid change. Kurokawa (1984) has suggested that over the next 15
years planning will take place for a third phase of educational reform. In
many of the countries represented in IEA the first phase occurred about
100 years ago with the establishment of universal primary education,
which was both free and compulsory. In some developing countries this
phase has been telescoped into a relatively few years. The second phase
took place after World War II and has been concerned with the
establishment of universal secondary education and the provision of
widespread opportunities for tertiary education. The extent to which
the countries involved in IEA studies have accomplished successfully this
second phase varies considerably, depending on the financial resources
available to them and the extent of their technological development.
However, we must recognize as Torsten Husén has warned us in his
challenging book, *The School in Question* (Husén, 1980) that universal
secondary education has been accompanied by very substantial problems
since some youth in developed countries display a marked alienation to
formal academic secondary education. It is evident that the future of

education in these countries does not lie in producing more of the same at the secondary and tertiary levels but in developing the more flexible approaches to teaching and learning which could be provided by the new technology. It is becoming clear that there are very significant rewards for those countries and those individuals who can remain at the forefront in scientific and technological research and development. For the future, it will not be just the learning that is achieved at school that determines a career at university and beyond, but rather the learning that is accomplished throughout a working life which is achieved by building upon the foundations laid down at the primary, secondary and tertiary levels. In the third phase widespread recurrent education programs will become a reality. The new frontiers of education will not exist in the secondary and tertiary institutions but in non-formal approaches to education. This is the scenario that faces education in IEA countries over the next 15 years, and we must consolidate and extend our provision and programs at the secondary and tertiary levels towards these ends. Since this relatively rapid movement towards the third phase of educational reform has been triggered off by recent scientific and technological developments, it is inevitable that science and technology should play a central role in the programs that evolve during this third phase.

The basic structure of the science curriculum of our secondary schools and universities was laid down in Germany and Britain during the latter years of the 19th and early years of the 20th Centuries. The emphasis in science education on experimental work would appear to have developed primarily in Britain and the United States at about this time. However, the 1930s, 1940s and 1950s saw, particularly in the United States of America, but also in many other countries the advance of the Progressive Education Movement and a weakening of coherent science courses in our schools. In the late 1950s and the 1960s, marked advances took place initially in the United States and Britain, but which subsequently reverberated around the world, in the fields of science and mathematics education. As a consequence it has become widely accepted that all students during their years of schooling should be studying both science and mathematics in courses that are appropriate for their aptitudes and stages of cognitive development.

In 1970, at a time which must now be seen as near to the middle of the period of curriculum reform in science education, the IEA conducted an International Study of Science Achievement in 19 countries. This study reported on the science curricula of the 19 countries and on the factors that were found to be influencing achievement in science not only between countries but also between schools and between students. A bench mark has been provided in those countries for further studies at regular intervals of the science curricula of the schools.

During the latter part of the 1970s interest in science education declined markedly. In many parts of the world there was a concern for a rapidly rising world population, fear of a nuclear war, and the consequences for the environment of uncontrolled industrial expansion. Science was seen by many to be the villain, and the reaction was to let science courses in schools decline. However, since 1981 there has been a marked turn around of interest in science education in many countries, but perhaps not all. The impact of scientific and technological development has been sudden and for many unexpected. These changes in technology are already influencing the ways in which we work and play. Although the electronic computer has been widely introduced into industry, business and also more recently the home, it is yet to have a significant influence on the classroom. Industrial robots are already used in some countries and are likely to become widespread. However, these are only two of the more obvious manifestations of technological change on our lives, that are based upon the rapid growth of science in recent decades. As a consequence there is a world wide shortage of highly skilled personnel who have a sound basic knowledge of science and technology and who have the flexibility to adapt to rapidly changing circumstances. The call is for a renewed interest in science education in schools.

There would appear to be three demands being made of science education. First, there is a need for all members of our societies to have a knowledge and understanding of the fundamental principles of science, in all its disciplines, physics, chemistry, biology, earth sciences, as well as of those sectors lying at the interfaces between these disciplines, that would provide a foundation for further learning in both science and technology at the post-secondary school level and at recurring stages throughout their lives. Secondly, there is a need for all members of our societies to understand the nature of the technological development that is currently taking place and the manner in which it could influence their lives in the office, the factory and the home. This is a task that must be undertaken primarily within science courses at school, because an understanding of technology is necessarily based on a knowledge and understanding of science. Thirdly, it is recognized that the environment in which we live is extremely delicately balanced, and that many effects arise at times of rapid societal and technological change which could displace this balance and could in the long term destroy our world. Again an understanding of the issues associated with the conservation of the environment are necessarily based on a knowledge and understanding of science, and cannot wisely be left to be covered in other areas of the curriculum of the schools. However, it is also necessary to recognize that the issues associated with both technological development and the environment are so great, that all that occurs in the schools is only an initial introduction. There must be a reliance on recurrent education programs to ensure that all members of our societies remain well informed on these issues.

The task for the Second IEA Science Study which is being conducted in 26 countries is to document both within each country and across the countries taking part, the state of science education programs in the schools in the years 1983–84. The major purpose of mapping the science curriculum in this way is to ensure that the developments that must be planned for the science curriculum in the future are built upon a soundly based knowledge of what is currently taking place in the schools in the wide range of countries involved in the study. For most countries it will be possible to make comparisons between the science curricula across countries at the three levels of the upper primary school, the middle secondary school and the terminal secondary school. There are very substantial benefits to be obtained from systematically planned comparisons across a wide range of countries because without such a framework for comparison, each country is limited at best, to superficial comparisons between itself and its immediate neighbours in a non-systematic way. Moreover, for 10 of the countries taking part in the Second IEA Science Study there is the possibility of making comparisons between the science curricula of the schools at the present time and in 1970, 14 years earlier. Thus the documented changes in the science curricula can be examined and can be used to inform the debate on the changes to be planned for science education in the future.

In conclusion, the purposes of this Second IEA Science Study which is currently in progress are:

1. to map the science curricula of the countries engaged in the study,
2. to develop a better understanding of the factors that influence the outcomes of science education, and
3. to make recommendations on ways in which the science curriculum and the conditions under which science is taught in the schools might be changed at a time when not only are new developments in science education being planned in a significant number of countries but also at a time when long term developments associated with the third phase of educational reform are being considered.

These are challenging tasks.

References

Ainley, J. G. *The Australian Science Facilities Program. A Study of Its Influence on Science Education in Australian Schools.* Hawthorn, Victoria: ACER, 1978.

Armstrong, H. E. *The Teaching of Scientific Method and other Papers on Education.* London: Macmillan, 1903.

Atkin, J. M. and Burnett, R. W. "Science Education". In R. L. Ebel (Ed.). *Encyclopedia of Educational Research.* (Fourth Edition). Toronto, Canada: Macmillan, 1969, pp.1192–1203.

44   *John P. Keeves*

Baez, A. V. *Innovation in Science Education — World Wide.* Paris: The Unesco Press, 1976.

Bruner, J. *The Process of Education.* Cambridge, Mass.: Harvard University Press, 1960.

Carroll, J. B. A model of school learning. *Teachers College Record,* 1963, **64**, 723–733.

Coleman, J. S. Methods and results in the IEA Studies of effects of school on learning. *Review of Educational Research,* 1975, **45**(3), 366.

Coleman, J. S. *et al. Equality of Educational Opportunity.* Washington: US Government Printing Office (2 Vols), 1966.

Comber, L. C. and Keeves, J. P. *Science Education in Nineteen Countries: An Empirical Study.* Stockholm: Almqvist and Wiksell and New York: Wiley (Halsted Press), 1973.

Conant, J. B. *On Understanding Science: An Historical Approach.* New Haven, Conn.: Yale University Press, 1947.

Fowler, H. S. *Secondary School Science Teaching Practices.* New York: The Center for Applied Research in Education, 1964.

Heyneman, S. P., Farrell, J. P. and Sepulveda-Stuardo, M. A. Text books and Achievement in Developing Countries: What we Know? *Journal of Curriculum Studies,* 1981, **13**, 227–246.

Heyneman, S. P. and Loxley, W. A. The Effect of Primary-School Quality on Academic Achievement across Twenty-nine High and Low Income Countries. *American Journal of Sociology,* 1983, **88**, 1162.

Husén, T. *The School in Question.* Oxford: Oxford University Press, 1980.

Ingle, R. and Jennings, A. *Science in Schools Which Way Now?* London: University of London, Institute of Education, 1981.

Jencks, C., Smith, M., Acland, H., Bane, M. J., Cohen, D., Gintis, H., Heys, B. and Michelson, S. *Inequality: A Reassessment of the Effect of Family and Schooling in America.* New York: Basic Books, 1972.

Keeves, J. P. *Educational Environment and Student Achievement.* Stockholm: Almqvist and Wiksell and Hawthorn, Victoria: ACER, 1972.

Keeves, J. P. *The Effects of the Conditions of Learning in the Schools on Educational Achievement.* IEA (Australia Report). 1974: **2**, Hawthorn, Victoria: ACER, 1974a.

Keeves, J. P. The IEA Science Project. In K. Hecht (Ed.) *Implementation of Curricula in Science Education.* Köln: Deutsche Unesco-Commission, 1974b.

Kelly, A. *Girls and Science: An International Study of Sex Differences in School Science Achievement.* Stockholm: Almqvist and Wiksell, 1978.

Kurokawa, Y. Human Resources and Economic Development. Paper presented at the Regional Seminar on the Contribution of Interdisciplinary Research to the Development of Education in Asia and the Pacific. 11 to 20 July 1984. Tokyo, Japan.

Lockard, J. D. *Twenty Years of Science and Mathematics Curriculum Development: The Tenth Report of the International Clearinghouse.* College Park, Maryland: International Clearinghouse Science Teaching Center, University of Maryland, 1977.

Marx, G. (Ed.) *Structure of Matter in the School.* Proceedings of the Fourth Danube Seminar, Balaton, Hungary, 10–12 October 1978. Budapest: Roland Eötvös University, 1979.

Pedhazur, E. J. *Multiple Regression in Behavioral Research: Explanation and Prediction.* New York: Holt, Rinehart and Winston, 1982.

Platt, W. J. Policy making and international studies in educational evaluation. In A. C. Purves and D. V. Levine, (Eds.). *Educational Policy and International Assessment.* Berkeley, Ca.: McCutchan, 1975, pp.33–59.

Rosier, M. J. Factors associated with learning science in Australian secondary schools. *Comparative Education Review.* 1974, **18** (2), 180–197.

Thorndike, R. L. *Reading Comprehension Education in Fifteen Countries.* Stockholm: Almqvist and Wiksell, and New York: John Wiley (Halsted Press), 1973.

Welch, W. W. Twenty Years of Science Curriculum Development: A Look Back. In D. C. Berliner (Ed.). *Review of Research in Education,* Vol. **7**, 1979, pp. 282–306.

The IEA Literature and Composition Studies and their Elucidation of the Nature and Formation of Interpretive and Rhetorical Communities

ALAN C. PURVES

Background

In 1964, at a point when the IEA First Mathematics Study was nearing completion, there was a clear sense that the IEA studies should continue and be expanded to other school subjects. One of the original members of IEA, A. W. Foshay of Teachers College, Columbia, thought it might be possible to study various aspects of mother-tongue learning, and encouraged by Torsten Husén, who has had a long interest in language and literature, he turned to colleagues at Columbia, one of whom was myself. Foshay's initial notion was that studies in the mother-tongue, particularly in the critical reading of literature and the rhetorical aspects of composition would give an insight into the national character.

Foshay's notion was not a new one; it followed from scholarship in the history of ideas, rhetorical history, and the history of literary criticism. Each of these disciplines had clearly demonstrated that there had existed in many countries and cultures deep shifts in the ways people approached literary texts, in the way they organized narratives and other types of writing, and the way they thought about various phenomena. Foshay argued that these shifts were reflected in the school curriculum and that the shifts had ramifications outside the language classroom. If a student learns that there is an appropriate way to discuss a literary text and an appropriate way to organize a composition, that student would transfer these styles of reading and writing into other areas of learning and even, perhaps, into everyday life. By studying these phenomena in school, one might gain an insight into some of these constituents of what we call culture in both a literary and an anthropological sense.

At the early meetings we discussed the issue and realized that we needed to make a choice between literature and composition because to study both would be too large an undertaking. Since my current interests lay in literature and since a study of reading comprehension was being undertaken by Professor Robert Thorndike, we decided to tackle literature first. A review of the previous research indicated that nothing quite like this had been undertaken, and that we were, to a certain extent charting new territory. We decided that the first step would have to be one of exploratory research.

Through the IEA contacts, we gathered a selection of compositions by secondary school students in Belgium, The Federal Republic of Germany, England and the United States. The students were asked to read one of the number of short stories (ones which existed in translated versions in the three languages) and to comment on the story. The students were given no more specific instructions. By this time we had acquired the services of a trilingual assistant, Victoria Rippere, who collaborated on the early phases of the study. What we noticed was that there appeared to be similarities in approach to writing about literature within classes and within countries, but the problem remained of defining those similarities. Over the course of 3 years, we developed a content-analytic scheme, which we called *The Elements of Writing about a Literary Work* (Purves and Rippere, 1968). This scheme was able to define what a student was writing about (such as a character, language, or literary devices) and the illocutionary force of the comment, whether it was personal testimony, descriptive, classificatory, interpretive, or evaluative. We were able to classify sentences and clauses of a student's writing about a literary text with an inter-rater reliability of .8.

Armed with this preparatory work, we took a proposal to an IEA meeting where, as Postlethwaite has remarked (Article 6) there was some scepticism. There was also some concern that a descriptive study was not enough; there should be some way of defining and measuring achievement cross-nationally. This aspect of a study we set about, but our main interest was in the descriptive part, and it is on this part that my chapter will dwell, for it is, I believe, from the descriptive aspect that the most fruitful insights about curriculum and evaluation have emerged. At the 1966 meeting of IEA in Hamburg, thanks in great measure to the encouragement of Torsten Husén and Gilbert De Landsheere, the literature study was formally launched with nine countries participating (ten educational systems since Belgium became divided into the Flemish and French-speaking systems). Although the study provided results about the achievement aspect and other measures that are worthy of note, I shall focus on the descriptive aspect of the study, since, together with a similar aspect of the study of Written Composition, it provides a point of continuity and a common theme, the theme of "community".

The Idea of Communities

The term "community" comes from the metaphor that Stanley Fish (1980) used so effectively to describe what happens in literature classes and may be broadened in its scope to encompass the larger world of language teaching. In describing literature instruction as the formation of "interpretive communities" (i.e., groups bound together by the way they perceive and interpret literary texts), Fish is continuing the post-structuralist trend in criticism that denies the authority for meaning to the text and to the writer but offers a counter to the extreme solipsism of the post-structuralists. His major thesis is that interpretation is bound by the norms and conventions of the community that an individual inhabits, which communities are to a great extent bounded by language, and particularly by a common semantic space. Fish's point is not novel; it has been a commonplace of linguistics since de Saussure (1916) and, later, Gumperz and Hymes (1974) and their depiction of speech communities and how people learn to be members of them.

To argue the position briefly, but in terms somewhat different from those of Fish, I would define a text as a linguistic utterance of a writer. Any linguistic utterance has two properties: one is a semantic, structural and stylistic core that is shared by the writer and many contemporary readers; the second is an overlay of associations held by the writer and not necessarily shared. This dichotomy is one that is again, a common-place of language study which distinguishes in systems of meaning the nucleus and the periphery (Ryabova, 1969). Recent research in schema theory (Goodman, 1984) indicates that the core and overlay exists at the level of the word, of course, but also at the level of larger units of discourse, such as paragraphs and stories. Earlier genre theory had espoused a similar position, that a reader was given a signal that a text was of a particular genre and so had certain expectations, which the text either fulfilled or denied.

But the issue is, as Fish observes, more complex still, for readers have long read texts with varied sets of presuppositions about how the text should be read. A philologist may look at a text differently than a moralist. In her recent *The Reader, The Text and the Poem* (1978), Louise Rosenblatt observes that readers may read a text "efferently" or "aesthetically" that is to take away a message or to take pleasure in the act of contemplating a text. Within the class of aesthetic reading exist several sub-classes, which Fish calls "interpretive communities." Communities share certain assumptions or what I. A. Richards (1929) called "stock responses" (such as the Marxists' assumption of the socio-political overtones of any work). These communities may be large or small; they may persist over long periods of time, and they appear to perpetuate themselves primarily through educational systems both formal and informal.

As readers, then, individuals inhabit communities which make meaning, and the potential variety of communities is vast given the number of possible aspects of a "text" that could be discussed and the number of approaches — personal analytic, classificatory, interpretive, and evaluative — that could be taken. A community intends to influence its members' very initial approach to a text and to guide their mental operations as they work through to an interpretation. Some of these communities might be determined by a general culture. For example, many European students reading William Carlos William's *The Use of Force* (in which a doctor fails to persuade a girl to open her mouth and finally forces it open and sees in his action a horrible violation) believe the doctor acts professionally throughout and criticize the girl. They appear to do so because the cultural norm holds that doctors are always right — even when brutal. Other communities, however, are determined by educational systems and individual teachers, as Fish demonstrates in his title essay, "Is there a text in this class?" which shows how he has channeled his students to be members of his community.

The Literature Study

Such a theory about communities needs verification, a description of what the cultural and educational differences are (if such there be) and an analysis of those factors might help define those differences. In the IEA literature study, we made up an inventory based on an analysis of the essays of students in several countries. The inventory (See Fig. 1) was presented to students three times, once in a questionnaire asking them to identify the five questions they thought were most important in dealing with literature in general, and twice more after they had read each of two short stories. We could, therefore, get a sense of which questions students thought would be most important in dealing with literature *in the abstract* and which of those questions were important after actually *reading* various stories. We gave the same twenty questions to the students' teachers. We also asked a group of university professors, curriculum specialists, and teacher trainers in each country to rate the questions as to their importance in teaching or in the curriculum in general.

These questionnaires, together with cognitive tests of comprehension and background and interest questionnaires were administered to two populations: the first included full-time students aged 14:00 to 14.11 years; the second, students in the pre-university year of secondary school (about age 18). The first population in most countries included students who were in some sort of general schooling. The countries involved in the study were Belgium (Flemish), Belgium (French), Chile, England, Finland, Iran, Italy, New Zealand, Sweden, and the United States.

110 Engagement with work:	Is this a proper subject for a story?
120 Involvement with form:	What emotions does the story arouse in me?
130 Involvement with content:	Are any of the characters in the story like people I know?
210 Perception of language:	Has the writer used words or sentences differently from the way people usually write?
220 Perception of literary devices:	What kinds of metaphors (or comparisons), images (or references to things outside the story) or other writer's devices are used in the story?
230 Perception of content:	What happens in the story?
240 Relation of form to content:	How is the way of telling the story related to what the story is about?
250 Perception of plot, structure or organization:	How does the story build up? How is it organized?
260 Perception of tone, attitude, and mood:	What is the writer's opinion of, or attitude toward the people in the story?
270 Perception—literary or generic classification:	What type of story is this one? Is it like any other story I know?
280 Perception—contextual classification:	When was the story written? What is the historical background of the story and its writer? Does the fact that the author is _____ tell me anything about the story?
300 Interpretation of past as key to the whole:	Is there any one part of the story that explains the whole story?
310 Interpretation of form:	Is there anything in the story that has a hidden meaning?
320 Interpretation of content:	How can we explain the way the people behave in the story?
330 Mimetic interpretation:	What does the story tell me about people I know?
340 Typological interpretation:	Does the story tell me anything about people or ideas in general?
350 Moral interpretation:	Is there a lesson to be learned from the story?
410 Affective evaluation:	Does the story succeed in getting me involved in the situation?
420 Evaluation of author's method:	Is the story well written?
430 Evaluation of author's vision:	Is the story about important things? Is it a trivial or a serious work?

Fig. 1. Response Preference Questionnaire
(Keyed According to the Elements of Writing about a Literary Work)

The results of the response preference measure (as it was called) were analyzed in a number of ways. The first analysis looked at consistency of selection of items across the three measures. The mean percent of the younger population in all countries selecting three or more of the same questions across questionnaires was 8.6 percent and selecting two or more of the same questions was 28.5 percent; for the older group, the percentages were 28.5 percent and 42.5 percent. These results indicated that students tended in general to become increasingly consistent in their selection of questions, which would mean that they tend increasingly to approach all texts from a single perspective.

Such a result does not negate the fact that students' critical approaches are influenced by the text. A multiple-discriminant analysis comparing the responses to three stories across countries and age groups was performed. Two of the stories varied considerably on a dimension that suggests that one was more difficult to understand than the other. A third differed from both these on eliciting more concern about the language, hidden meanings and the affective power of the story.

In terms of the national or community differences, the results showed that there were both a broad community of readers and national communities. Students in all countries generally rejected the questions "Is this a proper subject for a story?" and "Is anyone in this story like the people I know?" They generally found attractive the questions "Has anything in this story a hidden meaning?" and "What happens in the story?" Aside from these universal rejections and predilections, different countries seem to contain students with sharply different profiles of response. Two sets of questions form the coordinates on which one could plot the major differences between countries: the first coordinate would include an amphasis on point of view and personal interpretation (what does the story tell me about people like those I know?) and a subordination of evaluation of the meaningfulness of the work, and of the historical background. The second coordinate includes a strong emphasis on interpretation (character motivation, thematic interpretation, and moral interpretation), and a de-emphasis on form and structure. This coordinate could be said to form a "form-content" continuum; and the second coordinate, a "personal-impersonal" continuum (Fig. 2). Belgium and Italy are countries which emphasize the impersonal and formal; Chile, England and Iran emphasize the personal and content–oriented response. The United States students are concerned with content but not from a personal point of view.

At this point, then, one can conclude that preferences among responses are partially dependent on the text, but seemingly more dependent on what we might call the culture of the student, that patterns of preference become more sharply etched as students progress through secondary school. The question then remains as to whether

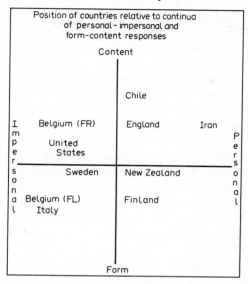

FIG. 2.

these patterns are learned in school. One way of determining that would be to see whether the students' preferences are those of the curriculum makers and the teachers. We found that in general, the preferences of the students and teachers are more similar than different. For the younger students, the average rank-order correlation between student and teacher is .35 (the lowest in Chile with −.05 and the highest Italy with .54); for the older students the average is .44 (Iran as the lowest with −.10 and Chile the highest with .71). The Iranian results are somewhat suspect on other grounds, so that if one were to exclude Iran, the average for the younger group would be .38 and for the older group .50. In any event, there is a clear indication that students agree with their teachers and tend to agree with them more as they get older. In the case of both student and teacher, the figures are based on the questionnaire responses and not based on response to a given story. In the three English speaking countries, the correlations are not as great between the 18-year-olds and their teachers as they are in Finland, or Chile; although the correspondence is strong in England (.44). A subsequent analysis of the New Zealand data showed that although the student's preferences differed from those of their teachers at the pre-university level, they matched the questions asked on University Entrance Examinations.

We had also asked experts in each of the countries as to where they would say the emphasis in the published curricula was placed with respect to the questions. As one might expect, there was disagreement among the experts, oftentimes between the more academically oriented experts and the more pedagogically oriented experts, but also between schools within the academic and the pedagogic groups. We also found that the experts tended to group the questions and to group them similarly, so that we could speak of four major approaches to the teaching of literature: formal–analytic, thematic, affective, and historical. Although there was disparity between the experts, teachers, and students in some countries, most notably in New Zealand; there was, in general, a remarkable congruence between groups and a strong trend for the teacher to act as the mediator between expert opinion and student protestation. The teacher, in short, tends to be a major force in influencing the student's choice of critical approach, and inducting the student into the interpretive community.

We have so far drawn a net of circumstantial evidence that leads us to the conclusion that whatever schools may fail to do they succeed in imparting to students a preferred way of approaching literary works. Older students tend to be more definite in their choices of responses than do younger ones; older students tend to agree more closely with teachers than do younger ones; differences between countries would seem to indicate that the differences are not entirely attributable to maturation (as regards reading interest, students tend to conform to an international age pattern rather than to national patterns across ages). These general trends support Fish's idea of interpretative communities and the force of educational institutions — curricula, examinations, and teachers — in inducting students into those communities. A cross-cultural study of instruction in literature, then, that examines what students say or write about literary texts, clearly supports the idea of interpretive communities that are larger than a single classroom, that may, in fact, be national.

The Written Composition Study

In 1980, IEA began a study of achievement in written composition, the second prong of Foshay's hypothesis. Again the study was strongly encouraged to attend to both critical and descriptive dimensions. For the latter, it would seem possible, by extension from the literature study that instruction in composition about general topics also produces communities that we might call "rhetorical communities". Support for such an hypothesis, appeared to be found in the case of composition in an academic discipline.

Instruction in any discipline is acculturation, or the bringing of the student into the "interpretive community" of the discipline. And there is evidence, mostly anecdotal, that each discipline is also a "rhetorical community", which is to say a field with certain norms, expectations, and conventions with respect to writing. One can clearly see the differences among disciplines if one looks at the scholarly journals, even though language courses (being taught by humanistically trained teachers) often imply that the style of literary research is applicable to many fields. Although any article has a beginning, a middle, and an end, the physical format will vary according to discipline as will the placement of certain kinds of material. In the humanities, the "review of research" either comes at the very beginning or, as is often the case, is sprinkled throughout the text. In the social sciences, the review of research clearly is the second in the article. In the sciences it occupies a minor role if it is there at all. Other obvious norms particular to disciplines exist in footnote style, in the use of external comment on the thesis, and the like. Sometimes these norms are unknown to secondary school teachers of composition and they do not adequately prepare their students for later work in other fields.

If rhetorical communities can be defined by discipline, which disciplines exert their force across languages so that a scientific paper in Finland resembles a scientific paper in Chile, can we also say of less specialized writing that there are national rhetorical communities? From the very beginning work on the IEA Study of Written Composition that hypothesis was pursued (Purves and Takala, 1982).

The idea of national styles of modes of writing is not a new one. Since the 1960s there has been an interest in "contrastive rhetoric," the study of differences in patterns of writing and organization. Most of that research, however, had examined the prose of writers learning a second language (Kaplan, 1966). Some studies had looked at literary styles as they change across geographical or temporal boundaries, but the IEA study provides a way of pursuing contrastive rhetoric using a systematically drawn sample of writing from an "average" population writing in the language of instruction.

The first problem, like that of the literature study was to create a standardized set of descriptors that could be used for a cross-cultural look at achievement in writing and its relation to national style or national rhetorical communities. The reader must be aware of a complication, however. There are two levels of description: one of writing or samples of writing; a second of criteria used to judge writing.

As an initial step, samples of essays were drawn in 1980 from secondary school students in Australia, England, Finland, Ivory Coast, Italy, Israel, Japan, Nigeria, New Zealand, Scotland, Thailand, and the United States. The students were generally able students from one or two classes. They were asked to write in class on the topic "My Native Town", a topic selected to be as non-directive as possible. If not written in English, the compositions were translated from the original language, the translator being asked to retain the style and flavour of the original and the translations being checked by bilingual teachers for fidelity to the original. If one were to examine the whole group of essays, one would notice a striking difference between countries and a striking similarity within countries. The following essays from Finland and Australia are to a certain extent exemplary of some of these differences: they have been selected as "typical" of a set of essays from one or two classes in each country (whether we are seeing class effects or national effects remains to be seen, although the whole Finnish sample came from two classes some 300 km apart — one rural, one urban).

FINLAND
MY HOME COUNTRY

My home village is Petajavesi which is situated in central Finland. Petajavesi has good connections by road to Keuruu, Jyvaskyla, Multia and Uurainen. Petajavesi is a small church village with 4000 inhabitants. The people of Petajavesi have clean nature and waters, two beautiful churches, the new and the old, the older church has received much admiration and fame even from afar in the world. A little to the side of the center there is the old Lemettila farm where every now and then in the summer tourists come to see the old-fashioned house and the emotional values held within it.

Modern times are seen also in Petajavesi, one can buy almost anything in the stores of which there are more than ten. The Recreation Hall which was completed a few years ago, has facilities for meetings and for sports and a library. There are two schools in the church village, the lower level and the upper level which also includes high school. Among places for further education, let us mention the School of Home Industry in Petajavesi. Speaking of industry, Petajavesi has its own bakery, shoe factory, plastic plant and a free-time clothing factory which is being built.

There are not enough jobs, but this new factory needs many female workers and it might improve the employment situation in Petajavesi.

There are also opportunities for hobbies, there are many different kinds of clubs and societies, a new skating rink, sports field, ski tracks and two sports halls.

AUSTRALIA
THE PLACE WHERE I WAS BORN

The road in which I was born is still lined by the Norfolk Island pines of my childhood. Sixteen years has thinned the rows considerably, but far more evident is the mark that time has left on the house. The old fir tree that once dominated the front garden, has since made way for a rose garden, and the iron gates that had at one time been so good to swing on, now stood, rusting on their hinges, badly in need of oil and a coat of paint. Creeper now grows over the house, to such an extent that it covers the gutters, whilst the concrete driveway that had been laid long before my arrival, is now cracked and uneven with moss growing between the slabs of concrete. Such is the place where I was born.

Childhood memories paint a different picture; the house was still young and in its prime, with the noise of a growing family to cover that of the cars outside. In the dead of night the ocean could be heard, pounding the rocks half a mile away. On a windy night the salty air would penetrate inside the house, and the smell would linger on throughout the next day.

The salt air is still apparent today, and the house murmurs of childhood noise. But the grass has grown long, and plans to widen the road threaten even the pines. But the ocean can still be heard, pounding the rocks half a mile away.

Clearly one needs to find some way of describing these differences and similarities as well as of providing a framework by which they could be compared as to quality. Carroll (1960) used the repertory grid technique and factor analysis to determine what aspects of prose readers noticed. He found six factors: (1) good-bad, (2) personal–impersonal, (3) ornamented–plain, (4) abstract–concrete, (5) serious–humorous, and (6) characterizing–narrating (or descriptive–narrative). Clearly Carroll's raters mingled evaluative and descriptive categories, but as he argues, factors 2, 3, 4, 5, and 6 can be supported by evidence from particular aspects of the text.

The analysis of essays on "My Native Town" from Australia, England, Finland, Ivory Coast, Italy, Israel, Japan, Nigeria, Scotland, Thailand and the United States suggests that some of Carroll's factors were likewise noted by three independent judges who sought to describe the dimensions of the differences they noted:

Personal–Impersonal. This factor depends primarily on the frequency of references in the text to the writer's thoughts and feelings about the subject.

Ornamented–Plain. This factor may also be defined as "figurative–literal" and alludes to the amount of metaphor and other figures of speech in the text.

Abstract–concrete. This factor is defined in terms of the amount of specific information, details, or references in the text.

Two of Carroll's factors, humorous–serious and characterizing–narrating, did not appear in our analysis: the first because there were few instances of humorous writing, but also, we suspect, because this factor contains an evaluative dimension. Carroll's characterizing–narrating factor appears to apply primarily to texts other than the kind called for by the assignment that allows for other modes such as exposition or argument. It is related, however, to the two other factors that were identified in the essay analysis.

Single–multiple. This factor refers to whether the text focuses on a single main point or is otherwise delimited or whether it treats of several related topics or appears to contain a number of diverse points around a central theme.

Propositional–appositional. This factor refers to the types of connectives that hold the main propositions of the text together, to its pattern of coherence. A propositional pattern uses such structures as the hypothetical (if–then), cause–effect, comparison–contrast, and classification-definition. An appositional pattern may use a temporal or narrative structure, a spatial or descriptive structure, an associational structure, or an additive structure (an accumulation of *ands*), and it often omits connectives and appears digressive.

Using these factors, then, one might characterize the essays from the ten countries (although such characterizations cannot yet be seen as definitive but illustrative of the coding system) as in Fig. 3. Clearly the essays can then be classified according to such a system. The system was also applied to another set on "What is a friend?" Clearly, too, this rating would be descriptive rather than evaluative. If a country's essays were rated consistently as, for instance, Australia — highly personal, ornamental, concrete, single, and appositional; or Finland — impersonal, plain, multiple and appositional, curriculum makers and teachers in either country might inquire whether such a style is to be desired or to be valued. The purpose of this study is to raise that issue, not to prescribe a set of values for all countries. The fact that the compositions come from "good" students suggests that these students have learned and are applying the norms of their rhetorical community. The question remains as to whether the virtues of each composition is desired.

	FACTOR				
	Personal	Ornamental	Abstract	Single	Propositional
Country					
Australia	High	High	Low	High	Low
England	Medium	Low	Low	Low	Low
Federal Republic of Germany	High	Low	Low	Low	Low
Finland	Low	Low	Low	Low	Low
Israel	High	Medium	Low	High	High
Italy	High	High	High	High	High
Ivory Coast	Medium	Low	Low	Low	Low
Japan	High	Low	High	High	Medium
Netherlands	High	Low	Low	Low	Low
New Zealand	Low	Low	Medium	Low	Low
Nigeria	Low	Low	Low	Low	Low
Scotland	Low	Low	Low	Low	Low
Thailand	High	High	Medium	Medium	Low
United States	Low	Low	Low	Medium	High

Fig. 3.

The Description of the Raters

The sample of the essays were given to two groups of bilingual raters. The first group consisted of beginning graduate students in various fields; the second group consisted of graduate students in comparative literature. The first group was asked to comment freely on the essays and the second was asked to rate the essays and comment on the strengths and weaknesses of each. Both groups were asked to use criteria that would apply to their native countries. The raters came from about seventeen countries — European, Asian, African, and Latin American.

The comments of the raters were analyzed and classified in the groupings found in Fig. 4. There are some analogies in the ratings to the descriptive factors, but most of the ratings have evaluative dimensions which would make them correspond more closely to Carroll's adjective scales. The personal and tonal categories have clear analogies to Carroll's scales; the structural and stylistic categories have descriptive counterparts (Fig. 5).

From this comparison we may conclude that evaluators make subtle discriminations within certain categories and that they employ all of Carroll's original factors except that of genre. A rating of an essay, therefore, allows for the possibility of more subtle distinctions among national styles than would a description. Defining national styles through ratings, however, bears with it the problem that one is dealing with perceptions or judgments of styles, not with actual styles. Nonetheless, the use of ratings by teachers and experts (if they are consistent in a country) could give one an idea of what aspects of a national style are approved by the educational establishment — if not approved, at least noticed.

From this preliminary work a scoring scheme has emerged for the major phase of the study. This scheme accounts for the emphases of the various cultures involved in the study. The compositions will be rated on their content, structure, and style and tone and the interest of the reader in the composition as general categories internationally defined. In addition, the participating centers will define their own criteria for adherence to grammatical and orthographical conventions, handwriting and neatness. The multiple scoring scheme allows for comparisons of score profiles within and across tasks, and for relating the profiles to the announced emphases in the curriculum. Thus a system that emphasizes content and grammar, for example, can be compared to one that emphasizes organization and style. The comparison can also help determine which set of emphases best produces writing that is of high quality across evaluative dimensions.

In addition to the scoring scheme's cross-cultural validity, the actual compositions may produce descriptive data about ways that students have of responding to different tasks. The tasks used in the study are

Alan C. Purves

Comments by Bilingual Raters

POSITIVE	NEGATIVE
I. Personal	
Appealing: enjoyable to read, good evocation of atmosphere; appeal to senses	Unappealing: cut and dry; flat; dryness of approach; lack of emotional appeal
Effective: appropriate; vivid; emphatic; eloquent; pertinent; good use of contrasts and comparisons; intimate picture gives reader the feeling of knowing town	Ineffective: unconvincing; not arresting; not strong enough; too much detail; irrelevant; not to the point; too many collateral subjects reduce impact; conclusion runs out
Original: stimulates, arouses curiosity; interesting; imaginative; spontaneous; freshness of feeling	Trite: cliched; commonplace; uninspired; mechanical; report-like; travelogue-like; guidebook style; encyclopedia; originality suppressed; banal; plastic image; student copied information dutifully; oleographic; sentimental, romantic, naive
Miscellaneous evocation of childhood memories, family atmosphere useful ideas aid to recall allusions to past self satisfaction	
II. Structural	
Concise: simplicity; straight to the point; maximum told in minimum of words; essential; efficient; trying to encompass many aspects in a nutshell; succinct; direct; neat and tidy	Wordy
Connected: transitions good	Disconnected: sentences unconnected; lists with no linking of ideas and/or sentences; like a catalogue; many short sentences; unsuccessful juxtaposition of topics; ending too abrupt
Developed: development of different levels of thought; thoroughness; well elaborated thoughts; examples to illustrate points	Undeveloped: no development of thought; ideas not elaborated; lacking breath of exposition; no development of argumentation; fragmentary treatment; no expansion of ideas; lack of adjectives to make situation and feelings real
Consistent: unity of style, ideas; unity between content and form; uniform; consistency of mood; repeated image at beginning and end give unity	Inconsistent
Focused: thesis + examples; thematic construction, well defined perspective	Unfocused

Fig. 4.

POSITIVE

Tight (overall structure): right order; sequences of paragraphs ordered; well organized; sequential development; clear vision of where going; unified expression; coherent structure; orderly and logical; ideas suitably paragraphed, paragraphs in harmony with statements

Miscellaneous
correct — appropriate approach to topic
development of inner and outer landscape
uneven distribution of ideas
topic balance
schematic
symmetry of thoughts

III. *Understanding*

Clear: Comprehensible

Detailed: full description

Informative: researched; excellent reportage; informed; attempt to cover many aspects; many ideas

Penetrating: expresses ideas with depth; reflective; associations; perceptive; evidence of thought, carefully thought out; penetrates below surface; result of meditation; sensitivity; ability to explore complexity; grasp of subject; ability to assimilate facts

Precise

IV. *Tonal*

Critical: exercise of judgment weight and decide benefits; balanced

Honest: lack of pretention, exaggeration; matter of fact; feelings expressed are true and sincere

NEGATIVE

Loose (overall structure): lacks cohesiveness; just a series of details with no purpose; lack of structure; lack of introduction, conclusion; unconnected, choppy paragraphs; essay jumps from point to point; difficult to follow sequence of thought; paragraphs too numerous; sentences misplaced; overlapping thoughts; misleading organization; piling ideas in one paragraph; unproportional paragraphs; no preordained structure; sloppy; random; broken distribution of material; disjointed impressions

Confused: obscure

Vague: poor description; not elaborated enough; unspecific

Uninformative: lack of information; too general; poor in content; sparse

Superficial: superficial generalizations; empty sentences; ability to reach only external striking aspects of reality; light handling of subject that requires broader treatment; no insights; simplistic approach

Hazy: imprecise

Uncritical: lack of critical judgment

Pretentious: dishonest linguistic quality

Fig. 4. continued

POSITIVE	NEGATIVE
Humorous: witty	Humorless
Personal: writer's impressions; voices opinions; subjective; deeply felt; nostalgic	Impersonal: no personal opinion or feeling; no point of view; cold, business-like; distant
Sophisticated: strong awareness of social and cultural structure	Unsophisticated: limited awareness of social realities
Miscellaneous	
enthusiasm of writer or lack of it	
negative attitude of writer	
fairness of giving judgment	
writer's strong sense of belonging	
socio-political expression	
writer's naivete	
writer's appreciation of importance of subject	
writer's disposition to escape into fantasy	
writer's modesty, shyness have touching quality	
irony	
melancholy	
writer's idealism	
no sense of audience	
philosophical	

V. *Stylistic*

POSITIVE	NEGATIVE
Fluid: graceful; flowing; articulate; natural flow	Labored: stiff; heavy; involved; contorted sentences; stiff parallelism; clumsy; stiff sentence connections
Formal: appropriate language	Colloquial: writing seems like speech
Metaphoric: color of milieu	Literal
Lively	Dull
Poetic: similar to literature; lyrical	Pseudo-poetic: artificial; grandiloquent
Subtle: lots of things suggested rather than told; indirect way to arouse feelings by linking sentiment to physical sensation	Simple: too straight forward; childish narrative
Varied (applies to words, sentence structures)	Repetitious: redundant; overused recurring symbol; monotonous; tautologies

	Carroll	Descriptors	Ratings
1. Evaluation			
	Good-Bad	———	Appealing Effective Original
2. Structure			
	———	Single-Multiple Logical-Analogical	Concise Connected Developed Consistent Focussed Tight
3. Personality			
	Personal–Impersonal	Personal–Impersonal	Critical Honest Personal Sophisticated
4. Style			
	Ornamented–Plain	Literal–Metaphoric	Metaphoric Formal Lively Poetic Varied Subtle
5. Content			
	Abstract–Concrete	Abstract–Concrete	Clear Detailed Informative Penetrating Precise
6. Tune			
	Serious-Humorous	———	Humorous
7. Genre			
	Characterizing–Narrating	———	———

FIG. 5. Juxtaposition of Descriptors and Ratings

drawn from a variety of cells within the domain of school writing (Fig. 6). The initial study of stylistic differences was limited to an expository–descriptive domain, but from the preliminary sample of compositions drawn from other domains, other dimensions of stylistic variation emerge.

One set of tasks is designed to elicit what many call functional writing, that is the writing of notes and letters in specific contexts — such as a letter of application or a note to the head of the school postponing an appointment. From the latter task come two examples (both translated) which illustrate a clear difference in approach.

Cognitive processing →		Reproduce		Organize / reorganize		Invent / generate
Dominant intention / purpose	Primary audience	Facts	Ideas	Events	Visual images, facts, mental states, ideas	Ideas, mental states, alternative worlds
To learn (meta-lingual)	Self				X	(shaded)
To convey emotions, feelings (emotive)	Self others	(shaded)			X	X
To inform (referen-tial)	Others	(shaded)			X	X
To con-vince / persuade (conna-tive)	Others	(shaded)			X	X
To enter-tain, delight, please (poetic)	Others	(shaded)				X
To keep in touch (phatic)	Others	(shaded)	(shaded)	(shaded)	(shaded)	(shaded)
Primary mode of discourse		Documentative discourse		Constative discourse Narrative Descriptive Explanatory		Exploratory discourse Interpretive Literary (Expository / argumentative)

Non-shaded areas include the primary cells of school writing instruction.
An X indicates a cell included in the IEA study of written composition.

FIG. 6. The Domain of Writing and School Writing

Mr Principal!

I would hereby like to inform you that I regret to be unable to attend our agreed appointment at 2 o'clock due to an urgent private matter. It is the funeral of a distant relative of which I have only recently been informed. I hope that you will understand my situation.

Sincerely,

Mrs. Headmistress:

Very respected madam, I write you to apologize myself for being unable to go to your office at the time you asked me to since something unexpected happened at home.
I will go to your office early tomorrow if you think it is appropriate like this, to give you the corresponding explanations.

With thanks,

At this point identifying the country of origin might be misleading because the sample from which these examples come was drawn to illustrate a range of performance rather than typicality. Nonetheless, inspection of the samples from the countries represented by these two notes indicates that the uniform practice in the first was to be rather direct and laconic, and in the second to be highly apologetic and almost obsequious. Certainly the second focuses more on the feelings of the reader and the first on the message of the writer. Such a pattern of difference also appears in the letter of application from the two countries.

To take another example, here are two compositions from two other countries in response to a task calling for a reflective composition on the generation gap:

Many young people find it difficult to talk and to understand middle-aged people.

This is a point of conversation that frequently arises in school and at home. Young people have a belief that the older generation are totally against them, and will not offer them the freedom they wish to have. On the other hand, the older generation believe the "youth of today" have an easy time of it. The type of phrase that has now become a cliche among older people is along the lines of, "it wasn't like that when I was a lad". This type of comment is one which annoys most young people.

The main reason why it annoys me is that it is so obvious, no-one expects the world to stay the same all the time, people have to adapt to changes. These changes therefore are bound to affect society, which then changes the way in which people are brought up. This type of statement is bound to cause conflict between young and old, and so the younger people are more reluctant to talk to their parents about problems which may have arisen at school or at home. Many parents find it very disconcerting that their children are afraid to talk to them about their problems, but the talkativeness of a child will usually be determined by how they were treated in their earlier years.

Another reason that children won't discuss things with their parents is that they consider themselves rebellious if they do their own thing, and can feel independent not having to ask their parents all the time. For a lot of young people it is quite "fashionable" to go against their parents wishes. Young people seem to have the idea that going against their parents means they are exercising their freedom, and showing they can live on their own.

I believe that conversation is probably the most important aspect of family life. I find that to discuss a problem with my parents makes me feel much more "grown-up" than to keep it to myself. For instance, recently I asked my parents for permission to be allowed to smoke in my own room. Admittedly they said no, and for a while I was very annoyed with them, but after a time I felt glad that I had plucked up courage to ask them, as if I now have any problems I know I can ask them without fear of being reprimanded. I believe there should be a strong bond of trust in any successful parent–child relationship.

The sort of parents I can't abide are those who aren't prepared to discuss anything at all. If the child asks about something which is very important to them, this type of parent will either consider the matter as trivial and tell the child so, or else reprimand the child for being so foolish as to do or to want such a thing. I believe that the problem of discussion between parents and children is hard to solve, as the parents will usually take a stubborn attitude where it is their children who are concerned, and the child will usually do the same.

The problem is one which has always existed, and I presume probably always will.

This composition takes a personal note and is opinionated or emotional in addressing the topic. The writer uses personal experience to support the argument. The composition does consider various aspects of the subject and finds that the matter is not one of simple good or bad. The ending is a bit abrupt, but one might well imagine that the pressure of time forced a quick concluding sentence. The writer has interpreted the assignment to restrict it to talk between parents and children, and such is certainly a permissable interpretation.

Adolescents and conversations, manners toward middle-age people.

Teenagers are hot tempered, hard headed unteachable: They like to take a risk; are not considerate. They have problems. Adults are fussy, grumbling, irritable and they like to preach. Sometimes they like to use authority. Teenagers and middle-aged people, thus, seem to move in the opposite direction. Their habits are incompatible. Age differences between these two groups of people is another cause for the problem.

Modern teenagers often refuse advice and preaching from others. It is hard to bring these two groups of people together. To familiarize teenagers with adults, we have to start at an early age and within the family. Because family is the first society of children. They will learn valuable things from families; from talking to manners, respects, and etiquettes. Parents with willing docile kids will find it easy to teach them also. But when they grow up, being in the teenage stage, the parents will find it difficult to teach them. Teenagers reject adults as their enemies. Adults are frightening devils. They do not want to get advice from adults. When they have no advice from adults, their actions often lack good ideas. They take actions on no reasons. This causes a lot of problems. At the end, adults are in turmoil.

Nowadays it is rare to find any teenagers who would like to see and consult with adults concerning education, finance, peer selection, or responsibilities. This is because adults often use authority, like to set up regulations and are too obsolete. Teenagers lack confidence in adults. They look at adults as having out of date ideas, living in a different era. Thus the teaching is not quite satisfactory. As a consequence, teenagers might turn to delinquency.

Modern teenagers should listen to advice from adults since they have good intentions. They consider us their off-spring. We should realize and think that we are growing up everyday. Such a matter is nothing if we are to be good leaders, have responsibility and are ready to give advice to off-spring in years to come. We should pay attention to adults now before there will be no adults to pay attention to.

This translated composition received a high score for style, for it is certainly nicely written with its parallel introduction and its use of imagery. The composition is less personal than the first and more dispassionate. But its argument progresses in a circular fashion, repeating the sense of the first paragraph in the second, third and fourth. It is more appositional and the first more propositional.

As one looks at other tasks in the preliminary set of compositions, one senses that there may be other differences as well. In writing narratives, for example, students from some countries tend to use dialogue much more than do students from other countries. This distinction may prove to be similar to Carroll's characterizing–narrating distinction.

One task that sought to capture these distinctions among communities directly was one that asked the students to write a letter of advice to a younger person coming to their school. The advice was to concern how to do well in writing. In addition to being rated, the compositions were to be analyzed for their content. A preliminary examination of that content analysis indicates that students from different countries are more similar then they are different and that their advice does not concern style and organization as much as it concerns manuscript form, spelling, grammar, and content, as well as such niceties as handing the paper in on time. Yet the limited sample suggests some differences between groups of students. Students in one system appear to stress originality, in another impressing the teacher by fancy style; in still another using a simple style so as not to "get into trouble."

It would appear that this task will probably inform us more than any other how students perceive the rhetorical community in which they have passed the novitiate but are not yet expert. As in the literature study I suspect there will be points of commonality between communities such as the importance of correctness in the mechanical aspects of writing and the importance of knowing the subject about which one is writing. But these points of commonality may well be overshadowed by the points of difference. Again, we suspect that these differences will be multidimensional, that they will encompass structure and style, that the patterns of any one community will vary significantly from those of another in at least one dimension, and that the differences among communities will be sharper as the children progress further through the educational system.

Conclusion

From both these studies, then, it appears that the curriculum in the mother tongue emphasizes both increasing the competence of students as readers or as writers and channeling the preferences of students as to the kinds of questions to ask about a literary text or to the structure and style of academic compositions. In both reading literature and writing compositions, one aspect of achievement may be defined as the cultivation of a set of habits. These habits may be seen in two studies as being habits of discourse. Beneath habits of discourse, however, are habits of mind; clearly in many different settings the educational system seeks to influence if not shape habits of the mind. The IEA studies of literature and written composition have, I believe, helped to portray the fact that curricula have this aim. The studies have shown that to a certain extent, the curricula succeed in achieving the aim. What is left to be explored is by what means the curricula succeed.

References

Carroll, John. "Vectors of Prose Style." T. A. Sebeok, ed., *Style in Language*, (Cambridge, MA and New York: Technology Press and John Wiley, 1960), pp. 283–292.

Fish, Stanley. *Is there a Text in this Class? The Authority of Interpretive Communities* (Cambridge, MA: Harvard University Press, 1980)

Kaplan, R. B. "Cultural thought patterns in inter-cultural education," *Language Learning*, **16** (1966), 1–20.

Goodman, Kenneth. "Unity in Reading," A. C. Purves and O. Niles eds., *Becoming Readers in a Complex Society* 83rd Yearbook of the National Society for the Study of Education, Part 1 (Chicago: National Society for the Study of Education, 1984), pp. 79–114.

Gumperz, J. J. and Hymes, D. *Directions in Sociolinguistics: The Ethnography of Communication.* (New York: Holt Rhinehart and Winston, 1974).

Purves, Alan C. *Literature Education in Ten Countries: International Studies in Evaluation 11* (Stockholm: Almqvist and Wiksell, 1973).

Purves, Alan, C. and Rippere, V. *The Elements of Writing about a Literary work, Research report* Number 9, Urbana, Illinois National Council of Teachers of English, 1968.

Purves, Alan C. and Takala, Sauli J., ed., *An International Perspective on the Evaluation of Written Composition*; Evaluation in Education: An International Review Series, Vol. **5**, No. 3, (Oxford, Pergamon Press, 1982).

Richards, I. A. *Practical Criticism.* (New York: Harcourt Brace and Co., 1929).

Rosenblatt, Louise, M. *The Reader, the Text, and the Poem: The Transactional Theory of the Literary Work*, (Carbondale, IL: Southern Illinois University Press, 1978).

Ryabova, T. V. "Mexanizm prozdenija reci po dannym a faziolozdi" *Voprosy porozdenija reci i obucenija jazyku* (Moskow: izd MGU, 1967), pp. 76–94.

Saussure, F. de, *Cours de linguistique general* (Lausanne: Payot, 1916).

Tornebohm, H. "Perspectives on Inquiring Systems." Department of Theory of Science, University of Gothenburg, Report No. 53, 1973.

Cross National Research in Mathematics Education

ROY W. PHILLIPPS

The link between IEA and cross national research in mathematics education is an integral part of the Association's history. In article 6. Neville Postlethwaite has pointed out that mathematics achievement was selected by IEA as the criterion measure for both the initial feasibility study and the first major research project in 1964. A second international study of mathematics (SIMS) was undertaken some 16 years later. The choice of mathematics as an area of study was influenced initially by the political and educational interest in the quality of mathematics and science education in the early 1960s as well as by the belief that the international nature of the symbols and conventions used in mathematics would assist in reducing between-language and between-culture difficulties when it came to constructing internationally valid tests.

The part played by Torsten Husén in the conceptualization and administration of the first mathematics study (FIMS) has already been alluded to in the Preface. Not only did Torsten Husén serve as chairman of the Association but he also played a leading role in the execution of the project and finally edited the two official international reports (Husén, 1967). In 1976 Torsten Husén again presided over the IEA General Assembly meeting in St. Andrews, Scotland where the formal decision was taken by IEA to embark on a second study of mathematics. His influence therefore spans the two major international empirical studies of mathematics education undertaken with fully representative samples of 13-year-olds and pre-university students.

The results from the first IEA study have been fully reported in the official volumes as well as in numerous articles, reports and papers at both the national and international levels (see Postlethwaite and Lewy, 1979).

It is anticipated that the results from SIMS will be reported by 1986 in three major volumes respectively covering a study of the national curricula, the data from the cross-sectional study, and data from the longitudinal study of the mathematics classroom. The intention of this chapter therefore is to contrast some aspects of these two major studies and to examine some of the preliminary data from the second study.

First IEA Mathematics Study

In the preface to the international report of the first study (*op. cit.*) Husén sketches the international milieu which surrounded the genesis of the first study as follows:

"A growing awareness of the important role that formal education plays in promoting — or hindering — social and economic developments together with the realization that few countries enjoy sufficient resources or man-power to satisfy the steadily growing demand for educational expansion have underlined the need for a searching and critical inquiry into the efficiency of present arrangements."

Thus the possibility of an empirical approach to such an enquiry on an international scale was recognized and accepted by IEA. The idea of using the world as a laboratory took on shape and meaning.

It was recognized that certain fundamental practices within education systems were not readily amenable to national experimentation. For example, it would not be easy for a country to experiment within its borders with different ages of entry. However, if cross-national variability existed the effects of early or later entry into the school system could be investigated.

Likewise controlling the retentivity of students in the system could be difficult. However, among the countries in IEA there was already a variety of retention rates in existence.

FIMS's Hypotheses

An examination of the hypotheses that were developed for the first study shows that they fall into three categories:

(a) Those dealing with school organization, selection, and differentiation.

(b) Those dealing with curriculum and methods of instruction.

(c) Those dealing with sociological, technological, and economic characteristics of families, schools and societies.

While the criterion measures were very clearly identified as mathematics achievement, attitudes towards mathematics education, and attitudes to education generally, the concomitant variables to be measured clearly indicated the researchers' interest in national systems of education rather than the strategies of mathematics education *per se*. It would seem that mathematics achievement was in some ways being viewed as a surrogate for a global measure of a nation's educational output. In contrasting the first and second mathematics studies it is important to appreciate that the thoughts and energies of the researchers in the first study were not solely directed towards the problems of mathematics education. This is not to say that efforts were not made to assess accurately the national mathematics curricula objectives and content or to devise internationally valid and fair mathematics achievement tests. A great deal of international consultation took place and all items were pilot tested and scrutinized by a specialist committee. While it was acknowledged that a complete curriculum coverage could not be achieved in the tests the final forms did represent a fair compromise of curriculum coverage for each country in relation to the time that schools in each country were prepared to devote to the testing programme.

The interest of IEA at that time in educational systems is further exemplified by the various summaries of results found in various reports. For example, Postlethwaite (Purves and Levine, 1975) lists some 17 main results from the study. Five of these relate to school systems such as the claim that the age of entry appeared to have little differential effect on mathematics achievement by the age of 13 years — a contention challenged by Shah (1971).

Three of the quoted results related to student characteristics. Low positive relationships were identified between attitudes to mathematics, and achievement, and positive relationships between interest in mathematics and achievement. The between-country correlations between achievement in mathematics and attitudes towards mathematics were consistently negative and for the younger populations surprisingly high.

Two results related to variables associated with teacher training which in general indicated that the more training a teacher received the better the student's achievement. This was especially true for the 13-year-olds. It was also shown that within-country correlations between teachers' perceptions of degree of freedom they were given within the school and student achievement was close to zero and often negative.

Under a rubric of learning conditions two findings were highlighted. High correlations were found between "opportunity-to-learn" mathematics and student achievement. Opportunity to learn in this context was measured by asking the teacher if the mathematics behind the actual item had been taught. A second result which appeared surprising was that hours spent on mathematics learning, i.e. instruction time plus homework, seemed to have only a weak association with achievement.

Variables related to the sex of the student highlighted the fact that, except possibly for the United States and Israel, more males than females studied mathematics and that boys scored higher than girls in all the populations tested. Boys also displayed more interest in mathematics than girls in all countries except for France and England. However, it was noted that where the learning conditions for boys and girls were more similar, such as in a comprehensive school, the differences in achievement were markedly reduced.

Social class was of interest on two counts. A pronounced socio-economic bias was evident in all countries in that the pre-university group differed from the 13-year-olds by being composed of a higher proportion of students whose fathers were in upper or middle-class occupations. It was also shown that when the level of instruction was held constant the place of the parents' residence (urban, rural) was, in general, not significantly related to mathematics achievement.

Reactions to the First Study

While researchers in the field of comparative education found much of interest in the reports of the study, as did research methodologists, there is little evidence to indicate that the study had any great effect on mathematics education around the world. It was perhaps unfortunate that it was left to the general media to interpret the initial results for teachers, mathematics educators and policymakers. The press, despite the efforts of the authors in the official reports to bury any cognitive comparisons deep in the text, played up the "olympic" nature of the results. This was particularly true within the United States where invidious comparisons were made in leading newspapers between US and Japanese students. Such sensationalism tended to antagonize mathematics' educators who sought explanations by examining and criticizing the methodology and the tests rather than searching for the positive messages contained in the report. For example, as far as the writer is aware no national "wrong answer" analyses were undertaken in any country. Such analyses may well have revealed national curriculum weaknesses, textbook misconceptions or teacher training gaps.

Secondary Analyses and FIMS Data Bank

In the hope that researchers would wish to conduct secondary analyses, the data were assembled into a documented data bank. Unfortunately very little use was made of the bank in its early years. Possibly the difficulties of accessing the material were responsible. The bank was reformatted in 1984 in preparation for secondary analyses for comparison purposes with the SIMS.

The Second Mathematics Study

Genesis of the Second IEA Mathematics Study

Following the first study of mathematics, IEA undertook an even more ambitious survey in six subject areas. The lessons learned from the mathematics study were put to good use in refining and improving the measures to be used. Improvements were made in general communications with National Centres as well as in the sampling procedures, manual preparation, data collection and data analyses. This cumulative inbuilt experience was available to the researchers involved with the second mathematics study.

The writer's link with the international management of IEA projects was during the last 3 years of the Six Subject Survey when he acted as Executive Director of IEA in Stockholm. It was in that capacity that he first came to value the help, wisdom and friendship of Torsten Husén as the Six Subject Survey was brought to a successful conclusion.

In the sentiments of Torsten it could be said that when the light at the end of the tunnel could be identified as daylight and not a train speeding towards us, then thoughts in the Stockholm office started to turn to the future of IEA. For a number of years IEA had been preparing and seeking backing for a number of rather complex new proposals in classroom environment, reading and pre-primary education. In 1975 it was recognized that the chances of finding funding for such new proposals at that time were virtually nil given that the educational research funding position had hardened in the United States and Europe.

The possibility of winding up IEA as an organization was being canvassed and this found support with some of the founding members who had carried the burden of arranging for the funding in the past. On the other hand there were other members who believed that IEA would have to be re-invented in the future if it was allowed to lapse. Particular support for this belief came from the Spencer Fellows — a relatively young group of 16 researchers who had had the opportunity of working for a year in Stockholm on the IEA data with the support of the Spencer Foundation based in Chicago, United States.

The first really determined effort to keep IEA as a viable organization and to undertake a second study of mathematics stemmed, I believe, from a meeting in my room in the University of Stockholm one cold bitter winter's afternoon when Zoltan Bathory of the National Institute of Education in Hungary, Kimmo Leimu of the University of Jyväsklä in Finland (both Spencer Fellows), and Robert Liljefors the National Technical Officer from Sweden joined me to try and identify what the basic criteria should be for any future project of IEA. Foremost on the list was the thought that IEA should capitalize on its known strengths — those of survey research. The knowledge and expertise were available as was the international network of experts that IEA could turn to for advice — the "IEA family." It was also acknowledged that many of the current popular educational debates centered on a concern for whether Johnny or Mary could count — "new mathematics" was under attack. The issue was well on the way to becoming politically and socially sensitive. It did not take any great wisdom to recognize that IEA had the only international data bank of achievement in mathematics collected just before the start of the "new mathematics" movement. The possibility of a before and 16-years-after study was a logical possibility. Unfortunately only 12 countries had taken part in the first study and the number of countries now interested in IEA had grown to around 30. Any proposal would also have to appeal to the new countries as well.

A third point emerged which gave the key. In the first study and the Six Subject Study one of the weaknesses related to the specification of a causal model had been the lack of a formal measure of prior achievement — the use of a surrogate for this factor had weakened the credibility of the model and its potential explanatory power. Any future study should, if possible, be longitudinal in nature over the school year. Further points related to the improvement of the opportunity-to-learn measure and the need to be able to link any teacher's data accurately to the class.

Torsten Husén readily endorsed this initiative and supported the proposal that it should be suggested that IEA undertake a second mathematics study. It was somewhat of a surprise to find all IEA countries endorsed the idea when initial expectations were that perhaps 8 countries might be interested and that such a small scale study may be able to keep IEA alive until research funding improved.

Organization for the Second Study

It is one thing for IEA Assembly members to agree that a proposal be prepared for a second mathematics study but quite another issue to have a proposal funded and organized. From the end of 1974 IEA had no project or institutional support apart from the goodwill of Torsten Husén's Institute of International Education, at the University of Stockholm. The New Zealand Department of Education had offered to support a small coordinating staff in Wellington if IEA wished to decentralize its activities. The General Assembly meeting at Rome in 1975 agreed, in principle, to the decentralization of its coordinating centres. Shortly afterwards the University of Sweden offered to support an international secretary to deal with general IEA issues and the New Zealand Department of Education set up a coordinating unit, consisting of the writer as International Coordinator for the Mathematics project and a clerical assistant.

A small grant from the J. R. McKenzie Trust in New Zealand enabled a search for futher funding to be made in the US where support from the Ford Foundation and the University of Illinois facilitated an international meeting of IEA representatives and mathematics educators. The proposal that resulted from this meeting was eventually funded in part by the National Institute of Education (NIE), Washington, the University of Illinois and the Department of Education, New Zealand. In the later stages assistance was also given by the Spencer Foundation, Chicago, National Institute for Educational Research (NIER), Japan, and, from 1982 onwards, the National Center for

Educational Statistics, Washington. This assistance together with informal support from many national centres and US universities epitomizes the collaborative nature and capacity of IEA. It should be noted though that the agency support came only after it was recognized that the second mathematics study would make a genuine attempt to address the problems of the mathematics educators rather than a further exploration of educational systems. The specialist committee that was established reflected this concern by its composition which included mathematicians, mathematics educators, research methodologists and psychometricians.

Rationale for the Second Study

From the outset it was agreed that the major aim of the study would be to examine the extent to which teachers contribute to the within and between national differences.

As a backdrop to this question the study's specialist committee recognized the need to investigate and describe the intended curriculum as provided by official syllabus statements or in some cases through the recommended textbooks. In implementing the curriculum, however officially prescribed, teachers make many personal judgements as to what actually gets taught to a particular class or child and this may vary greatly to what was officially intended. The measurement of this implemented syllabus was also important. Again what mathematics curriculum is actually received by students may also vary from the implemented curriculum. The criterion measures therefore set out to assess the achieved curriculum.

The factors and the many associated variables which were thought to influence the teaching-learning processes were included in the questionnaires for students, teachers and schools. The design also allowed for countries to administer the cognitive and attitudinal measures at the start of the school year. For those countries electing to take part in this longitudinal aspect of the study there were detailed questionnaires which investigated the teaching of five specific mathematics topics — e.g. common and decimal fractions; ratio, proportion and percentage; measurement; geometry; integers and algebra.

Some Preliminary Results from SIMS

While at this time it is not possible to give a full resumé of the results from the second study it is possible to examine some of the preliminary data from the intended, implemented and achieved curriculum areas.

The Intended Curriculum

As a starting point for a broad description of the importance assigned by individual countries to various topics in their mathematics curricula, a comprehensive international list of possible topics was drawn up. Countries were asked to add any topics not already on the list and to assign importance ratings to each topic at three behavioral levels, e.g. computation, comprehension and higher abilities (application and analysis). The responsibility for these judgements rested with the National Mathematics Committees. As well as providing a basis for the selection of the test items these ratings were used in identifying the official curriculum for each country.

While the national ratings of importance enabled the development of a grid which reflected the international consensus and guided the selection of test items, it is less clear as to the utility of the national ratings in describing the national curriculum in a quantitative way. Tables 1 and 2 display the consensus international grids for the respective populations. Population A is the modal grade of 13-year-olds and Population B is all students taking 5 or more hours per week of mathematics in the final grade (e.g. grade 12 or its equivalent), of secondary school.

Considerable time and effort has been devoted to attempting to quantify the importance ratings that countries gave to the mathematics topics in their syllabuses. While uncertainty does remain over the universality of any interpretation, given to any clustering of countries by curriculum, the SIMS curriculum report will present some interesting possibilities.

Appropriateness Ratings

On the assumption that the international grid was a reasonably accurate picture of the "international curriculum" and that the cognitive items contained in the test forms mirrored this international consensus, a rating of the appropriateness or acceptability of each item for a country's curriculum was sought from the National Mathematics Committees. (Since making these judgements some countries have claimed their ratings really reflected whether or not the item was acceptable or not giving a slight nuance to the intended meaning of the word appropriate). Very few countries expressed any reservations about the items or the balance of emphasis between the topics to be tested. Where a small group of countries (France, Belgium and Netherlands) expressed doubts about a possible bias against their curriculum, a special set of items was added to each population's test forms to redress this imbalance.

The percentage of items (within a content area) deemed appropriate/ acceptable by each country are shown in Figs 1 and 2. Figure 1 considers only the items used in the cross-sectional aspect for Population A i.e. 157 items.

As well 7 items which did not fit comfortably into the formally defined sub-tests for Population B are not considered in Fig. 2. These formally

TABLE 1.
Population A. The International Grid

Content Topics		Computation	Comprehension	Application	Analysis
000	**ARITHMETIC**				
	001 Natural numbers and whole numbers	V	V	V	I
	002 Common fractions	V	V	V	I
	003 Decimal fractions	V	V	I	I
	004 Ratio, proportion, percentage	V	V	I	I
	005 Number theory	I	I	–	–
	006 Powers and exponents	I	I	–	–
	007 Other numeration systems	–	–	–	–
	008 Square roots	I	I	–	–
	009 Dimensional analysis	I	I	–	–
100	**ALGEBRA**				
	101 Integers	V	V	I	I
	102 Rationals	I	I	I	I
	103 Integer exponents	I_s	–	–	–
	104 Formulas and algebraic expressions	I	I	I	I
	105 Polynomials and rational expressions	I	I_s	–	–
	106 Equations and inequations (linear only)	V	I	I	I_s
	107 Relations and functions	I	I	I	–
	108 Systems of linear equations	–	–	–	–
	109 Finite systems	–	–	–	–
	110 Finite sets	I	I	I	–
	111 Flowcharts and programming	–	–	–	–
	112 Real numbers	–	–	–	–
200	**GEOMETRY**				
	201 Classification of plane figures	I	V	I	I_s
	202 Properties of plane figures	I	V	I	I
	203 Congruence of plane figures	I	I	I	I_s
	204 Similarity of plane figures	I	I	I	I_s
	205 Geometric constructions	I_s	I_s	I_s	–
	206 Pythagorean triangles	I_s	I_s	I_s	–
	207 Coordinates	I	I	I	I_s
	208 Simple deductions	I_s	I	I	I
	209 Informal transformations in geometry	I	I	I	–
	210 Relationships between lines and planes in space	–	–	–	–
	211 Solids (Symmetry properties)	I_s	I_s	I_s	–
	212 Spatial visualization and representation	–	I_s	I_s	–
	213 Orientation (spatial)	–	I_s	–	–
	214 Decomposition of figures	–	–	–	–
	215 Transformational geometry	I_s	I_s	I_s	–

Table 1 continued

Content Topics	Behavioral Categories			
	Computation	Comprehension	Application	Analysis
200 PROBABILITY AND STATISTICS				
301 Data collection	I_s	I	I	–
302 Organization of Data	I	I	I	I_s
303 Representation of data	I	I	I	I_s
304 Interpretation of data (mean, median, mode)	I	I	I	–
305 Combinatorics	–	–	–	–
306 Outcomes, sample spaces and events	I_s	–	–	–
307 Counting of sets, (P (A B), P(A B), Independent events	–	–	–	–
308 Mutually exclusive events	–	–	–	–
309 Complementary events	–	–	–	–
400 MEASUREMENT				
401 Standard units of measure	V	V	V	–
402 Estimation	I	I	I	–
403 Approximation	I	I	I	–
404 Determination of measures: areas, volumes, etc.	V	V	I	I

V = very important in all countries
I = important in all countries
I_s = important for some countries.

TABLE 2.
Population B. The International Grid

Content Topics	Behavioral Categories Computation	Comprehension	Application	Analysis
1. SETS, RELATIONS AND FUNCTIONS				
1.1 Set notation	I	I	–	–
1.2 Set operations (e.g., union, inclusion)	I	I	–	–
1.3 Relations	–	–	–	–
1.4 Functions	V	V	V	I
1.5 Infinite sets, cardinality and cardinal algebra (rationals and reals)	–	–	–	–
2. NUMBER SYSTEMS				
2.1 Common laws for number systems	I	I	I	–
2.2 Natural numbers	I	I	I	I
2.3 Decimals	I	I	I	I
2.4 Real numbers	I	I	I	–
2.5 Complex numbers	V	I	I	I
3. ALGEBRA				
3.1 Polynomials (over R)	V	V	V	I
3.2 Quotients of Polynomials	I	I	I	–
3.3 Roots and radicals	V	V	I	–
3.4 Equations and inequalities	V	V	V	I
3.5 System of equations and inequalities	V	V	V	I
3.6 Matrices	I_s	I_s	I_s	I_s
3.7 Groups, rings and fields	–	–	–	–
4. GEOMETRY				
4.1 Euclidean (synthetic) geometry	I	I	–	–
4.2 Affine and projective geometry in the plane	–	–	–	–
4.3 Analytic (coordinate) geometry in the plane	I	I	V	I
4.4 Three-dimensional coordinate geometry	–	–	–	–
4.5 Vector methods	I	I	I	I
4.6 Trigonometry	V	V	V	I
4.7 Finite geometries	–	–	–	–
4.8 Elements of topology	–	–	–	–

Table 2 continued

Content Topics	Behavioral Categories Computation	Comprehension	Application	Analysis
5. ANALYSIS				
5.1 Elementary functions	V	V	V	V
5.2 Properties of functions	V	V	V	I
5.3 Limits and continuity	I	I	I	–
5.4 Differentiation	V	V	I	I
5.5 Applications of the derivative	V	V	V	I
5.6 Integration	V	V	V	I
5.7 Techniques of integration	V	V	I	I
5.8 Applications of integration	V	V	V	I
5.9 Differential equations	I_s	I_s	I_s	I_s
5.10 Sequences and series of functions	–	–	–	–
6. PROBABILITY AND STATISTICS				
6.1 Probability	V	V	I	–
6.2 Statistics	I	I	I	–
6.3 Distributions	I	I	I	–
6.4 Statistical inference	I_s	I_s	–	–
6.5 Bivariate statistics	–	–	–	–
7. FINITE MATHEMATICS				
7.1 Combinatorics	I	I	I	–
8. COMPUTER SCIENCE	I_s	I_s	I	–
9. LOGIC	–	–	–	–

V = very important in all countries
I = important in all countries
I_s = important for some countries

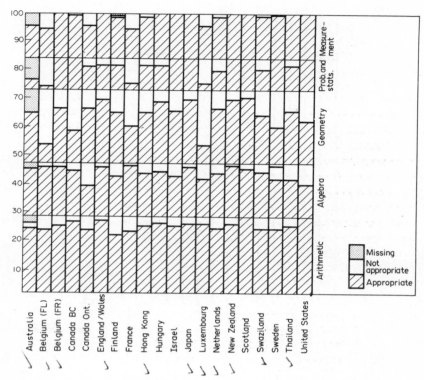

Fig. 1. Population A. Proportion of Items Appropriate by Sub-test and Country

defined sub-tests are asterisked in Table 4 and together consist of 129 discrete items.

An examination of these figures shows clearly that it is important to consider the appropriateness ratings, which signpost variations in the formal curricula between countries, when making any international comparisons. While a good international consensus exists for Algebra the same could not be said for Geometry, hence any comparisons above common item level for Geometry could well be meaningless, when considered across all countries.

Implemented Curriculum

One of the principal measures of the implemented curriculum relies on the "Opportunity-to-Learn" measures. Teachers were asked to respond to the following questions in respect to each item in the test battery for the class in the sample:

Roy W. Phillipps

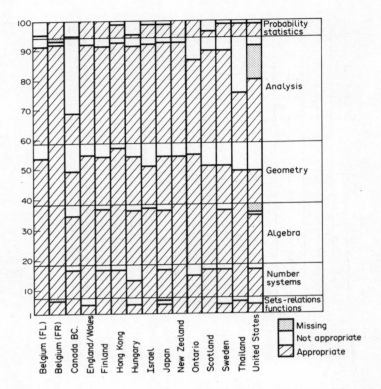

FIG. 2. Population B. Proportion of Items Appropriate by Sub-test and Country

What percentage of the students from the target class do you estimate will get the item correct without guessing?

1   Virtually none
2   6–40 percent
3   41–60 percent
4   61–94 percent
5   Virtually all

(This item was included to focus the teachers' attention on the difference between how a class may react to an item as opposed to whether the mathematics behind the item had been taught).

During this school year did you teach or review the mathematics needed to answer the item correctly?

1   No
2   Yes

If in this school year you did not teach or revise the mathematics needed to answer this item correctly, was it because

       1   it had been taught prior to this school year?
       2   it will be taught later (this year or later)?
       3   it is not in the school curriculum at all?
       4   for other reasons?

Unfortunately not all countries were able to ask these questions of their teachers. These questions will allow a number of approaches to developing O–T–L measures. In Tables 3 and 4 the O-T-L scores displayed simply represent the weighted ratings for sub-scores derived from the teachers' judgements of whether or not the mathematics had been taught or not up to the time of rating. As with the appropriateness ratings, O-T-L should also be considered whenever international comparisons are being made. Students who have not been given an opportunity to study a topic cannot be expected to score well. Any comparisons across countries should therefore be tempered by a consideration of this index.

Achieved Curriculum

Sub-test Scores

Population A

Five major sub-scores have been identified from the items used. Table 3 lists these weighted scores as percentages together with the standard errors and the appropriateness ratings and the opportunity-to-learn measures again expressed as percentages. Figure 3 gives a plot of the median of the international means was well as the upper and lower quartiles of country means. The extremes in each case represent the mean of the country with highest or lowest score respectively.

Population B

Table 4 lists data for 11 scores together with their standard errors, appropriateness ratings and opportunity-to-learn measures, the latter two expressed in percentage form. If the six scores for Sets, Relations and Functions; Number Systems; Algebra; Geometry; Analysis; and Probability and Statistics are considered they account for 129 of 136 items administered at Population B without any overlap of items. The 7 items not included consisted of several items which were originally intended to form a sub-score on finite mathematics and an item that turned out to have an element of ambiguity about it.

Roy W. Phillipps

Population A: Weighted Sub-test Scores, Standard Errors, Weighted OTL and Appropriateness (%)

	No. of items	Belgium (Fl)		Belgium (Fr)		Canada (BC)		Canada (Ont)		England/Wales	
Arithmetic	(46)	58.0	1.4	57.0	1.8	58.0	1.3	54.5	0.9	48.2	1.3
		84.8	76.3	91.3		95.7	82.6	84.8	86.6	97.8	78.0
Algebra	(30)	52.9	1.7	49.1	2.0	47.9	1.4	42.0	0.8	40.1	1.3
		93.3	72.5	93.3		86.7	84.9	56.7	69.7	93.3	62.7
Geometry	(39)	42.5	1.1	42.8	1.5	42.3	1.2	43.2	0.8	44.8	1.2
		25.6	30.7	76.9		43.6	48.3	76.9	48.6	87.2	53.8
Probability & Statistics	(18)	58.2	1.5	52.0	1.7	61.3	1.3	57.0	0.9	60.2	1.1
		11.1	38.7	0.0		94.4	46.9	77.8	60.9	83.3	68.8
Measurement	(24)	58.2	1.3	56.8	1.5	51.9	1.3	50.8	0.9	48.6	1.2
		66.7	83.5	100		95.8	76.5	79.2	83.6	100	79.9

	No. of items	Japan		Luxembourg		Netherlands		New Zealand		Nigeria	
Arithmetic	(46)	60.3	0.4	45.4	1.3	59.3	1.1	45.6	1.2	40.8	1.1
		93.5	84.7	93.5	79.2	87.0	81.5	93.5	67.3		78.7
Algebra	(30)	60.3	0.5	31.2	1.7	51.3	1.2	39.4	1.1	32.4	0.7
		93.3	83.4	73.3	51.6	80.0	73.0	96.7	62.2		72.6
Geometry	(39)	57.6	0.4	25.3	0.8	52.0	1.0	44.8	1.0	26.2	0.7
		87.2	51.2	23.1	35.4	76.9	66.5	87.2	59.4		64.5
Probability & Statistics	(18)	70.9	0.4	37.3	1.3	65.9	0.9	57.3	1.1	37.0	1.0
		100	75.5	22.2	32.4		31.8		59.5		63.7
Measurement	(24)	68.6	0.4	50.1	1.1	61.9	1.0	45.1	1.1	30.7	0.9
		100	94.7	79.2	81.7	87.5	82.4	100	70.1		71.0

Key: Mean   SE
     %
     APP   OTL
     %   %

Table 3 continued

Finland		France		Hong Kong		Hungary		Israel	
45.5	1.0	57.7	0.5	55.1	1.4	56.8	1.5	49.9	1.5
80.4	75.5	82.6	86.2	91.3		93.5	91.2	91.3	70.5
43.6	0.9	55.0	0.8	43.2	1.2	50.4	1.6	44.0	1.6
76.7	69.8	96.7	86.5	80.0		90.0	91.1	76.7	79.4
43.2	0.8	38.0	0.5	42.5	1.0	53.4	1.4	35.9	1.3
69.2	38.6	53.8	42.7	69.2		84.6	86.1	74.4	42.5
57.6	1.0	57.4	0.6	55.9	1.4	60.4	1.3	51.9	1.5
83.3	51.9	27.8	50.3	83.3		83.3	85.5	0.0	52.0
51.3	0.9	59.5	0.4	52.6	1.4	62.1	1.2	46.4	1.3
91.3	70.0	62.5	92.1	91.7		100	97.3	100	63.3

Scotland		Swaziland		Sweden		Thailand		U.S.A.	
50.2	0.5	32.3	1.4	40.6	0.9	43.1	1.3	51.4	1.2
100		87.0	84.9	87.0	65.9	91.3	85.8	100	84.3
42.9	0.7	25.1	1.5	32.3	0.8	37.7	1.0	42.1	1.2
90.0		83.3	87.3	75.9	44.8	73.3	82.7	63.3	67.9
45.5	0.6	31.1	1.3	39.4	0.8	39.3	0.9	37.8	0.9
89.7		64.1	79.7	48.7	34.6	71.8	57.4	59.0	43.6
59.3	0.5	36.0	1.7	56.3	1.1	45.3	1.0	57.7	1.1
100		88.9	82.8	100	46.7	77.8	56.3	94.4	70.4
48.4	0.7	35.2	1.3	48.7	1.0	48.3	1.1	40.8	0.9
100		87.5	92.3	95.8	66.5	100	86.4	100	75.3

TABLE 4.

Population B: Weighted Sub-test Scores, Standard Errors, Weighted OTL and Appropriateness (%)

Sub-test	No. of items	Belgium (Fr)	Belgium (Fl)	Canada (BC)	England	Finland	Hong Kong
Sets, Relations & Functions	(7)*	4.62 0.13 / 100	5.00 0.10 / 85.7 90.9	3.34 0.12 / 100 65.3	4.30 0.07 / 71.4 48.1	5.40 0.09 / 100 87.9	5.57 0.11 / 100
Number Systems	(17)*	7.49 0.26 / 100	8.13 0.19 / 100 79.7	7.33 0.22 / 88.2 75.3	10.09 0.13 / 100 74.2	9.63 0.18 / 100 90.2	13.20 0.26 / 94.1
Algebra	(26)*	14.38 0.41 / 100	15.95 0.31 / 100 91.6	12.20 0.36 / 84.6 82.4	17.15 0.16 / 100 85.7	17.88 0.20 / 96.2 92.4	20.37 0.37 / 100
Equations & Inequalities	(12)	6.62 0.19 / 100	7.16 0.16 / 100 85.7	6.18 0.16 / 83.3 80.9	8.42 0.09 / 100 82.7	8.30 0.12 / 100 92.6	9.46 0.17 / 100
Geometry	(26)*	9.81 0.35 / 76.9	11.03 0.29 / 100 81.9	7.83 0.30 / 57.7 49.9	13.36 0.14 / 84.6 69.3	12.46 0.22 / 80.8 78.9	16.94 0.36 / 92.3
Analytical Geometry	(7)	3.01 0.13 / 85.7	3.55 0.12 / 100 84.0	2.68 0.11 / 71.4 51.1	4.28 0.05 / 100 78.7	3.58 0.09 / 100 94.0	5.38 0.11 / 100
Trigonometry	(8)	3.55 0.20 / 100	4.07 0.14 / 100 95.0	2.68 0.16 / 100 92.8	4.94 0.06 / 100 92.6	4.16 0.12 / 100 96.0	5.99 0.13 / 100
Analysis	(46)*	19.75 0.63 / 93.5	21.03 0.53 / 95.7 87.8	9.67 0.48 / 30.4 32.8	26.45 0.29 / 95.7 85.3	25.12 0.52 / 93.5 86.5	32.76 0.88 / 97.8
Functions	(19)	9.86 0.28 / 100	11.23 0.22 / 94.7 93.3	7.49 0.31 / 89.5 70.8	11.99 0.14 / 89.5 75.5	13.07 0.19 / 100 90.9	14.72 0.32 / 94.7
Calculus	(27)	11.14 0.36 / 88.9	11.30 0.33 / 92.6 85.2	3.65 0.28 / 0.0 11.7	15.48 0.20 / 92.6 87.0	13.31 0.34 / 88.9 82.6	18.45 0.56 / 100
Probability & Statistics	(7)*	2.70 0.10 / 28.6	3.01 0.11 / 100 46.4	2.69 0.12 / 14.3 28.7	4.46 0.06 / 100 61.3	4.03 0.12 / 100 86.7	5.08 0.10 / 85.7

Sub-test	No. of items	Hungary		Israel		Japan		New Zealand		Scotland		Sweden		Thailand	
Sets, Relations & Functions	(7)*	2.47 / 71.4	0.10 / 44.7	3.59 / 100	0.16 / 32.1	5.53 / 71.4	0.07 / 94.7	5.03 / 100	0.09 / 84.7	3.53 / 100	0.11	4.11 / 71.4	0.07 / 60.3	3.64 / 85.7	0.11
Number Systems	(17)*	4.75 / 58.8	0.22 / 55.0	7.84 / 94.1	0.26 / 58.6	11.69 / 94.1	0.18 / 80.1	8.60 / 100	0.23 / 90.1	6.63 / 88.2	0.18	10.56 / 94.1	0.14 / 87.3	5.60 / 94.1	0.20
Algebra	(26)*	11.67 / 92.3	0.38 / 86.7	15.70 / 96.2	0.40 / 69.2	20.32 / 92.3	0.25 / 99.6	14.72 / 100	0.32 / 92.6	12.45 / 100	0.24	15.58 / 92.3	0.21 / 89.5	9.96 / 100	0.37
Equations & Inequalities	(12)	6.34 / 100	0.18 / 91.9	7.93 / 100	0.21 / 65.4	9.66 / 83.3	0.10 / 99.8	7.51 / 100	0.16 / 88.1	6.73 / 100	0.12	8.28 / 100	0.11 / 92.5	5.12 / 100	0.16
Geometry	(26)*	7.85 / 80.8	0.28 / 73.5	9.00 / 69.2	0.38 / 44.1	15.72 / 80.8	0.26 / 89.3	11.14 / 80.8	0.25 / 75.0	10.87 / 69.2	0.22	12.60 / 69.2	0.14 / 65.7	7.74 / 73.1	0.24
Analytical Geometry	(7)	2.61 / 100	0.11 / 81.6	2.83 / 100	0.17 / 53.3	4.99 / 100	0.08 / 92.9	3.29 / 100	0.10 / 70.7	3.19 / 85.7	0.08	4.07 / 71.4	0.06 / 74.0	2.15 / 85.7	0.08
Trigonometry	(8)	2.50 / 100	0.13 / 96.9	4.39 / 100	0.15 / 97.4	5.20 / 100	0.11 / 99.8	3.84 / 100	0.14 / 95.8	3.95 / 87.5	0.10	4.59 / 100	0.08 / 97.4	2.31 / 100	0.11
Analysis	(46)*	11.87 / 93.5	0.50 / 67.1	20.69 / 95.7	0.75 / 79.2	30.70 / 97.8	0.65 / 91.8	22.16 / 97.8	0.52 / 92.6	14.53 / 89.1	0.41	23.51 / 89.1	0.37 / 94.1	12.13 / 47.8	0.37
Functions	(19)	7.45 / 100	0.29 / 73.5	10.37 / 100	0.33 / 70.8	14.22 / 89.5	0.21 / 95.1	11.20 / 100	0.23 / 87.6	8.06 / 94.7	0.23	11.62 / 89.5	0.12 / 84.3	7.26 / 89.5	0.26
Calculus	(27)	5.54 / 88.9	0.27 / 59.1	10.80 / 92.6	0.46 / 71.9	16.98 / 96.3	0.42 / 89.4	12.63 / 96.3	0.34 / 93.5	7.61 / 88.9	0.28	12.62 / 85.2	0.26 / 80.9	5.76 / 22.0	0.14
Probability & Statistics	(7)*	2.01 / 28.6	0.08 / 26.9	2.63 / 85.7	0.15 / 36.7	4.93 / 85.7	0.07 / 81.7	4.06 / 100	0.12 / 86.4	3.19 / 42.9	0.08	4.48 / 85.7	0.07 / 75.0	2.39 / 85.7	0.09

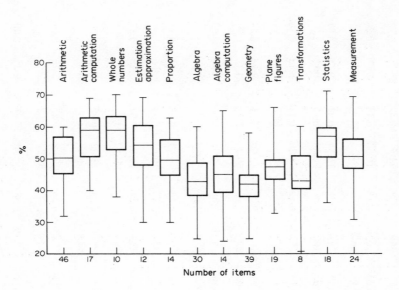

Fɪɢ. 3. Population A Plots Showing Medians and Quartiles of Country Means
as well as Highest and Lowest Country Means

Retentivity

When making international comparisons at Population B level there is
a further caveat in addition to appropriateness and opportunity-to-learn
to be considered, namely the retentivity of students within the system. As
can be seen from the figures in Table 5 these do vary considerably from
country to country.

Algebra Sub-scores

The appropriateness ratings identify the content of the algebra sub-
tests as ones where the items have considerable support from most
countries. At Population A level Canada (Ontario) and the USA
indicated that more than a third of the items were outside their normal
curriculum but for all other countries at least about 75 percent of the
test was appropriate or acceptable. Only Canada (British Columbia)
expressed any real reservation at Population B with an 85 percent
appropriateness rating.

Some discrepanices do occur though between Appropriateness ratings
and the teachers' "Opportunity-to-Learn" measures. For example, the
England/Wales National Committee considered 93 percent of the items
appropriate but the teachers report that only 63 percent of the students
had been taught the sub-test content before or at the Population A level.
Large discrepancies also appear for Luxembourg and Sweden. The cause

TABLE. 5.

Percentage of Population B age cohort retained in school system and the percentage of that retained cohort taking mathematics courses as defined for Population B

Country	% of age cohort in school	% of age cohort in school taking Pop B mathematics
Belgium (Fl)	65	9–10
Belgium (Fr)	65	9–10
Canada (BC)	82	30
Canada (Ont)	36	19
England	17	6
Finland	59	15
Hong Kong	23	8
Hungary	50	50*
Israel	60	6
Japan	87	12
New Zealand	17	11
Scotland	33	15
Sweden	24	12
Thailand	8	?
USA	75	10–12

*Note. Total cohort included as all students are required to take aptitude based courses in mathematics. About 7% of the target population take advanced courses.

of such mismatches may well lie in teacher unfamiliarity with the official syllabuses or, as has been suggested by one country, an over-reliance by the teachers on textbooks which fail to mirror the objectives and intent of the actual syllabuses.

Two countries, Japan and Netherlands, which were among the higher scoring countries in the algebra sub-test at Population A display quite different patterns of class or school mean score distributions. Figure 4 gives the stem and leaf patterns for these two countries revealing a pattern of "national mastery" for Japan while the Netherlands' pattern probably reflects the variety of school types and curricula within their system. It should be noted that the Netherlands' sample was not fully representative in that 20 percent of the students in the Population were excluded from the sample. These students were in the school type which catered for the weaker students.

The Algebra sub-test contained 30 items at the Population A level. A sample of 10 of these items has been selected here to illustrate the range of items and results to some of the algebraic concepts.

(Each plot, e.g. the top Japanese score 26.3, is a class mean).

Japan
Stem leaf   #   *Box Plot*

Stem	leaf	#	Box Plot
26	3	1	0
25	6	1	0
24			
23	3	1	0
22	3	1	I
21	011112334458	12	I
20	00023334556778889	17	I
19	00111111113333444555666677777888899	35	+-----+
18	0111122223334445555566666666666778888999	40	✫--+--✫
17	0000001111122222333344445555666667777888888999	46	I I
16	111233344455678888889999	24	+-----+
15	1123556769	10	I
14	136789999	9	I
13	0266789	7	0
12	7	1	0
11	1	1	0

    ----+----+----+----+----+----+----+----+----+-

Multiply stem leaf by 10✫✫+01

Netherlands
Stem	leaf	#	Box plot
27	2	1	I
26	1469	4	I
25	06	2	I
24	024557	6	I
23	0134778	7	I
22	1133347788	10	I
21	0012228	7	I
20	11134456778999	14	I
19	0278	4	I
18	12235677889	11	+ ----- +
17	23559	5	I I
16	0112223334567779	16	I I
15	00011233445566678	17	I + I
14	01122344446777889	17	✫ ----- ✫
13	145556	6	I I
12	0122234557778899	16	I I
11	01135679	8	I I
10	0023467899	10	I I
9	0001223444789	13	I I
8	000011112233344456777889999	27	+ ----- +
7	0013455556888999	16	I
6	0123566789	10	I
5	33468	5	I
4	06	2	I
3	49	2	I

    ----+----+----+----+----+----+----+--

Multiply stem leaf by 10✫✫+01

Fig. 4. Stem and Leaf Diagrams for Japan and Netherlands for Population
A Algebra Sub-score

The solution of 6 of the items depends largely on the capacity of the student to comprehend and manipulate directed numbers. Apart from Japan no country could claim any degree of national mastery of the ability to subtract one negative number from another as is illustrated by Example 1. It is interesting to note from the distractor patterns that random guessing is not taking place. Examples 2 and 3 which required the product of two negative numbers produced results which tended to indicate, except for Sweden, a sizeable proportion of each sample had learned the rule and could respond correctly to Example 2. However when in Example 3 an additional step of substitution was called for there was a marked reduction in correct answers as can be seen from the item analysis statistics. Example 4 had the added complication of needing a translation from a verbal form before the mathematics could be performed. Whatever the reason this item proved very difficult in all countries except the Netherlands — where there are no mountains!

As indicated in the third Japanese National Report (Sawada, 1983), the use of the number line concept in teaching directed number operations seems to be a useful strategy. This is one of the hypotheses being investigated in the longitudinal study. Examples 5 and 6 are two items which relate to the use of the number line. The results shown in Example 5 would seem to indicate that not all classes are familiar with the concept.

The solution of simple equations, which might be considered an important objective for algebra teaching at this level, was tested by Examples 7 and 8. The principal error, as is revealed by the distractor pattern in Example 7, appears once again to be associated with the ability to handle directed numbers.

Only in Israel and Japan could more than 50 percent of the students make a correct response in Examples 9 and 10 which tested the understanding of zero in operations.

Population B Algebra Items

The 26 items in this sub-test are characterized by the fact that all the National Mathematics Committees endorsed 17 of the items as appropriate. One country had reservations about 4 of the items and a further 3 items were rated inappropriate by 2 countries and 5 countries found 2 of the items inappropriate for their country.

Table 6 lists the 17 items deemed appropriate in all countries and indicates those countries where a correct response by at least 75 percent of the sample was achieved. Also listed are those countries where less than 30 percent could respond correctly. Three countries — Scotland, Belgium (Fr), Hong Kong — did not collect O-T-L data from teachers.

Roy W. Phillipps

```
Code 113
(−6) − (−8) is equal to
        A      14
       *B       2
        C      −2
        D     −10
        E     −14

* = correct answer
```

Country	A	B	C	D	E	Omit
Belgium (Fl)	7.6	50.7	10.6	1.7	27.7	1.8
Belgium (Fr)	7.8	50.6	15.4	1.5	17.3	7.4
Canada (BC)	13.0	46.9	9.9	1.5	26.1	2.7
Canada (Ont)	12.2	41.4	15.3	1.8	27.6	1.7
England/Wales	12.5	35.6	24.6	1.0	25.7	0.8
Finland	10.5	40.3	28.9	2.7	17.1	0.5
France	5.4	70.4	12.1	0.4	10.2	1.5
Hong Kong	15.1	42.5	19.8	3.3	18.1	1.0
Hungary	11.1	42.7	14.4	0.6	27.2	4.3
Israel	10.1	45.7	14.7	1.7	20.3	7.4
Japan	5.1	71.5	10.2	1.1	11.2	1.1
Luxembourg	5.7	47.0	14.9	1.9	14.6	15.9
Netherlands	8.0	40.0	10.3	2.3	38.0	1.6
New Zealand	12.8	29.2	17.5	1.9	36.3	2.4
Nigeria	19.1	25.4	19.5	6.1	22.2	8.0
Scotland	15.0	39.0	17.0	1.0	24.0	3.0
Swaziland	14.6	25.2	29.6	2.3	23.5	4.8
Sweden	12.0	22.2	24.6	5.8	32.5	3.0
Thailand	23.0	32.4	20.6	1.2	22.4	0.4
USA	9.6	38.6	21.9	3.2	25.1	1.5

EXAMPLE 1.

```
┌─────────────────────────────────┐
│           Code 012              │
│   (−2) × (−3) is equal to       │
│           A     −6              │
│           B     −5              │
│           C     −1              │
│           D      5              │
│          *E      6              │
│                                 │
│     * = correct answer          │
└─────────────────────────────────┘
```

Country	A	B	C	D	E	Omit
Belgium (Fl)	17.8	4.5	2.2	3.2	67.2	5.0
Belgium (Fr)	22.0	3.0	3.5	2.6	64.2	4.7
Canada (BC)	22.2	3.9	0.9	3.5	68.0	1.6
Canada (Ont)	26.5	4.9	2.2	4.1	61.3	1.2
England/Wales	32.8	11.5	5.8	4.3	45.0	0.6
Finland	22.9	3.0	1.7	3.0	69.2	0.3
France	15.5	2.2	0.5	3.0	77.4	1.4
Hong Kong	35.8	4.2	3.7	3.5	51.5	1.2
Hungary	23.6	3.6	1.5	3.8	66.9	0.8
Israel	11.9	3.3	2.5	4.3	76.0	2.0
Japan	10.5	1.3	0.9	1.6	85.2	0.3
Luxembourg	23.6	4.7	2.5	3.2	50.9	15.1
Netherlands	21.9	2.7	1.2	2.0	71.5	0.8
New Zealand	30.7	11.2	5.5	6.4	45.5	0.9
Nigeria	28.4	5.2	1.9	4.1	58.6	1.7
Scotland	22.0	8.0	4.0	5.0	59.0	2.0
Swaziland	53.4	7.8	5.0	1.9	26.9	4.9
Sweden	55.8	11.4	8.6	3.9	19.6	0.8
Thailand	24.1	4.3	2.7	5.9	62.6	0.2
USA	29.9	6.4	4.3	3.7	54.3	1.4

EXAMPLE 2.

```
              Code 115
    If x = −3, the value of −3x is
           A      −9
           B      −6
           C      −1
           D       1
          *E       9

    * = correct answer
```

Country	A	B	C	D	E	Omit
Belgium (Fl)	18.4	11.0	7.6	6.0	46.7	10.4
Belgium (Fr)	18.8	9.8	4.6	6.1	50.7	10.0
Canada (BC)	21.6	10.2	5.2	4.9	50.5	7.7
Canada (Ont)	29.1	13.1	5.5	4.6	45.3	2.5
England/Wales	37.5	15.9	5.2	3.3	33.1	5.3
Finland	19.4	15.6	8.0	5.2	49.3	2.7
France	26.6	4.7	2.8	2.5	56.9	6.4
Hong Kong	33.3	16.7	9.2	8.0	30.8	1.7
Hungary	26.9	8.4	2.7	4.4	47.5	10.3
Israel	22.8	9.7	4.4	3.9	37.9	21.3
Japan	9.9	11.9	3.9	6.6	63.0	4.8
Luxembourg	20.7	12.5	2.4	2.8	27.0	34.6
Netherlands	19.3	9.9	7.0	7.3	52.4	4.2
New Zealand	29.2	18.2	8.4	9.8	32.4	2.1
Nigeria	19.5	24.2	8.2	6.1	33.3	9.0
Scotland	26.0	12.0	5.0	5.0	46.0	6.0
Swaziland	31.7	15.5	7.6	6.5	15.2	23.6
Sweden	28.4	29.3	13.9	10.8	13.1	4.5
Thailand	33.9	13.9	10.0	9.6	32.2	0.3
USA	27.1	16.7	7.2	8.6	37.3	3.0

EXAMPLE 3.

Code 013

The air temperature at the foot of a mountain is 31 degrees. On top of the mountain the temperature is −7 degrees. How much warmer is the air at the foot of the mountain?

A	−38 degrees
B	−24 degrees
C	7 degrees
D	24 degrees
*E	38 degrees

* = correct answer

Country	A	B	C	D	E	Omit
Belgium (Fl)	5.0	6.2	3.0	20.5	64.1	1.2
Belgium (Fr)	10.3	9.0	3.7	18.4	43.0	15.5
Canada (BC)	3.6	4.9	2.4	27.6	58.0	3.5
Canada (Ont)	7.2	9.7	3.4	26.9	50.9	2.0
England/Wales	8.6	12.4	3.3	24.5	48.8	2.5
Finland	6.5	10.4	5.3	34.8	40.7	2.2
France	6.7	6.1	1.6	30.0	52.3	3.3
Hong Kong	5.6	8.8	9.1	30.1	42.5	3.7
Hungary	4.9	7.1	0.7	29.9	56.2	1.3
Israel	16.3	8.2	3.0	26.8	34.2	11.5
Japan	4.1	5.1	2.1	26.4	60.7	1.5
Luxembourg	9.3	8.0	3.2	25.4	35.6	18.5
Netherlands	3.9	3.4	2.3	16.2	72.1	2.3
New Zealand	7.5	9.6	5.1	23.3	52.6	2.0
Nigeria	18.9	16.3	5.2	25.4	12.6	21.3
Scotland	8.0	7.0	4.0	21.0	56.0	4.0
Swaziland	12.1	14.0	6.0	15.7	12.3	39.8
Sweden	9.8	10.7	4.8	23.8	46.9	4.0
Thailand	8.9	24.9	6.0	38.1	21.6	0.4
USA	7.5	11.5	6.8	28.3	43.1	2.9

EXAMPLE 4.

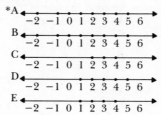

Code 082

The set of integers less than 5 is represented on one of the number lines shown below. Which one?

*A
$-2 \ -1 \ 0 \ 1 \ 2 \ 3 \ 4 \ 5 \ 6$

B
$-2 \ -1 \ 0 \ 1 \ 2 \ 3 \ 4 \ 5 \ 6$

C
$-2 \ -1 \ 0 \ 1 \ 2 \ 3 \ 4 \ 5 \ 6$

D
$-2 \ -1 \ 0 \ 1 \ 2 \ 3 \ 4 \ 5 \ 6$

E
$-2 \ -1 \ 0 \ 1 \ 2 \ 3 \ 4 \ 5 \ 6$

* = correct answer

Country	A	B	C	D	E	Omit
Belgium (Fl)	46.3	14.6	11.9	10.4	13.3	3.4
Belgium (Fr)	33.8	10.2	10.5	12.1	17.0	16.3
Canada (BC)	65.6	8.9	4.9	7.3	7.9	5.5
Canada (Ont)	56.7	12.7	8.7	10.7	8.9	2.4
England/Wales	32.6	8.6	24.3	11.2	15.4	8.1
Finland	49.5	11.9	11.8	9.8	14.5	2.7
France	58.1	12.4	4.7	5.3	11.3	8.0
Hong Kong	22.6	15.7	19.1	17.9	18.0	6.3
Hungary	43.1	8.6	13.3	2.8	14.9	17.5
Israel	30.7	13.5	9.2	4.8	15.4	26.4
Japan	53.7	13.3	3.0	5.2	21.6	3.3
Luxembourg	27.5	1.5	8.6	4.2	12.9	45.3
Netherlands	55.3	12.2	6.1	7.1	15.9	3.6
New Zealand	54.9	14.3	8.2	10.5	10.0	1.8
Nigeria	9.7	7.7	28.1	11.9	13.5	29.8
Scotland	49.0	12.0	10.0	8.0	12.0	7.0
Swaziland	14.4	11.8	20.0	8.5	10.4	34.8
Sweden	27.6	10.7	13.8	13.0	28.9	5.8
Thailand	39.5	21.4	10.7	10.9	17.1	0.3
USA	47.4	14.9	13.5	11.7	11.4	1.0

EXAMPLE 5.

```
                        Code 014
                  —o———— o———— o—
                  −10      0      10
          Which of the following sequences of numbers
          is in the order in which they occur from left to
          right on the number line?
                  A      0, ½, −1

                  B      0, −1, ½

                 *C      −1, − ½, 0

                  D      −1, 0, ½

                  E      − ½, −1, 0


          * = correct answer
```

Country	A	B	C	D	E	Omit
Belgium (Fl)	4.4	5.4	56.8	17.0	10.6	5.8
Belgium (Fr)	7.1	5.0	53.8	14.4	6.3	13.4
Canada (BC)	5.5	6.8	46.6	12.8	8.2	20.1
Canada (Ont)	9.1	9.2	45.6	16.5	14.4	5.2
England/Wales	8.6	7.2	51.3	16.2	7.0	9.9
Finland	4.7	5.8	67.6	12.4	6.4	3.2
France	4.7	6.0	34.8	12.1	7.6	34.6
Hong Kong	10.5	10.0	46.4	16.9	13.2	3.1
Hungary	4.7	7.0	63.3	9.5	8.5	7.1
Israel	7.8	3.4	69.3	4.8	5.8	8.8
Japan	4.5	5.6	67.1	10.4	10.9	1.5
Luxembourg	4.5	5.5	20.8	10.3	4.3	54.6
Netherlands	2.1	1.9	86.9	4.5	3.9	0.8
New Zealand	8.4	9.5	49.6	16.7	12.0	3.8
Nigeria	16.7	15.0	23.4	11.6	9.6	23.5
Scotland	7.0	5.0	64.0	13.0	6.0	5.0
Swaziland	20.7	11.7	33.3	8.8	9.4	16.0
Sweden	6.8	9.3	37.6	35.3	5.2	5.9
Thailand	9.6	11.1	34.8	17.7	26.1	0.7
USA	9.3	9.7	51.8	12.6	11.0	5.7

EXAMPLE 6.

```
┌─────────────────────────────────┐
│           Code 151              │
│    If 5x +4 = 4x −31, then      │
│    x is equal to                │
│           *A      −35           │
│            B      −27           │
│            C       3            │
│            D      27            │
│            E      35            │
│                                 │
│    * = correct answer           │
└─────────────────────────────────┘
```

Country	A	B	C	D	E	Omit
Belgium (Fl)	44.8	17.4	9.2	8.4	7.9	12.4
Belgium (Fr)	39.5	16.3	10.8	9.3	7.2	16.9
Canada (BC)	17.9	20.2	16.8	17.1	5.9	22.3
Canada (Ont)	13.0	19.1	26.7	20.2	7.8	13.1
England/Wales	22.4	23.5	20.4	17.3	8.5	8.2
Finland	18.1	23.7	22.6	20.7	7.6	7.4
France	41.5	17.4	12.1	7.3	6.0	15.8
Hong Kong	24.4	23.0	17.6	19.1	11.6	3.9
Hungary	45.6	17.4	9.3	8.4	6.3	13.2
Israel	22.6	15.0	7.9	15.3	5.9	33.2
Japan	57.8	11.5	9.7	6.9	10.0	4.2
Luxembourg	20.1	12.2	6.0	7.3	4.0	50.5
Netherlands	30.7	21.2	13.8	14.0	10.3	10.2
New Zealand	14.3	25.6	26.7	19.5	9.8	4.3
Nigeria	24.8	25.7	12.7	14.6	10.9	11.7
Scotland	26.0	20.0	15.0	14.0	11.0	14.0
Swaziland	9.3	15.8	19.6	17.4	14.7	23.5
Sweden	13.4	24.0	25.1	21.1	9.1	7.2
Thailand	15.5	29.0	22.0	18.7	12.9	1.9
USA	20.1	20.4	24.3	20.6	8.9	5.9

EXAMPLE 7.

```
                Code 018
      If 6x −3 = 15
        then 6x = 15 −3  (i)
        and 6x = 12      (ii)
        and x    = 12    (iii)
                    6
        and x   =   2    (iv)
      The error in the above reasoning,
      if one exists, FIRST APPEARS in
      line
              *A      (i)
               B      (ii)
               C      (iii)
               D      (iv)
               E      None of these,
                      there is no error.

      * = correct answer
```

Country	A	B	C	D	E	Omit
Belgium (Fl)	55.2	9.6	12.0	4.8	10.0	8.6
Belgium (Fr)	54.8	5.9	6.5	5.4	16.1	11.3
Canada (BC)	44.9	10.0	12.3	5.7	15.5	11.7
Canada (Ont)	37.6	10.6	16.8	6.2	24.3	4.6
England/Wales	40.1	12.7	12.0	5.2	24.3	5.8
Finland	36.3	14.9	20.0	8.0	17.1	3.9
France	58.0	7.7	9.9	4.3	11.7	8.3
Hong Kong	48.6	9.1	12.6	7.6	20.6	1.4
Hungary	59.2	18.2	6.1	2.9	11.6	2.1
Israel	49.6	12.9	7.7	5.9	11.4	12.5
Japan	76.8	3.2	7.7	2.6	9.1	0.6
Luxembourg	32.3	5.7	8.0	2.1	15.2	36.7
Netherlands	53.1	10.8	13.1	5.0	14.2	3.9
New Zealand	35.8	14.5	16.4	8.1	21.9	3.3
Nigeria	36.8	11.0	6.7	8.2	30.1	7.1
Scotland	45.0	12.0	14.0	4.0	20.0	6.0
Swaziland	17.5	10.2	10.0	9.8	38.5	14.1
Sweden	29.1	14.4	19.6	8.6	23.6	4.8
Thailand	39.0	18.6	14.0	10.9	16.1	1.4
USA	41.8	13.2	14.8	10.4	17.4	2.5

EXAMPLE 8.

Code 086

If $\dfrac{4x}{12} = 0$, then x is equal to

*A	0
B	3
C	8
D	12
E	16

* = correct answer

Country	A	B	C	D	E	Omit
Belgium (Fl)	43.2	27.3	12.2	5.3	2.4	9.7
Belgium (Fr)	47.5	35.4	3.9	2.9	1.6	8.7
Canada (BC)	56.5	30.5	4.3	1.2	0.6	7.0
Canada (Ont)	51.8	33.8	6.2	3.5	1.4	3.4
England/Wales	36.0	42.9	9.1	6.1	3.8	2.3
Finland	45.9	36.8	8.0	6.0	1.8	1.5
France	55.8	33.0	2.6	2.3	0.6	5.6
Hong Kong	43.2	41.1	8.8	3.6	1.6	1.4
Hungary	42.5	46.2	3.1	2.3	1.6	4.4
Israel	56.8	25.6	4.6	2.7	1.4	8.9
Japan	50.0	42.1	3.5	2.8	0.5	1.2
Luxembourg	26.2	37.3	3.5	2.0	0.7	30.4
Netherlands	39.3	47.1	5.4	3.8	0.9	3.6
New Zealand	48.8	31.7	9.7	6.0	2.8	1.1
Nigeria	18.6	69.2	4.3	2.9	2.0	3.4
Scotland	36.0	46.0	7.0	4.0	2.0	4.0
Swaziland	27.2	46.6	9.2	4.4	3.8	9.2
Sweden	26.5	48.7	13.5	5.5	3.3	2.4
Thailand	35.4	41.1	13.0	6.1	3.7	0.6
USA	46.8	31.0	9.3	6.5	3.3	3.1

EXAMPLE 9.

$$
\begin{array}{c}
\text{Code 053} \\
\text{When } x = 2,\ \dfrac{7x + 4}{5x - 4} \text{ is equal to}
\end{array}
$$

A	11
*B	3
C	$\dfrac{11}{5}$
D	$\dfrac{9}{5}$
E	$\dfrac{7}{5}$

* = correct answer

Country	A	B	C	D	E	Omit
Belgium (Fl)	9.4	48.3	10.8	10.5	7.5	13.4
Belgium (Fr)	7.1	55.8	7.4	5.9	8.4	15.4
Canada (BC)	6.8	59.2	9.6	6.3	3.9	14.3
Canada (Ont)	7.3	61.1	11.9	8.0	6.3	5.4
England/Wales	13.7	47.7	17.4	8.0	6.4	6.9
Finland	12.3	52.2	14.5	10.0	7.5	3.5
France	4.4	55.5	7.9	5.7	9.6	16.8
Hong Kong	8.4	53.6	14.7	11.9	8.5	2.7
Hungary	9.7	58.3	14.3	3.4	3.7	10.9
Israel	6.8	48.4	14.4	2.5	2.9	25.1
Japan	7.0	62.5	6.0	5.3	14.8	4.4
Luxembourg	10.1	35.2	9.2	3.1	6.9	35.4
Netherlands	8.2	64.6	8.7	7.5	5.2	5.9
New Zealand	12.4	42.6	20.0	12.4	8.4	4.2
Nigeria	15.0	38.0	13.2	9.0	13.1	12.2
Scotland	12.0	56.0	15.0	7.0	4.0	5.0
Swaziland	16.8	19.1	21.4	8.4	9.3	25.2
Sweden	11.8	38.6	20.1	15.2	8.6	5.7
Thailand	19.2	38.9	22.9	9.2	8.4	1.4
USA	12.1	53.5	13.5	10.3	6.1	4.4

EXAMPLE 10.

Roy W. Phillipps

TABLE 6.

Population B. Algebra Sub-test Items Deemed Appropriate in all Countries

Code No.	Stem	Correctly answered by 75% or more	OTL %	Correctly answered by less than 30%	OTL %
004	$3a^{1/2} \times 3a^{-1/2}$ is equal to	Hong Kong	–	Hungary Thailand USA New Zealand Israel	100 96 100 100 96
005	Which of the following points lies in the region bounded by the lines $y = 1$, $y = x$, and $x + y = 6$.	England/Wales Finland Japan	90 98 100	Thailand	82
006	The curve defined by $y = 3x(x - 2)(2x + 1)$ intersects the x-axis only at the points . . .	England/Wales Belgium (Fl) Finland Hong Kong Japan Canada (Ont)	98 97 100 – 100 90	Thailand	31
008	P is a polynomial in x of degree m, and Q is a polynomial in x of degree n, with $n < m$. The degree of polynomial $(P + Q)(P - Q)$ is			*ALL* except Hong Kong, Finland, and Japan.	
017	The number of pairs of integer values of x, y which satisfy $x + y < 4$, $x > 0$, $y > 0$ simultaneously is	Japan	100	Thailand	77
019	Which of the following, $(x - 1)$, $(x - 2)$, $(x + 2)$, $(x - 4)$ are factors of $x^3 - 4x^2 - x + 4$?	Belgium (Fl) Finland Hong Kong Japan Canada (Ont)	77 92 – 100 74	–	
021	 According to the graph, $ax + b > cx^2$ when			*ALL* except Hong Kong and Japan	

Table 6 continued

Code No.	Stem	Correctly answered by 75% or more	OTL %	Correctly answered by less than 30%	OTL %
036	$P(\pi) = \dfrac{n^3 - 2n^2 - n + 2}{n^2 - 1}$ P(n) is not defined for	Belgium (Fl) Belgium (Fr) Canada (Ont) Finland Hong Kong Israel Japan New Zealand USA	99 – 92 99 – 96 99 99 99	–	
050	Two mathematical models are proposed to predict the return y, in dollars, from the sale of x thousand units of an article (where $0 < x < 5$). Each of these models, A and B, is based on different marketing methods. model A $y = 6x - x^2$ model B $y = 2x$ For what values of x does model B predict a greater return than model A?	–		–	
051	A piece of wire 52 cm long is cut into two parts and each part is bent to form a square. The total area of the two squares is 97 cm². How much longer (in cm) is a side of the larger square than a side of the smaller square?	–		–	
066	The solution set for the equation $(1 - 2x)(2 + x) = 0$ is . . .	*ALL* except Hungary & Thailand		–	
067	If x is a real number. then y, defined by $y = \sqrt{x^2 - 1}$, is a real number for	Finland Hong Kong Israel Japan	100 – 93 100	–	
079	If $2x^2 - 12x + 9 = 2(x - a)^2 + b$, then	England/Wales Finland Hong Kong Japan	96 99 – 100		

Table 6 continued

Code No.	Stem	Correctly answered by 75% or more	OTL %	Correctly answered by less than 30%	OTL %
080	If $x > 0$, $y > 0$, and $x \neq y$, then $\dfrac{1}{\sqrt{x} - \sqrt{y}}$ is equal to . .	Finland Hong Kong Japan	100 – 100		
081	If x and y are real numbers for which x can you define y by $\qquad\ldots\ldots\ldots$ $y = \dfrac{x}{\sqrt{9 - x^2}}$	–		Canada (BC) New Zealand Scotland USA	96 100 – 99
082	For the equation $x^2 - 5x + 6 = 0$	All countries	–		
097	A freight train travelling at 50 kilometres per hour leaves a station 3 hours before an express train which travels in the same direction at 90 kilometres an hour. How many hours after leaving will it take the express train to over-take the freight train?	Hong Kong Japan	– 100	–	

Algebra Anchor Items

Population A

The Algebra sub-test contains 7 items which were administered in the first IEA Mathematics Study and one item (113) which had been used as an open-ended item in the first study. These 8 items are listed in Table 7 with their appropriateness and O-T-L ratings, where available, from the second study. Any interpretation of a positive or negative change would need to take account of the emphasis the mathematics behind these items is given in the current curricula.

Population B

Two items, 082 and 095, unchanged from the first study were included in the second study while a further three were included in a slightly modified form. Item 081 was modified to make the correct response mathematically correct by changing ' x < −3 and x > 3' to 'x < −3 or x > 3'. Item 020 in its original form had two correct responses and it may be difficult to assess whether the changes have made the new version intrinsically easier. Most countries display improved results on

TABLE 7.
Population A. Algebra Anchor Items

Code 113
$(-6) - (-8)$ is equal to

A	14
B	2
C	-2
D	-10
E	-14

(Note: open-ended in 1st Study)

Country	Pop 1B 1st Study Score %	Pop A 2nd Study Score %	Appropriate*	OTL %
Belgium (Fr)	47.8	56.9	√	–
England/Wales	37.9	34.4	√	89
Finland	47.7	39.9	√	98
France	32.6	71.4	√	99
Israel	35.2	41.1	√	92
Japan	62.3	72.0	√	100
Netherlands	30.4	37.6	√	90
Scotland	37.1	39.5	√	–
Sweden	25.0	22.5	√	59
USA	28.9	40.7	X	94

* √ Appropriate; X Not appropriate

Code 015
Simplify: $5x + 3y + 2x - 4y$

A	$7x + 7y$
B	$8x - 2y$
C	$6xy$
D	$7x - y$
E	$7x + y$

Country	Pop 1B 1st Study Score %	Pop A 2nd Study Score %	Appropriate*	OTL %
Belgium (Fr)	71.1	76.8	√	–
England/Wales	51.0	48.8	√	88
Finland	11.7	54.0	√	93
France	42.6	78.9	√	97
Israel	42.7	66.7	√	88
Japan	39.1	73.7	√	80
Netherlands	41.8	65.5	√	91
Scotland	51.5	52.7	√	–
Sweden	14.6	35.2	√	58
USA	26.2	30.3	√	54

* √ Appropriate; X Not appropriate

Table 7 Continued

Code 120

The symbol P ∩ Q represents the   A   (P ∩ Q) ∪ R
intersection of sets P and Q and the   B   P ∪ (Q ∩ R)
symbol P ∪ Q represents the union   C   P ∩ (Q ∪ R)
of sets P and Q. Which of the   D   (P ∩ Q) ∩ R
following represents the shaded   E   (P ∪ Q ∩ R
portion of the diagram

Country	Pop 1B 1st Study Score %	Pop A 2nd Study Score %	Appropriate*	OTL %
Belgium (Fr)	17.2	46.3	√	–
England/Wales	18.6	28.3	√	39
Finland	9.6	26.1	√	76
France	13.4	36.2	X	93
Israel	18.5	26.8	√	69
Japan	34.9	36.9	√	55
Netherlands	6.8	32.2	√	63
Scotland	16.9	27.9	√	–
Sweden	19.4	23.1	√	18
USA	23.2	24.9	X	84

* √ Appropriate; X Not appropriate

Code 148

Which of the following is FALSE
when *a*, *b*, and *c* are different
real numbers?

    A $(a + b) + c = a + (b + c)$
    B $ab = ba$
    C $a + b = b + a$
    D $(ab)c = a(bc)$
    E $a - b = b - a$

Country	Pop 1B 1st Study Score %	Pop A 2nd Study Score %	Appropriate*	OTL %
Belgium (Fr)	39.1	56.5	√	–
England/Wales	31.4	33.5	√	40
Finland	31.9	37.2	√	78
France	30.7	62.3	√	99
Israel	53.5	44.8	X	78
Japan	59.4	59.3	√	57
Netherlands	27.0	33.8	X	76
Scotland	34.8	33.9	√	–
Sweden	18.8	21.8	X	28
USA	39.5	36.2	√	66

* √ Appropriate; X Not appropriate

Table 7 continued

Code 016

Soda costs *a* cents for each bottle, but there is a refund of *b* cents on each empty bottle. How much will Henry have to pay for x bottles if he brings back y empties?	A	ax + by cents
	B	ax − by cents
	C	(a − b)x cents
	D	(a + x) − (b + y) cents
	E	none of these

Country	Pop 1B 1st Study Score %	Pop A 2nd Study Score %	Appropriate*	OTL %
Belgium (Fr)	42.8	37.7	√	–
England/Wales	35.0	38.6	√	58
Finland	34.6	35.9	X	59
France	30.7	40.2	√	60
Israel	44.3	49.2	√	73
Japan	58.8	61.5	√	97
Netherlands	35.7	44.7	√	51
Scotland	39.4	36.8	√	–
Sweden	22.5	30.5	X	31
USA	28.4	30.5	√	42

* √ Appropriate; X Not appropriate

Code 017

If P = LW and if P = 12 and L = 3, then W is equal to

A	$\frac{3}{4}$
B	3
C	4
D	12
E	36

Country	Pop 1B 1st Study Score %	Pop A 2nd Study Score %	Appropriate*	OTL %
Belgium (Fr)	61.6	74.0	√	–
England/Wales	61.4	56.6	√	82
Finland	47.9	54.4	√	85
France	40.6	89.6	√	97
Israel	65.0	59.3	√	83
Japan	76.7	81.6	√	94
Netherlands	50.2	67.7	√	87
Scotland	62.0	63.3	√	–
Sweden	45.2	44.0	√	48
USA	66.2	68.3	√	89

* √ Appropriate; X Not appropriate

Table 7 continued

Code 086

If $\frac{4x}{12} = 0$, then x is equal to

A	0
B	3
C	8
D	12
E	16

Country	Pop 1B 1st Study Score %	Pop A 2nd Study Score %	Appropriate*	OTL %
Belgium (Fr)	33.2	51.8	√	–
England/Wales	33.1	34.4	√	83
Finland	30.4	43.7	√	81
France	26.7	56.5	√	92
Israel	27.9	61.6	√	86
Japan	37.0	50.6	√	99
Netherlands	18.9	37.5	√	80
Scotland	30.3	35.8	√	–
Sweden	18.7	26.1	Missing	74
USA	38.1	48.4	√	80

* √ Appropriate; X Not appropriate

Code 118

$\frac{x}{2} < 7$ is equivalent to

A	$x < \frac{7}{2}$
B	$x < 5$
C	$x < 14$
D	$x > 5$
E	$x > 14$

Country	Pop 1B 1st Study Score %	Pop A 2nd Study Score %	Appropriate*	OTL %
Belgium (Fr)	45.2	41.1	√	–
England/Wales	39.2	34.6	√	30
Finland	29.6	32.8	√	28
France	27.3	27.7	√	67
Israel	38.2	33.7	√	77
Japan	35.2	45.8	√	20
Netherlands	20.4	37.6	√	65
Scotland	34.2	34.8	√	–
Sweden	30.3	33.1	√	48
USA	36.1	44.2	X	57

* √ Appropriate; X Not appropriate

TABLE 8.
Population B. Algebra Anchor Items

Code 082
For the equation $x^2 - 5x + 6 = 0$
A   there is no solution
B   there is exactly *one* solution
C   there are exactly *two* solutions
D   there are exactly *three* solutions
E   there are *more than three* solutions

Country	Pop 3A 1st Study Score %	Pop B 2nd Study Score %	Appropriate*	OTL %
Belgium (Fr)	96.2	89.8	√	99
England/Wales	97.1	94.9	√	98
Finland	93.1	97.1	√	100
Israel	97.0	94.1	√	67
Japan	92.5	97.3	√	100
Scotland	98.1	79.9	√	–
Sweden	94.3	92.8	√	100
USA	67.6	79.7	√	83

* √ Appropriate; X Not appropriate

Code 095
When $(1 + p)^6$ is expanded, the
coefficient of p^4 is
A   6
B   10
C   15
D   20
E   30

Country	Pop 3A 1st Study Score %	Pop B 2nd Study Score %	Appropriate*	OTL %
Belgium (Fr)	63.5	36.0	√	73
England/Wales	83.3	72.4	√	96
Finland	66.3	56.6	√	96
Israel	57.3	41.9	√	50
Japan	75.2	80.1	√	97
Scotland	59.2	28.6	√	–
Sweden	53.3	49.9	√	84
USA	33.6	33.3	√	83

* √ Appropriate; X Not appropriate

Table 8 continued

Code 051

A piece of wire 52 cm long is
cut into two parts and each part
is bent to form a square. The
total area of the two squares
is 97 cm^2. How much longer
(in cm) is a side of the larger
square than a side of the smaller
square?

A	4
B	5
C	9
D	14
E	20

Country	Pop 3A 1st Study Score %	Pop B 2nd Study Score %	Appropriate*	OTL %
Belgium (Fr)	69.5	39.6	√	84
England/Wales	72.9	60.1	√	91
Finland	56.8	47.7	√	94
Israel	94.1	38.5	√	59
Japan	64.7	62.7	√	100
Scotland	65.7	53.8	√	–
Sweden	80.3	55.3	√	94
USA	41.9	35.7	√	89

* √ Appropriate; X Not appropriate

Code 081

If x and y are real numbers,
for which x can you define y by

$$y = \frac{x}{\sqrt{9 - x^2}}$$

A	All x except x = 3
B	All x except x = 3 and x = −3
C	x < −3 or x > 3
D	−3 < x < 3
E	x < 3

Country	Pop 3A 1st Study Score %	Pop B 2nd Study Score %	Appropriate*	OTL %
Belgium (Fr)	51.7	54.9	√	100
England/Wales	65.9	47.4	√	90
Finland	49.4	60.1	√	100
Israel	58.3	46.3	√	94
Japan	56.6	57.4	√	97
Scotland	46.0	24.3	√	–
Sweden	62.9	43.1	√	99
USA	30.3	25.5	√	99

* √ Appropriate; X Not appropriate

Table 8 continued

Code 020
x and y are real numbers. The
product of the matrices

$$A = \begin{pmatrix} 1 & x \\ 0 & 1 \end{pmatrix} \text{ and } B = \begin{pmatrix} 1 & 0 \\ y & 1 \end{pmatrix}$$

is commutative *only if*

A	x = 0
B	y = 0
C	x = y
D	x = 0 or y = 0
E	x = 0 and y = 0

Country	Pop 3A 1st Study Score %	Pop B 2nd Study Score %	Appropriate*	OTL %
Belgium (Fr)	22.2	28.9	✓	97
England/Wales	14.5	32.7	✓	57
Finland	10.8	9.7	X	6
Israel	11.3	4.0	X	2
Japan	23.7	57.6	✓	99
Scotland	20.5	26.0	✓	–
Sweden	7.9	21.0	X	9
USA	21.7	13.1	✓	53

* ✓ Appropriate; X Not appropriate

this item. A third item 051 was changed from an open-ended item to a multi-choice item with an alteration to the stem as well. The mathematics behind the item however remains the same.

The interpretation of any change scores in Table 8 for these items between FIMS and SIMS as well as taking note of the caveats of appropriateness and O-T-L must for Population B include a consideration of the changes in composition of the defined population.

Conclusion

While a paper of this length can only give a glimpse of the data included in two such massive studies the potential for in-depth analyses and for secondary analyses can be seen. To assist researchers towards this goal IEA has taken special care to build a documented data bank as part of each project. This bank will be available in 1986 to researchers around the world in the hope that many secondary and possibly meta analyses will be undertaken.

References

Husén, Torsten. (ed) International Study of Achievement in Mathematics, A Comparison of Twelve Countries, Vols I–II Stockholm: Almqvist & Wiksell; and New York: John Wiley & Sons, 1967.
Postlethwaite, T. Neville and Lewy, Arieh. Annotated Bibliography of IEA Publications (1962–1978). Stockholm: IEA, University of Stockholm, 1979.
Purves, A. and Levine, D. (eds) Educational Policy and International Assessment. Berkeley, Cal.: McCutchan Publishing Co., 1975.
Shah, Sair Ali. The Relationship between "Age of Entry" and Achievement of 13-Year-Olds p. 121–123 *J. Res. Math. Ed.*, Vol. **2**, No. 2, 1971.
Sawada, T. Mathematics Achievement and Teaching Practice in Lower Secondary Schools (Grade 7). Second International Mathematics Study. National Report of Japan Vol. **3**, NIER, Tokyo, 1983.

International Comparisons of Cognitive Achievement

JAMES S. COLEMAN

Introduction

Prominent among the accomplishments of Torsten Husén has been his initiation and nurturance of the IEA studies of international comparative achievement. These studies were initiated in the 1960s for mathematics achievement, and have expanded enormously since then, both in number of countries participating and in areas of achievement investigated.

The IEA mathematics study (Husén, 1967) was one of the pioneer studies of education to study effects of schooling by examining not inputs into schools but achievement outputs. It transcended the others in a major respect: they were confined to a single country, while the IEA studies were international, allowing cross-national comparisons. Yet I believe this property of IEA has been insufficiently exploited, with the result that the impact of IEA studies on educational policy — admittedly great in a few countries — has been less great than the potential of the data allows. This paper will be an attempt to demonstrate this in a small way, using the results of the early 1970s testing of science and reading comprehension. Before carrying out the analyses, I will review briefly the history of systematic attempts to find differential effects of different schools on cognitive achievement, beginning in the 1960s.

A Brief Overview of Work on School Determinants of Achievement

One of the early attempts to find a systematic relation between the inputs into a school and the achievement that comes out of it was initiated by the Civil Rights Act of 1964 in the United States, and published as *Equality of Educational Opportunity* in 1966. This study examined cognitive achievement at five grade levels, studying over 700,000 students at schools representative of the whole breadth of American elementary and secondary education. But very surprisingly, there was little relation between the usual measures of quality of input and achievement. It was found instead that the principal factors in their

111

effect on achievement among all those measured were characteristics of the student's family background — parents' education, socioeconomic status of the family, number of siblings, parents' interest in the child's education and in the written word, and similar background factors. These results have become so common now that it becomes even an embarrassment to restate them. Another set of variables which ran a poor second to the student's own background in their effects on his achievement, but they were nevertheless stronger than the school inputs which were measured: the backgrounds of other students in the school. If a boy or girl was in a school with other students from more educationally-oriented backgrounds, he or she performed better.

Hardly measurable were the effects on achievement of variations in resources brought to schools by school boards, principals, and teachers.

At about the same time, Gilbert Peaker had found similar results, using similar methods, in his analysis for the Plowden Report in England. Subsequently, many studies in the United States found similar conclusions about the greater effect of variations in family background than of variations in school characteristics. The reports of the six-subject survey of IEA, following the expert guidance of Peaker, found results that did not differ extensively. Few, if any, identifiable inputs into schools could be found that brought consistently higher achievement.

More recently, there have come to be results which indicate a somewhat different state of affairs. Stephen Heyneman and William Loxley have shown that in less developed countries, there is something of a reversal: resource inputs to schools make large differences in achievement, with the familiar family background characteristics playing a smaller role (Heyneman and Loxley, 1983).

In my own work, I and my colleagues have compared public high schools in the United States with high schools in the private sector, and have found achievement differences that cannot be explained by variations in backgrounds or prior achievement of students in the different sectors, with some indications that these differences may be explained by variations in academic demands and disciplinary level (Coleman, Hoffer and Kilgore, 1982). Using measures of achievement growth over the last 2 years of high school as a criterion, we have pursued this further, finding strong effects of the academic demands on achievement levels (Hoffer, Coleman and Greeley, 1985).

A Reanalysis of Some IEA Data

International achievement comparisons were hardly possible before the extraordinary IEA studies, which had their intellectual and institutional origins in Stockholm under the guidance of Torsten Husén. Beginning with the 1960s testing of achievement in mathematics among 13-year-olds and secondary school seniors, continuing with the six-subject survey in the 1970s, to a second testing of mathematics and science achievement in the 1980s, these studies are without precedent or parallel in international comparative social research.

What I propose to do in this analysis is to point the way to a use of the IEA studies to learn about the effects of variations in schooling, a use that is different from those to which the IEA data have been put in the past. This use involves several essential elements:

(a) Looking for the effects of variations in schooling, not by comparisons *within* a country, as has been the principal form of analysis of IEA data, but by comparisons *between* countries.

(b) Using a younger cohort as a control for an older cohort, to examine what happens over a definable period of school. I will use the 10-year-old cohort as a control for the 14-year-old cohort, thus examining differences among countries in upper elementary school. I will then use this to predict something about the different outcomes to be found in secondary school, and will test this with achievement of students in their last year of secondary school.

(c) I will look at *relative* changes in two areas of achievement in different countries, to gain an idea of the relative emphasis placed on these two different areas. The two areas are science achievement and reading comprehension.

I want to emphasize that the analysis I will carry out is not extensive or sophisticated or highly technical. I have not carried out new tabulations with the original data, but use merely the published data from two volumes of the six-subject study, the volume on science achievement (Comber and Keeves, 1973) and the volume on reading comprehension (Thorndike, 1973). I want to emphasize also that none of the elements of the analysis that I am suggesting with this example are new for the IEA studies. In the first mathematics study, Gilbert Peaker carried out a between country analysis (Husén, 1967, vol. **II**, chap. 2), and other between-country analysis have been carried out since.

Younger cohorts have been used as controls for older cohorts in several analysis, to obtain measures of growth (see, for example, Thorndike, 1973, p. 145, and Comber and Keeves, 1973, p.120). So this is also not new. Similarly, relative achievement in different areas have been examined. For example, in the six-subject study, comparison between reading comprehension, science achievement, and literature achievement are carried out by Thorndike (1973, chapter 10).

However, I will argue that the overall strategy, the combination of the various aspects of the analysis, *is* new, and that it offers the opportunity to learn new things about the functioning of educational systems, and the effect of that functioning on students who pass through those systems. In the first graph, Fig. 1, are plotted the achievement scores of 10-year-olds in science and in reading comprehension. These are the number of items correct out of 40 items in the science test and the number correct out of 40 items on the reading test. (An adjustment for guessing was applied to the raw scores by the authors). The data are for all countries that administered both reading and science tests at ages 10 and 14, excluding two less developed countries, Chile and India. The scores are taken from Table 7.2, p. 159, in the science volume and Table 8.1, p. 124, in the reading volume.

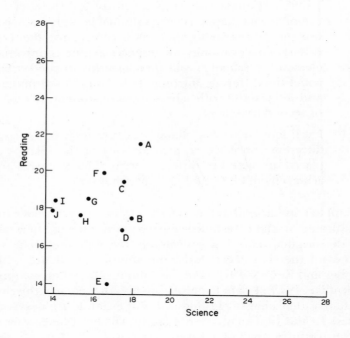

FIG. 1

The points in Fig. 1 show some scatter, with one country, country A, highest in both areas of achievement, but no country lowest in both areas. Country E, lowest in reading comprehension, is a little above average in science, while the two countries especially low in science, I and J, are about average in reading. A caveat should be entered, however, about reading. Since the ten countries had eight different languages, the reading comprehension tests were necessarily different. Although extensive attempts were made to have them fully comparable, there is not the same degree of comparability as in the science test, which had the same items in all countries.

Figure 2 takes the points of Fig. 1 as starting points for ten arrows, with each arrow ending at a point representing the achievement of the 14-year-olds in that same country. (Data are taken from Table 7.2, p. 159, in the science volume, and Table 8.2, p. 125, in the reading volume.) In all countries but two, essentially a whole cohort was in school. In those two, 83 percent (in country F) and 55 percent (in country E) of the cohort were still in school for the age-14 test.

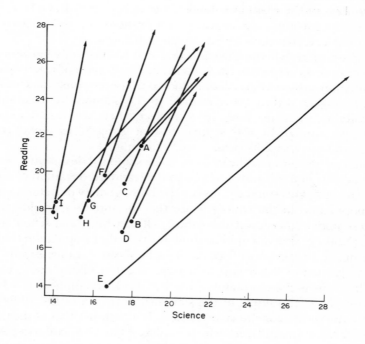

Fig. 2

These test scores do not represent performance on the same items at ages 10 and 14. The science test was in fact 80 items long at age 14, rather than 40 items as in the other tests. Thus, nothing can be determined here about absolute levels of growth, and I shall not attempt to draw any such conclusions.

But what is striking about Fig. 2 is the two different directions taken by the arrows. The arrows for countries A, E, G, and I are nearly parallel, heading off the right, showing a high growth in science relative to that in reading comprehension. Countries B, C, D, F, H, and J are also nearly parallel to one another, showing less growth in science relative to that in reading. There are also differences in the overall amount of growth, with country A having the shortest arrow, and country E having by far the longest. The variations in the growth in science have produced by age 14 a much wider achievement variation among countries than is true for the 10-year-olds. On the other hand, the achievement variation among countries in reading is much *less* than it was at age 10.

The very striking differences between the two sets of countries in the directions of these arrows suggests that something different is going on in the upper elementary grades of these two sets of countries — that is, between ages 10 and 14. It is as if the schools in countries A, E, G, and I are concentrating on science, while those in countries B, C, D, F, H, and J are concentrating on reading comprehension, or perhaps more generally in verbal skills or humanistic education.

I raised to myself the question that if this were so, what other indicators would we expect to find of such intensification of teaching on one or the other subject? One place to look is in the variation in achievement in the subject within the country. If the schools in a country are intensifying their teaching in a subject, then we would expect an increased spread in the scores in that subject, as some students progressed very rapidly, while others did not.

This can be measured by looking at the standard deviation of scores of 14-year-olds in the country *relative* to the standard deviation of scores of 10-year-olds. This standardizes for the homogeneity or heterogeneity of the population in the county, since the 10- and 14-year-olds are both representative samples of the cohort, all of which is in school at those ages. (Nothing similar could be done for the other population tested, the students in the last year of secondary school, since countries vary widely in the fraction of the cohort in school, and thus taking the test.)

When this is done, obtaining the standard deviation of the 14-year-olds' scores as a multiple of the standard deviation of the 10-year-olds' scores, the result is as shown in Table 1. In the upper half of the table are data for the four countries which I will call Group I, countries A, E, G, and I, whose growth in science relative to that in reading was high. In the lower half are the data for the six countries which I will call Group II, countries B, C, D, F, H, and J, whose growth in science relative to that in reading was low.

The reading comprehension standard deviations of 14-year-olds are very little greater than those of 10-year-olds. Furthermore, this is very little different in the two sets of countries. The conjecture stated earlier does not hold true for reading comprehension: the countries in the lower half of the table, Group II, show no greater increase in the spread of reading comprehension scores than do those in the upper half, Group I.

The story is very different, however, for science scores. The countries whose growth in science achievement was *high* relative to that in reading

TABLE 1

Standard Deviation of 14-Year-Olds' Scores in Each Country, Relative to Those of 10-Year-Olds, for Two Sets of Countries, in Reading Comprehension and in Science Achievement

	Country	(SD14)/(SD10) Reading	Science
Group I	A	1.03	1.60
	E	1.01	1.59
	G	1.03	1.66
	I	1.04	1.69
Group II	B	1.05	1.26
	C	1.01	1.29
	D	1.00	1.25
	F	1.06	1.19
	H	1.07	1.32
	J	0.94	1.24

TABLE 2

Average Science Achievement Scores of the Highest 1 Per Cent of the Cohort of the of Age of Last-Year Secondary Students in Group II Countries and in Group I Countries

	Country	Score
Group I	G	51.6
	I	50.7
	A	49.5
	E	48.0
Group II	H	47.1
	C	46.0
	D	45.8
	B	39.8
	F	38.2
	J	36.2

show much greater increases in spread of students' science scores within the country than do those in which relative growth in science was low.

What this suggests is that the essential differences in the upper elementary schools in these two groups of countries is not in their intensity of teaching in reading but in their intensity of teaching in science: the countries of Group I begin to teach science intensively to at least some of their students by the time they are 14. This has two results: it increases the overall country scores in science at age 14, and it increases the spread among students — presumably a spread between those students who are receiving the intensified teaching in science and those who are not (or perhaps merely a spread between those students who respond to the more intense work and those who do not).

This conjecture is reinforced by the growth in scores and in spread for two countries not included here which administered the science test at ages 10 and 14, but not the reading test. They had growth in science of 8.8 and 9.2, comparable to that of the Group I countries' average growth of 7.2 (in contrast to the Group II countries' average growth of 2.7); and the standard deviations of their 14-year-olds' scores were also high relative to the 10-year-olds' scores (1.55 and 1.92 respectively).

We can ask a further question. What is the later impact of this early attention to science in later school? It appears that the Group I countries begin to concentrate the attention of some of their students on science at least by age 14, while the Group II countries do not. Does this produce an elite at the end of secondary school that is more proficient in science than their counterparts in countries where this early intensification on science does not occur?

The answer is given in Table 2, which gives the science achievement scores of the top 1 per cent in each country, for the Group I countries and the Group II countries. As the table shows, the relation is striking: the scores of the top 1 percent of science achievers in all Group I countries are higher than the scores of the top 1 percent of science achievers in any Group II country. (One of the two additional countries mentioned above, which would fall into Group I according to its gain in score and standard deviation, administered the upper secondary test. The average score of its top 1 percent is 45.0, placing it 2.1 items below the highest Group I country). Thus the early intensified attention to (or perhaps specialization in) science in Group I countries before age 14 results in a higher-achieving scientific elite at the end of secondary school than found in Group II countries.

Conclusion

This rather simple analysis that I have carried out with the published IEA data suggests that there may be much more potential in analyses that compare countries than has yet been realized. One reason for the potential richness of the data for increasing our knowledge of the effects of schooling lies in the very design of the IEA project: it covers educational systems that differ from one another in some ways that schools within a single country do not. Thus the range and kind of variation to be found among schools in the IEA data is far greater than would be found in single country studies. Effects of major variations in school systems in achievement can themselves be major; but to find these requires breaking out of the country-by-country analyses that have been widely used in IEA reports. The example I have reported here is intended to exemplify some of the benefits of even a rather simple and straightforward analysis of the sort I am advocating.

There may be some interest in the identities of the Group I and Group II countries. They are:

Group I	A	Sweden
	E	Hungary
	G	England
	I	Scotland
Group II	B	Belgium (Flemish
	C	Finland
	D	USA
	F	Italy
	H	Netherlands
	J	Belgium (French)

References

Coleman, James S., *et al. Equality of Educational Opportunity.* Washington: U. S. Government Printing Office, 1966.
Coleman, James, Thomas Hoffer and Sally Kilgore. *High School Achievement: Public, Catholic, and Private Schools Compared.* New York: Basic Books, 1982.
Comber, L. C. and John P. Keeves. *Science Education in Nineteen Countries.* Stockholm: Almqvist and Wicksell, 1973.
Hoffer, Thomas, James Coleman and Andrew Greeley. "Achievement Growth in Public and Catholic High Schools," *Sociology of Education,* 1985. Vol. **58**, No. 2, pp. 74–97.
Husén, Torsten, ed. *International Study of Achievement in Mathematics,* v.I,II. Stockholm: Almqvist and Wicksell, 1967.
Heyneman, Stephen, and William Loxley. "The Effect of Primary School Quality on Academic Achievement Across Twenty-Nine High- and Low-Income Countries", *America Journal of Sociology,* 1983, Vol. **88**, No. 6, pp. 1162–1194.
Thorndike, R. L. *Reading Comprehension Education in Fifteen Countries.* Stockholm: Almqvist and Wicksell, 1973.

Organizing Cross National Research Projects

T. NEVILLE POSTLETHWAITE

This article follows four articles reporting cross national studies in mathematics education, science education, reading and written composition education. All of these studies have been organized by the International Association for the Evaluation of Educational Achievement (IEA). IEA is the largest organization undertaking cross national research in education and has been doing such research for over 25 years. Since Torsten Husén has been involved with IEA for the period of its existence and was Chairman from 1962 to 1978 and since I was coordinator from 1962 to 1972 and have been Chairman since 1978, it would seem to be appropriate to base this article on lessons culled from working in and with IEA.

The article will deal with the selection of themes for international research, organizing country participation, major technical problems, organizational structure for the conduct of such studies, fund raising and accounting, and publication and dissemination. In some cases, it will be important to include a historical dimension, since there are differences between the beginning of the first project when all participants are highly committed and 25 years later when "routine" procedures have taken over.

Selection of Research Themes

At the beginning of IEA the persons representing the participating twelve research centers very quickly settled on measuring and explaining variation in mathematics achievement as their first major research project. Maths was selected because attention was being paid to the reform of mathematics education at that time — the early 1960s — and it was anticipated that it would be easier to test mathematics achievement internationally than any other subject. Once the mathematics study was finished it was, of course, logical to examine whether the kinds of educational findings using one educational outcome — mathematics — held in other subjects or not. Thus, cross-sectional surveys were mounted in Reading Comprehension, Literature, Science, French as a

Foreign Language, English as a Foreign Language, and Civic Education. Reading, Science and the Foreign Languages were easily agreed upon. There was much discussion about the possibility and meaningfulness of testing in Literature. On the principle of "when in doubt, do some pilot work" pilot work was conducted. As a result of the pilot studies, as well as the ingenuity and tenacity of the persons working on the Literature Committee, it was decided to go ahead, although with some reluctance. Civic Education was also in doubt and subject to pilot work. Of the ten countries interested in participating in the study, it was discovered that there was remarkable similarity in terms of both the attitudes considered desirable and interest across participating countries in wishing to have estimates of how the "working" of certain societal institutions were perceived by students. Hence, Civic Education was included in the so-called six-subject survey. It must be borne in mind that it was not only the measurement of achievement at certain school levels which was undertaken but also an analysis of the determinants (in school and out of school) of such achievement.

Whereas the mathematics study had involved twelve countries, twenty-one participated in the six-subject survey, although not all countries participated in every subject area. Participation ranged from eight countries in French as a Foreign Language to nineteen countries in Science.

It was during the six-subject survey that suggestions from outside the IEA membership began to be made to IEA about the sorts of evaluation and research projects it might undertake. Such suggestions came from World Bank and UNESCO personnel but, interestingly, never from OECD (Organisation for Economic Co-operation and Development) staff. As the membership of IEA increased, more research centers joined which were directly dependent upon or even belonged to Ministries of Education. Pressure increased to undertake work perceived to be of direct utility to Ministries of Education.

In 1979 there were fourteen different proposals for new studies. By then IEA also had over 30 member institutes. These two facts forced IEA to create a mechanism for the selection of studies. A "Future Activities" committee was formed. It was a sub-committee of the representatives of all research institutes which were members of IEA. The composition of the committee was such that all continents were represented, including developed and developing countries. The "Future Activities" committee established the following criteria to judge whether or not IEA should undertake a study:

— Is it likely to add to knowledge *and* help improve practice;
— Does it use proven methodology;
— Are more than five countries interested in participating;
— Is IEA the most appropriate organization to undertake the study;
— Is international funding likely to be forthcoming.

In practice, the last criterion is hardly ever discussed since if the first four criteria are met it is — often over optimistically — assumed that international funding will be forthcoming.

Selection is undertaken in two or more steps. The first step is to review a three- to ten-page document describing the overall idea of the proposed study. A yes or no decision is taken. For example, in 1979 eight of the fourteen proposals were turned down at the very first review. If the idea receives a positive response, a small *ad hoc* committee is formed. It typically has five members, one of whom is an experienced IEA worker, and the other four are eminent persons in the field of study being proposed. Some of them may or may not be IEA members. The *ad hoc* committee has the task of producing a very detailed proposal. This process can take from 1 to 3 years. When the proposal is ready, it is brought back to the "Future Activities" committee and IEA. There is typically a 2-year waiting period before the project actually begins. This waiting period is used for national and international fund raising. In 1985, the task of the Future Activities Committee was taken over by the IEA Standing Committee.

The selection mechanism works well but there is one difficulty. Even after acceptance the *ad hoc* steering committee members often wish to rewrite the proposal to make it "better" for grant-giving agencies.

Rather than wait for proposals to be made to IEA, it might be desirable for IEA to set up its own continuous polling mechanism, not only of Ministries of Education but also of educational research institutions and scholars. This remains to be seen.

Country Participation

Officially it is a research institution which is a member of IEA and not a country. IEA is a non governmental organization. The problem of defining what a "country" is arose early in IEA's history. In the first mathematics study the National Foundation for Educational Research in England and Wales was a member. So was the Scottish Council for Research in Education. This was defended, at that time, on the grounds that they were research institutes representing administratively separate and different education systems. Belgium was also in the mathematics study. But, between the mathematics study and the six-subject survey, what had been one system of education became two separate systems of education: Flemish speaking Belgium and French speaking Belgium. Thus, two Belgiums have participated in IEA work since that time. Then, the province of Ontario in Canada applied to participate in IEA's work. To begin with, IEA wanted all of Canada to join, but this proved to be impossible. Thus, a "rule" was developed to indicate that research institutes representing up to two separate systems of education within a nation (i.e. defined politically) may be members of IEA. However, as soon as there are three or more systems represented within a nation, the research centers involved must agree on which one of them will represent all of them in the IEA General Assembly. This "rule" was made in order to keep the General Assembly meeting manageable and "fair". If one did not have such a "rule", it would be possible to imagine representatives from each of the Canadian provinces and Australian states and territories, for example, being on the General Assembly together with only one representative from France, one representative from Indonesia and so on. Although the rule may seem clumsy, it does allow maximum participation. Nevertheless, as IEA increases its membership in terms of more research institutes representing nations, more problems about the fairness of representation will surely occur.

One misconception about IEA is that it selects countries for specific research projects. This is not so. Research institutes representing systems of education decide whether to participate or not. Thus, once a project is given the green light by IEA, each existing member of IEA decides whether or not to participate.

Through informal contacts the project is made known to research centers in other countries. Agencies such as the World Bank also help in making the project known. The absence of active recruiting has the advantage that institutions join because they want to join and because they think participation in the project will be useful to their institutes and countries. There is then a built-in motivation. On the other hand, it is quite possible that certain institutes which would wish to join a project never hear of it.

By 1985 there were about forty countries participating in IEA. As the number of institutes has increased, it has become more difficult to control the quality of research. Some persons have been in favor of actively recruiting more countries on the grounds that all countries should have the opportunity of profiting from participation in IEA's research projects. Others have felt that to add more countries would severely jeopardize the quality of the research. A point of balance would seem to have been arrived at. At the end of this article there is a list of the participating institutes as of 1985. Those asterisked are not members of the IEA General Assembly. They have opted to participate in one project and not to be full members of IEA.

One final point about country participation is worthy of mention. It is usually the case that in any one project there are developed and developing countries including countries from Europe, North America, Africa, Asia and Australasia. The variation may not cover all systems of education in the world but must be close to it. In this sense, any generalizable results for a project could probably apply to most, if not all, countries in the world.

Major Technical Problems

The major steps in designing and conducting a research project are:

— a clear statement of aims
— a research design
— sampling plan
— instrument construction

— data collection and recording
— data analysis
— writing reports.

When a project officially begins, the first event is a meeting of those persons from the participating centers who will be in charge of the day to day work. The person at each center in this role is known as the National Research Coordinator (NRC). The NRCs review in detail the proposal worked out by the *ad hoc* steering committee together with the members of the steering committee, whose membership overlaps considerably with that of the *ad hoc* steering committee. The background and experience of the NRCs from the different research centers varies a great deal. Each major step is reviewed. Of particular importance is the detailed *conceptualization* of the study in terms of the variables to be included and the models to be tested. Given the various ways in which the NRCs perceive the problem, the sharing of ideas can be extremely valuable. However, time is needed for talking through the ideas. Just to arrive at a series of path models where discussion is needed on every arrow takes time. The great danger is that all sorts of variables may be thrown into the project without the planners thinking through the theoretical basis for inclusion. The result can be a massive "fishing" exercise, in which the host of variables are sifted to identify the more important from the less important in terms of predicting a certain criterion, rather than a "hunting" exercise in which models are confirmed or rejected or where there is a to-ing and fro-ing between the initial model and the data with successive modifications of the model until a model is confirmed.

The basic *research design* usually remains the same as that proposed by the *ad hoc* steering committee, although theoretical elegance has often to be tempered by the practical conditions of what the NRCs say is actually feasible within countries in terms of testing, especially testing time.

Survey sampling in education is not very well understood or practised in most countries. Several IEA persons have experience in both the theory and practice of such sampling so that NRC discussions are usually focussed on equivalence of terminology when describing the school systems so as to arrive at a definition of target populations in order to have comparable populations. The actual sampling of the target populations is much more a matter of teaching and learning aided by a good sampling manual.

The goodness of the *measures* in terms of objectivity, validity, unidimensionality and reliability is, as in any project, of great importance. Often, the Steering Committee members or selected NRCs are responsible for the first draft of measures. Each NRC then examines each question in terms of the appropriateness for his or her system of education. Occasionally, it is necessary to use slightly different questions in each country in background questionnaires (student, teacher or school principal) in order to yield the equivalent international information required for the dimension being measured. For cognitive-achievement measures, the first step is to undertake a content analysis of actually what is meant to be learned by the target population in each country. In science, mathematics, and foreign languages what is meant to be learned in all countries (developed and developing) is remarkably similar, particularly at the junior secondary school level (grades 7 and 8). About 90 percent of the objectives are the same, although sometimes with differing degrees of emphasis. It is the set of common objectives which are taken for the international test. The way in which the content analysis is done (examinations analysis, textbook analysis, teacher committees and so on) will depend on the system of education. Each NRC must decide on the most valid way of undertaking the content analysis for his system.

It is sometimes argued that because cultures and systems are different it is meaningless to try and *compare achievement*. IEA's point of view is that it is meaningful to compare achievement where the objectives are the same. However, it should be noted that each NRC is expected to ensure that additional national questions are produced for the objectives which are in the national curriculum and which are not in the international test so that what is tested in any one system of education covers what is meant to have been learned by the target population in that country. A frequent distinction is made among the intended curriculum, the implemented curriculum and the achieved curriculum. The intended curriculum is that described as a result of the content analysis. However, it is clear that individual teachers will include and exclude certain objectives from the intended curriculum and give different emphases to the various objectives. A measure known as "Opportunity to Learn" is an attempt to obtain from each teacher in the sample the extent to which the teacher has taught the objectives included in the international test. This is a measure of the implemented curriculum. In this way, target-population achievement can be compared on the basis of either the intended or implemented curriculum.

For subjects such as Literature or Written Composition, students' performance can be compared for each of a series of dimensions typically used to examine Literature and Written-Composition achievement. In Written Composition, the establishment of a common scale for comparison between countries is not an easy matter but, in a sense, is not different from the case of a single examining board in a country judging essays where there is more than one school of thought about what good essay writing is. For a given target population, a 5-point scale is established and raters from each country are trained to rate to this scale where there is prior agreement on what quality of essay constitutes each point on the scale.

It is to be noted that IEA has not attempted cross national measures of achievement in subjects such as history, art, music, and religion, because of the wide range of differences that may obtain in judgements about what constitutes proper curriculum content in such fields.

Pilot work — that is, conducting preliminary try-outs of the measuring instruments — is essential and takes time. Constructing measures that "work" internationally typically takes more time than doing it only nationally. It is important that the results of pilot work in the different countries is reviewed by all the NRCs such that consensus criteria are worked out to judge when a measure is good enough to be used internationally.

Data collection can take different forms in different countries. Data collection manuals are written but sometimes with alternative procedures set down on the basis of what the NRCs say is feasible. Typically, data collection should take place as near as possible to the end of the school year, but the interval before the end of the school year will vary from system to system. In longitudinal studies the system for tracing students will vary depending on whether or not the system requires residential registration and the maintenance of national registers. NRCs can learn from each other on the basis of their various experiences.

Within each participating research center there are usually, but not always, routine procedures for *recording data*. Each IEA project produces its own international code book; and however the data are recorded in each national center, it is imperative that the data are handed in for international data processing in the specified international format. It is interesting that in the early days of IEA this was not a particular problem, but by the early 1980s there were many errors. The international code books were correct, but there was a great deal of sloppiness on the part of NRCs. There was no particular pattern to the amount of poor recording exhibited. Some experienced centers displayed good recording and others poor recording. Some new centers were good and others poor. Both developed and developing countries spread across the whole spectrum of good to poor recording. This is also true of National Centers replying to queries about their data from the International Center. More attention is being given to this aspect but it is not entirely clear why there is such variation in performing what is not a difficult task.

Data analyses are undertaken both internationally and nationally. The international data-processing center undertakes the specified international analyses for the international report, and each NRC undertakes the desired national analyses for a national report.

Structural Organization

(i) *Structure as the Need Arose*

No particular preplanning about structural organization was undertaken at any one point in the time in the history of IEA. Rather, decisions were taken as the need arose. When the first mathematics study was undertaken 1961 to 1966, the heads of centers met once or twice a year. It was they who developed the instruments, and at every meeting there was more work to accomplish than was possible in the time available. However, it was realized that some sort of central unit was required to undertake all of the day-to-day international coordination. Funding was required for this. The University of Chicago (the National Center for the USA) received a grant from the US Office of Education. The coordinator and his secretary were located at the UNESCO Institute for Education in Hamburg, since it was thought at the time that a UNESCO umbrella would facilitate the participation of some countries. For various reasons, there was a strong feeling that this loose association of research institutes should be able to receive money. For this to happen, the association had to become a legal entity. On the advice of UNESCO, a legal association was then created under Belgian law. Funding was thereafter applied for to several grant-giving agencies and the funds were granted. According to the new statutes, the accounts of the association had to be audited by an international auditor, so the services of Price Waterhouse were obtained. In 1979 Ernst & Whinney became the international auditors.

In the first mathematics study the international data processing was undertaken at the University of Chicago by Dr. Richard M. Wolf, an assistant of Professor Benjamin Bloom. The six-subject survey involved a massive amount of data processing. During the pilot work, the data processing was undertaken at one of the national centers. Once the large scale full runs began, the data-processing center was moved to New York, as required by the US agency granting the funding.

It was really at the beginning of the six-subject survey that organizational structure became necessary. Two main changes occurred. First, there were six different subject areas instead of one and, second, the heads of centers who had also been the workers in the first mathematics study were no longer going to be the workers; they wished to appoint other members of their staffs to do the work so that NRCs came into being. Given that each of the six subjects involved different kinds of measures and methods, special committees for each subject became necessary. In effect, relatively small committees were formed (5 to 7 persons), and these became the Steering Committees for each project, a mechanism which continues to exist. The NRCs for any one project became important, and these formed the Study Committee which was subordinate to the General Assembly. In a sense, this already created a two tier hierarchy. The heads of centers formed the General Assembly which took all major decisions on projects to be undertaken, financing, staffing, publication policy and the like but delegated the detailed running of a project to the NRCs, Steering Committee and International Coordinating Center.

(ii) *Centralization vs. Decentralization*

One major unresolved aspect of the organization is the extent to which it should be centralized or decentralized. Until the mid-1970s it was highly centralized. Thus, for the six-subject-area study there was one international coordinating center and one international (at one time split into two) data processing center. The staff were full time and paid from international funds. In the mid-1970s the second mathematics study began, with one international coordinating center for that study located in New Zealand. Then, as a second project began (Classroom Environment), a second international coordinating center was established in Canada for that project. As this pattern continued, by 1985 there were international coordinating centers in New Zealand, Canada, the USA, Finland, Australia, and the UK. It is unclear why this policy emerged, but by 1984 there was a strong move to recreate more centralization. It was proposed that there be one IEA headquarters office for the coordination of all of IEA and one international data processing center which would be minimally responsible for the editing, sorting, and filing of all incoming data from national centers for all projects. The headquarters could also conduct various multivariate analyses for specific projects. Both central institutions require funding. Specific project money is difficult to raise. Central "overhead" funding is extremely difficult to raise, a point to be taken up later.

(iii) *Structure by the Mid-1980s*

By the mid-1980s the structure of IEA was as follows:

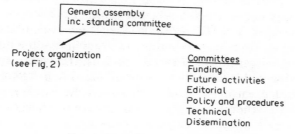

FIG. 1. Overall Structure of IEA

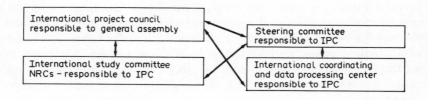

Fig. 2. Organizational Structure for any one IEA Project

The *General Assembly* consists of the heads (or nominated representatives) of each participating research institution which is participating actively in a project and has joined the IEA General Assembly. It is also possible to have individual members of the General Assembly. The General Assembly is responsible for all IEA activities. It meets once a year. The *Standing Committee* is a committee of the Chairman and six other members elected by the General Assembly. Its function is to take decisions on behalf of the General Assembly between General Assembly meetings.

The *International Project Council* (IPC) for any one project consists of the heads (or their representatives) of those research institutions participating in the project. It is possible to have on the IPC representatives of research institutes which have opted to participate in that project but have not opted to be member of the IEA General Assembly. An example would be the Institute for Science and Mathematics Education Development in the Philippines which is clearly a relevant institute to participate in Science but would not be relevant for any arts projects. In general, a research institute in IEA is the major national educational research institute for a country and is able to participate in any of the IEA projects. Occasionally it may not wish to participate or may feel that it doesn't have the competent staff for that project. In this case, it is expected to contact another institute in the country which may be more competent and/or willing to participate. The new institute would be a member of the IPC for that project but not a member of the General Assembly. The IPC is responsible for ensuring that high quality work is conducted within the budget and timetable agreed upon.

The *Steering Committee* and *International Coordinating Center* are the two bodies working internationally full time. Their task is to interact with the NRCs in order to ensure that all work is carried out. All are responsible to the IPC and General Assembly. Apart from the structure for any one project, there were certain *overarching committees* created by the General

Assembly for Funding, Future Activities, Policy and Procedures, Editorial and Publications, Technical, and Dissemination. Again, each committee was established as the need arose. Similarly, some committees which were established were discontinued once they had fulfilled their purpose.

Problems of Organization

(i) *Role of General Assembly members*

As IEA has expanded, various problems have arisen. In some institutes the head is not an experienced researcher. As more institutes within a country have become involved in different projects, the link between the General Assembly member and the various NRCs in some countries has become weak. Some General Assembly members do not meet regularly with all their NRCs.

The research projects undertaken by IEA are decided on by the IEA General Assembly, and — as can well be imagined — the input of any one member is usually in direct proportion to his professional ability. At least, this has been the experience to date. Before a project can be launched it needs the backing of the various members' national Ministries of Education or national funding agencies for educational research. It can occur occasionally that senior members of Ministries or funding agencies are guilty of secondary ignorance (i.e. they don't realize that they don't know something). This is not altogether surprising since many educators are ethnocentric and believe that their own system is best or, if not best, at least best for their tradition and culture. They do not know (or sometimes do not care to know) how a particular problem is tackled in other countries. Or, they do not recognize that they have a problem on their hands because a problem only exists for them if questions are raised in parliament or by teachers or by parents in sufficient numbers. This condition of secondary ignorance requires that all IEA General Assembly members be able to educate (in a diplomatic way) the senior members of their ministries or fı funding agencies — an educational assignment that is not always feasible.

(ii) *Developing Countries*   .

Countries are often labeled as "developing" and "developed" or "industrialized". Occasionally, some of the researchers from "developed" countries feel that by allowing more "developing" countries into IEA, the standards of IEA's research work will be lowered. There is no evidence for this because, in practice, "quality" of work is monitored; and where any country does not meet certain standards, it is either allowed to withdraw its data or have its data included in the international reports but accompanied by statements about the quality of the data. In some cases, the "developed" country researchers are more or less ignorant about research in "developing" countries. This changes as the researchers work together on a common project.

(iii) *Cultural Imperialism in Research*

Some developed-country researchers (and curiously, always those who have not worked in IEA) accuse IEA of cultural imperialism in research. The argument is that IEA has a majority of "developed"-country representatives, that the research is *only* empirically conceived, thus exluding other research approaches in the "developing" countries, and that the conceptualization is only Western. However, it should be noted that no research institute joins a project unless it wishes to do so. Any five countries can join together to run a project, and they could all be developing countries. The research methodology used should always be appropriate for the research questions asked, and the research contribution of each member is usually in direct proportion to his or her experience and ability in research.

(iv) *Commitment to the Work*

Another problem is the commitment to international cooperation in this kind of work. In the first mathematics study the twelve research institute heads were undertaking pioneering work. Their commitment was total. One wonders as more institutes have joined if some join only in terms of what they will get out of the study. The notion that commitment in terms of input to all aspects of a study and interest in international cooperation in research is of importance if a large organization is to undertake good quality research. Such commitment may be lacking, and one problem is how to increase and maintain it. However, let it not be thought that commitment does not usually exist. All of the General Assembly members, Steering Committee members, and many of the International Coordinators donate their services absolutely free. Many General Assembly members have gone out of their way to raise money within their countries to host General Assembly meetings, Steering Committee meetings and NRC meetings. International Coordinating centers are housed free-of-charge in some member institutes. Indeed, if the work of IEA had to be fully paid, the budget would be so enormous that IEA would not exist.

Associated with the problem of commitment is the acceptance of democratic procedures. It has occurred that after agreements have been arrived at by the General Assembly or by the NRCs, particular individuals do not hold to these. For example, in the six-subject survey it was agreed that one sample would be drawn for Reading, Science and Literature and that where a country was participating in all three subject areas all children would be tested in all three areas. One country agreed to this and upon returning home unilaterally went ahead and drew two separate samples, one for Reading Comprehension and Literature and one for Science. In some cases, it occurs that a research institute joins a project after a year or two of operation. It is in the first 2 years of a project that the ground rules are established and major decisions taken on a series of technical procedures. In some cases, the tests have already been established for the particpating countries. If a research institute joins late, it must necessarily accept the procedures and instruments already established by the other research institutes. If the new institute cannot accept such procedures and instruments, it should not join. It has, occasionally, occurred that an institute joins late and then wishes to have everything changed. This can be extremely disruptive and damaging. Much depends on the tact of the IPC chairman and International Coordinator in dealing with such cases.

(v) *Personnel*

Good research experience, tact, diplomacy, the ability to listen and learn, administrative skill, and in some cases fund-raising ability are all qualities required in all IEA personnel. It will be readily admitted that not all persons possess all qualities. However, the chairpersons of IPCs and Steering Committees and International Coordinators should possess as many as possible of the skills.

The selection of such persons is critical. Although some mistakes have been made, they have been rare. But when they have occurred they have had a negative effect on project work. Two skills which appear rare are the ability to listen and the ability to motivate committee members to work between meetings. Very often if, for example, a Japanese or French colleague is struggling to say something in English, he usually has something important to say. If, however, the chairman is a person having been immersed in quick-firing US research debates, he may not have the patience or sensitivity to listen carefully. This can have negative effects on the morale of the group. Some colleagues have a mentality of working only when they attend meetings. However, the hard work must go on between meetings. The meetings have to be used for arriving at consensus. When committee members do not work between meetings, this can play havoc with the preplanned timetable.

(vi) *International Coordinating Center* (ICC)

For any one project, the ICC is the heart of the total organization system. IEA had one coordinator and one secretary for the first mathematics study. In 1967 this increased to one executive director (a fancy title for the coordinator), a chief secretary, a bookkeeper and several typists. The coordinating center is the secretarial office and central post office for the project. Once the project committee has given

T. Neville Postlethwaite

the detailed instructions, it is up to the coordinator to ensure that each
detail is accomplished on time and, where possible, the coordinator
should help control the quality of the work. It is wise to develop a flow
chart for each part of the exercise. This shows what must be
accomplished each month and how one piece of work feeds into
another. Separately, there should be a document indicating who is
responsible for each task. The coordinator must not only know which
member of the committee has to produce what, when, and how, but also
must ensure it is circulated to whomever it must go. Whereas there may
be 5 or 7 members of the committee, there can be over 30 National
Centers in a project. Each National Center has its timetable, and the
coordinator must ensure that each National Center hands in what it is
meant to hand in on time and that it does so to the appropriate person.
For example, in IEA surveys a sampling manual is written explaining in
detail the principles and practice of probability sampling. The coordinator must ensure that deadlines exist for the manual arriving at the
National Centers and for when National Centers will hand in their
sampling plans to the sampling referee. This latter timetabling often
requires some negotiation with National Centers. Negotiation, in turn,
means that the coordinator needs good rapport with each National
Center. It often means that he should be fluent in the world's major
international languages. Although English is the agreed-upon language
of communication in the IEA, the person who is designated a particular
task in a National Center will not necessarily speak English. This is
particularly true in French- and Spanish-speaking countries. The
coordinator must know when to chase, cajole, charm or "kick" National
Center personnel to ensure that deadlines are kept. It is clear that
deadlines are of utmost importance. If the committee does not keep to
its deadlines, this can jeopardize the whole project since National
Centers typically receive their funding for the national data collection
from their Ministries of Education, and Ministries can become very
angry — to the point of cancelling a project — if their planned budgets
suffer. If a National Center does not keep to its deadlines, the
international data processing cannot run as planned so that all of the
data are not analyzed and ready for write-up. This is also an aspect
which the committee chairmen cannot emphasize enough.

   In IEA's history the coordinator has always been responsible for
writing the manuals for the National Centers, for school coordinators,
for test administrators and for data processing. The coordinator does
not have to write them all by himself but must ensure that the various
bits are written and fit logically together. The writing of manuals —
especially those for National Centers — is not an easy matter, but it is a
skill which can be learned.

   The international data-processing center is usually a part of the international coordinating center. Where it has not been so or where the data processing center has been split (cleaning of data and production of univariates at one location and multivariate analyses at another location) there have been problems of communication and long delays. Unfortunately, funding constraints have often required data-processing be split, but whenever possible this should be avoided.

Detailed preplanning is not only necessary for the totality of a project but is particularly needed for the data-processing stage. Checks on the accuracy of data-recording should be built in at National Centers, such that all data coming into the international center are clean — a rare occurrence.

As can be seen, organization is necessary; but to arrive at an ideal organization that is adequately funded is not an easy matter.

Funding

There are two aspects to international-research funding — national funding and international funding.

National funding for any specific project is raised by the participating research institute for that country. In most cases this is from governmental sources although, in some countries, it is from private foundations. In the case of developing countries, the participating institutes often raise their money from bilateral aid agencies or private foundations outside their countries, typically from the USA, the Federal Republic of Germany, and Japan. It is, of course, up to the IEA General Assembly or IPC member to "sell" the project to the appropriate national grant-giving agencies. It sometimes happens that the IEA Chairman is called upon to reinforce the worthwhileness of a project with the national authorities. In the 1960s, it was IEA-international which raised the funding for NRCs to attend NRC meetings. As money became tight, this became impossible and now it is up to participating institutions to finance the participation of their personnel in international meetings. In some cases — East European countries and developing countries — raising such funds is either extremely difficult or impossible, so that IEA international has to attempt to cover the travel fares.

International funding is required to pay for the international coordinating centers, for meetings of the Steering Committee, and for helping participating institutes with international travel costs which they are unable to cover. The very first grant for the first mathematics study was extremely difficult to raise. The money for the six-subject area was easier, partly because of the potential of the study and partly because the mid- to latter-60s were the halcyon days for funding educational research. The first study was financed solely from United States sources. The six-subject study was financed from British, German, Swedish and

US government and private foundation sources. When IEA decided to undertake a second mathematics study in 1976, funding money was in short supply. Indeed, it was somewhat of a hand-to-mouth existence. By the beginning of the 1980s funding became somewhat easier but there was still not enough for what was required. However, by the mid-1980s, international funding came from private sources in Germany, Japan, the Netherlands, the USA, and a bilateral agency in Canada. In some cases, international coordinating costs were subsidised by the host institutes. Steering Committee meetings, NRC meetings and General Assembly meetings were often held at participating institutions, and the participating institutions covered the cost of board and lodging.

Two points are worthy of note. The first is that IEA has received no direct continuous governmental funding. The second is that there are no membership fees. It has often been suggested that IEA should have membership fees and that these should be used to finance all international costs. In 1985 there were four ongoing projects. At that time an international coordinating center cost about US$ 250,000 per year i.e. for four projects the total international coordinating center costs were 1 million US dollars per year. With forty participating institutions, this would mean membership fees of US$ 25,000 per year per institute, assuming that all institutes participated in all projects, which is not the case. Hence, some institutes would have to pay more. Certain institutes from developing countries or Eastern European countries would be unable to pay such money. Even some industrialized countries would be unable to raise such fees. There would also be the danger of creating first- and second-class membership if differential fees were introduced. This would be against the aim of having equal participation in cooperative research projects.

Approaching governments for funding of the international budget has proved singularly unsuccessful. Governments already pay to such multilaterial agencies as UNESCO and OECD and think that those agencies should be conducting the type of educational research work carried out by IEA.

All funding is raised on a project basis. There is no overall headquarters, which is run voluntarily by the Chairman and his secretary in Hamburg with the help of a part-time secretary in Sweden. Overhead costs must surely be the cheapest of any international organization. But, as IEA membership increases it is becoming urgent to: create a headquarters to ensure coordination of all projects; help new institutes to learn the IEA ropes; centralize data-cleaning facilities; provide more help to some developing countries; produce saleable proposals; raise money; and ensure good dissemination of all results. The prospect of raising such money is poor, so that one wonders about the advantages and disadvantages of institutionalizing an international educational research organization.

Finally, as with any research funding, there is the problem of grant-giving agencies changing their foci of interest, of being prepared to pay some types of costs and not others, and of the ethnocentricity or sometimes ignorance of the referees used for making recommendations in such agencies. The reporting to agencies often has to be undertaken in different formats at different times of the year. This, plus all the accounting, is a full-time job for one person. The most difficult task is raising money for travel to international meetings. Many grant-giving agencies are, quite rightly, not prepared to fund travel costs to meetings where persons read "academic" papers to each other. However, the agencies' way of dealing with this is to have a blanket ruling on no money for travel. Yet, the IEA Steering Committee and NRC meetings are workshops with more work than time to accomplish the work. Such meetings in cooperative research are critical, but ensuring full attendance is greatly constrained by lack of travel money.

Publications and Dissemination

Although the training aspect of international research, whereby researchers learn from each other, can be of great importance, the visibility of the worthwhileness of such research is usually judged from its publications. The audiences for research results are policy makers (a small audience), other researchers, teacher educators and teachers.

Both international publications and national publications result from IEA studies. The international publications include data from all participating countries and generalizations about education across countries as well as descriptions of differences between countries and the determinants of such differences. National publications are prepared by the participating institutes for national consumption.

Several problems arise with international publications. These are concerned with the size of the audience and a publisher being prepared to have small runs, mass distribution to teachers, data being included in or excluded from the publication, and the question of authorship.

Researchers tend to write technical reports. This is important, in that the research community should be able to judge the soundness of the research. However, at best, such reports will sell one-thousand to fifteen-hundred copies. Policymakers often want a short report. In a sense, their researchers should compile such a report for them but perhaps the press release issued by the international organization could help in this matter. An international report should certainly be issued for teacher-educators but where the research jargon is cut to a minimum; and, it should concentrate on those results of most interest to teacher-educators and teachers. IEA has not been very successful with its publications in that the reports for the researchers and teacher-educators have been combined into one report. In the halcyon days of research funding, it was possible to persuade a grant-giving agency to subsidize the printing costs. By the mid-1970s this was no longer the case, and a publisher is often reluctant to take on any publication which is likely to sell fewer than two thousand copies.

IEA has often thought that a mass dissemination of results to all schools in each participating country in a research project would be desirable. The *set* materials produced conjointly by the New Zealand and Australian Council for Educational Research present a basic idea which could be used. Again, such mass distribution needs funding, and the materials need to be tried out and revised before going to teachers. Above all, they must be visibly useful to teachers.

One problem that has arisen concerns the possibility of a participating research center withdrawing its data from a publication at the last minute. In some developing countries the participating institutes must receive ministerial permission before their results can be published. It is always possible that a Minister may think that the results put his government in a poor light and will refuse permission to publish.

Since the results cannot be known before the analyses are completed, this risk must always be run. Although it is possible to have a participating institute agree that if it participates in a project its results should be published, it is not realistic to require such a commitment since governments and Ministers change; and if a new Minister refuses the right to publish, there is little the head of a participating institute can do when his or her job is dependent on the Minister. It is worth noting that all NRCs and heads of institutes have made a practice of checking the draft of the international publication very carefully before the manuscript is finalized.

The decision about whose name should appear as the author is sometimes a problem. Different cultures have different practices. In some countries, there is a tradition of the head of the institute being listed as the "author" even though he has not been involved in the research at all. In other countries, it is only those who write the manuscript who appear on the cover sheet as the authors but their names are listed in order of their seniority in the institute. In others, it is the person who has written most whose name is on the cover. After having experienced some difficulties, IEA decided that the author or editor hierarchy should be in terms of the amount of writing by each person except where the NRCs, international coordinating staff, and the members of the Steering Committee had all agreed on an order or an overall editor.

No international manuscript goes to the publisher until the Editorial Committee has passed it. This often requires that the editor of any volume revise until the Editorial Committee is satisfied. The Editorial Committee's function is to ensure the highest possible quality of research reporting.

Continuous Review

It is important that an international research body review its work and its organization or else have it reviewed by outsiders on a regular basis. As an example, several questions are listed below from an internal review session held in August, 1984.

As a basis for discussion the following was assumed: "IEA is a voluntary association of national institutes for educational research which engages in an organized form of international cooperation based on professional interests. The work builds upon the full and active participation of the member institutes and individuals, who are expected to share their wisdom in conceiving and conducting multinational education studies with common interests and design. Furthermore:

— IEA is *not* the kind of international organization which could constitute a political arena for handling issues of societal ideologies, North–South differences, or religious concerns. There are other organizations for these purposes.
— IEA is *not* a funding agency; rather, it is a fund-seeking agency.
— As far as the aims and quality of work are concerned, it is the members of IEA (i.e. the national institutions and individuals) who are responsible for initiating, monitoring and correcting action within the organization. And most importantly, they are responsible for the action itself."

The questions about IEA's operation included:

1. How can IEA ensure that every individual in IEA makes the fullest possible contribution?
2. What should be the form of IEA's responsibility? To the world community of educators? For improving educational theory and practice? In improving research competence in the different countries? In influencing policymaking in different countries?
3. How can IEA's mode of operation be improved for choosing worthy research topics, improving the research methodology used, and undertaking certain support pilot studies?
4. Structurally, should IEA be centralized or decentralized?
5. Is the number of persons now in an international coordinating center appropriate or are additional services required?
6. Does a participating research institute function well? What improvements could be made?
7. How is the NRC's work organized? Should an NRC be full time or part time? (Why are letters not answered? Why are problems

sometime raised at a late stage? Why are consensus agreements not adhered to?)
8. What improvements can be made in procedures for:
    (a) decision making;
    (b) project development;
    (c) project implementation;
    (d) project completion.
9. Is the present distribution of responsibilities adequate?
10. Does the working language (English) present a problem?
11. Should IEA remain a non governmental organization?
12. Should membership fees be charged?

Conclusion

On the basis of 25 years of experience of IEA, what pointers could be given to others wishing to launch international research projects? The following are some, but surely not all, of the main points to look out for.

1. Ensure that the project chosen has high priority in the participating countries and ensure that all heads of centers — and/or National Research Coordinators — are highly motivated to participate and have a say in the overall design and instrument construction.
2. Choose the "prime-movers" very carefully — both the head of projects committees and the international coordinator.
3. Plan in absolute detail and realistically, and ensure that each person knows (and feels responsible for) what he/she has to produce when and how. All persons must know (in fact they should have been partly responsible for) the detailed plans and timetable. To inculcate this sense of responsibility (social? cultural?) is very important. "Loners" are dangerous in a team exercise.
4. Foresee, where possible, problems of a substantial and interpersonal kind and plan how to deal with them.
5. Seek to teach the persons involved to listen to others, to be humble and hard-working. Try to get away from ethnocentrism and prima-donna-ship.
6. Attempt to discover the personal aspiration of the various individuals involved, and try to match the reward to the aspiration.
7. Ensure that key persons have the ability to unite team members to tackle a common problem, and delegate tasks appropriately. (This is not learned easily).
8. As far as possible, ensure that full-funding is available from the beginning of a project.
9. Recognize that the members of the team must:
    (a) accept not to be a prima-donna and selfish.

(b) often accept routine tasks.
(c) accept hard discussion and criticism.
(d) work hard in meetings and *between* meetings.
(e) accept that some members of the team will not produce as much as others

Throughout a project the leader must set standards of quality of work and ensure that he or she surpasses, or at least reaches, these standards and that all other members do likewise.

Participating Research Institutes in IEA

Australia:
Australian Council for Educational Research
P.O. Box 210
Hawthorn, Victoria 3122

Belgium (Fl):
Seminarie en Laboratorium voor Didactiek
Pasteurlaan 2
9000 Gent

Belgium (Fr):
Laboratoire de pédagogie expérimentale
Université de Liège au Sart Tilman
4000 Liege 1

Canada (BC):
Faculty of Education
2125 Main Mall
University Campus
University of British Columbia
Vancouver, BC M5S 1V6

Canada (Ontario):
Ontario Institute for Studies in Education
252 Bloor Street West
Toronto, Ontario M5S IV6

Canada (Québec):
INRS-Education
2383 Chemin Ste-Foy
Ste-Foy Québec G1V 1T1

Chile:
Universidad de Chile
Dirección General Académica y Estudiantil
Alameda Bernardo O'Higgins 1058
Santiago

England & Wales
National Foundation for Educational Research in England and Wales
The Mere, Upton Park
Slough, Berks. SL1 2DQ

Finland:
Institute for Educational Research
University of Jyväskylä
Yliopistonkatu 9

T. Neville Postlethwaite

France: Institut National de la Recherche Pédagogique
                 29, rue d'Ulm
                 75230 Paris Cedex 05

Germany: Max-Planck-Institut für Psychologische
                    Forschung
                 Leopoldstr. 24
                 8000 München 40

Ghana: Ghana Education Service
                 P.O. Box M. 45
                 Accra

Hong Kong: School of Education
                 University of Hong Kong
                 Hong Kong

Hungary: Orszagos Pedagogiai Intezet
                 Gorkij Fasor 17–21
                 H-1071 Budapest

Indonesia: Balitbang Dikbud
                 Jl. Jenderal Surdirman
                 Tromol Pos 297 KBY
                 Jakarta

Israel: School of Education
                 Tel Aviv University
                 Ramat Aviv
                 Tel Aviv

Italy: Centro Europeo dell'Educazione
                 Villa Falconieri
                 00044 Frascati

Japan: National Institute for Educational Research
                 6-5-22 Shimomeguro 6-Chome
                 Meguro-ku
                 Tokyo

Kenya: Bureau of Educational Research
                 Kenyatta University College
                 P.O. Box 43844
                 Nairobi

Korea: Korean Educational Development Institute
                 20-1 Umyeon-Dong
                 Gangnam-Gu
                 Seoul

*and (for Science):   National Institute for Educational Research and
Training
25–1 Samchung-Dong
Chongro-Gu
Seoul

Luxembourg: Institut Pédagogique
route de Diekirch
Walferdange

*Mexico: Subsecretaria de Planceación Educative
Dirección General de Evaluación
Anil 571 60 Piso
Granjas Mexico
Mexico CP 08400

Netherlands: Technische Hogeschool Twente
Vakgroep Onderwijskunde
Postbus 217
7500 AE Enschede

New Zealand: Department of Education
Private Bag
Wellington

Nigeria: International Centre for Educational Evaluation
University of Ibadan
Ibadan

*Norway: The International Learning Cooperative
Rosenhof Skole
Dynekilgatan 10
0 569 Oslo 5

*Papua New Guinea: Education Department
University of Papua New Guinea
P.O. Box 320 University
Port Moresby

Peoples Rep. of
China: Central Institute for Educational Research
10 Bei Huan Xi Lu
Beitaipingzhuan
Beijing

*Philippines: Institute for Science and Mathematics
Education Development
University of the Philippines
Pardo de Tavera St.
Diliman
Quezon City

Poland:	Instytut Ksztalcenia Nauczycieli ul. Kokotowska 16/20 00–561 Warszawa
Scotland:	The Scottish Council for Research in Education 15 St. John Street Edinburgh EH8 8JR
Singapore:	Institute of Education 469 Bukit Timah Road Singapore 1025
Sweden:	Institute for International Education University of Stockholm S–106 91 Stockholm
Thailand:	National Education Commission Ministry of Education Sukhothai Road Bangkok 3
USA:	Teachers College Columbia University New York, NY 10027
*Zimbabwe:	Department of Curriculum Studies University of Zimbabwe P.O. Box MP 167 Mount Pleasant Harare
and:	Ministry of Education and Culture P.O. Box 8022 Causeway

* = member of project only; not member of General Assembly.

Training and Cooperation

The International Seminar for Advanced Training in Curriculum Development and Innovation

BENJAMIN S. BLOOM

This article is dedicated to Torsten Husén who did so much to make this international seminar possible as well as effective.

Introduction

UNESCO sponsored a meeting of experts on curriculum of general education in Moscow, USSR in January, 1968. This 7-day meeting was attended by 33 experts from 22 countries. I was the co-chairman of this conference.

The major proposals for international and national action in the report of this meeting included the following:

1. *National Centers for Curriculum Development and Research*

   The process of curriculum construction is a very complex one requiring a variety of experts to participate in the development of specifications, learning materials, evaluation procedures and educational research. The most effective curricula are now being developed by those nations fortunate enough to possess curriculum centers with appropriate teams of experts.

   It is *recommended* that Member States of UNESCO be helped in the creation of national centers for curriculum development and research through initial financial support, consultants, training opportunities and dissemination of information. The major effort of UNESCO should, however, be directed to relating the knowledge and experience available in some countries to the support of other countries in this work.

2. *Exchange of Experience*

   The various procedures associated with curriculum development constitute an educational technology which is well known in theory, but less well exemplified in practice. The number of national centers engaging in curriculum development is, however, growing and it is the opinion of the meeting that current procedures could

145

be refined and better practices realized, if there were an interchange of information about the techniques that have been
evolved.

The meeting *recommends* for consideration by UNESCO the
problem of how the interchange of experience of curriculum
development might be facilitated. In particular, the meeting invites
UNESCO to consider the possibility of bringing together for a
training session of a month or more, followed by other meetings at
regular intervals, national teams, the members of which would
thereby get to know one another, and so establish a network of
communication which would make knowledge available.

3. *Assistance in Curriculum Development and Evaluation*

It is *recommended* that frequent systematically organized meetings
of curriculum experts be held to assist in the evaluation and
development of curricula. Such meetings should be conducted at
international, regional, and national levels.

A curriculum is not static, either in its content or in its methods.
It must be under continuous review and revision, preferably by
teachers working with experts in the field. Curriculum reform
commissions should be permanent bodies concerned also with the
preparation of materials and retraining of teachers. Curriculum
reviews should be systematically planned, rather than *ad hoc*.
Further, as new methods and techniques are evolved for curriculum development, for evaluation, and for learning and instruction,
there must be machinery for disseminating knowledge about them
between and within countries.

It is further *recommended* that UNESCO assist by organizing
international and regional meetings of curriculum experts and by
encouraging and aiding national authorities to develop their own
procedures and programmes.

4. *Training of Specialists in Curriculum Development*

It is *recommended* that assistance be given to countries to establish
or expand the systematic training of educational specialists in the
field of curriculum development, and, when advisable to assist
groups of countries having similar problems in the organization of
regional courses for this purpose.

Following the Moscow meeting, the staff of UNESCO invited me to
submit a plan for a six to nine week training program and seminar which
would be in harmony with the first two recommendations of the Moscow
meeting. Such a plan was submitted in the summer of 1968 and
considered in great detail by selected members of the UNESCO staff at a
meeting with me and other experts in this field. It was agreed that these
ideas with some revision might form the basis for further planning
meetings and that efforts should be made to secure the interest of

prospective faculty members, various ministries of education, and appropriate sources of funds.

At a later meeting of the Unesco General Council, approval was given to this training program and support was pledged from Unesco in the amount of $15,000. A steering committee consisting of R. Dave (India), T. Husén (Sweden), J. Sandven (Norway), and B. Bloom (USA) was appointed to insure that the faculty selected would be the best one possible. This steering committee was also given the responsibility of reviewing the national applications for participation in the training program and determining the applications to be approved in the light of the strength of the present organizations of the curriculum centers and their plans for the future and with due regard to the qualifications of the proposed teams to participate in the training.

I discussed the proposed training program with funding agencies in Europe and the US and received pledges of support in the amount considered necessary in the original budget proposed to Unesco. Unfortunately, the program which was to be offered in the summer of 1969 was delayed until the summer of 1971. This meant that many changes had to be made in the funding and the conditions under which the program would be held.

In view of the many difficulties in conducting this program under Unesco auspices, it was finally decided to invite International Association for the Evaluation of Educational Achievement (IEA) both to administer the program as well as to take full responsibility for it. This decision was taken in December, 1970 after it was envisaged that sufficient funds could be secured to provide for faculty costs, material, and travel and living costs for teams of curriculum specialists from nations which satisfied all the conditions for participation but were unable to fund it fully because of various economic conditions.

Aims of the Seminar

Given the view of the Moscow meeting that curriculum centers provide a *systematic* approach to curriculum development including studies of national needs and values, evaluation of the effects of specific changes in the curriculum, and teacher training, it was considered likely that the large majority of countries could profit from improvements in their curriculum work as well as from a training program for the key persons in their curriculum centers.

Each country must organize its curriculum work along the lines it regards as most relevant for its special conditions. Some countries will have highly centralized curriculum centers while others will attempt to provide for decentralized curriculum work. Some will place their curriculum work in the Ministry of Education; others will create National Centers located in some relation to the Ministry, the institutions

Benjamin Bloom

of higher education, and the public-supported schools; while others will regard curriculum work as a series of special contract projects to be supported by public and private funds.

However it is organized, each country will have to provide for four functions:

1. *The Determination of the Specifications for the Curriculum*

This will include the content and objectives of the curriculum. This function requires a series of value decisions based on available evidence in the country, studies made of specific social and educational needs in the nation, expert opinions, and a body of theory and research on learning. This is the most fundamental set of problems in curriculum development and each nation may learn from the experience of other nations with these problems.

2. *The Development of Learning Material and Instructional Procedures*

This function requires highly skilled workers who can create materials and procedures which will serve the functions specified for the curriculum. It also includes the trying out of the materials and procedures under appropriate conditions with students and teachers in order to find ways of improving them and to determine the limitations and advantages of each set of materials and techniques. This stage in curriculum development constitutes a technology which can be shared by all and which can be improved in a systematic way from year to year.

3. *The Evaluation of the Effectiveness of Learning Material and Instructional Procedures*

This function involves the careful use of evidence to determine the extent to which the curriculum has the intended effects on students. This stage in curriculum development includes the creation of appropriate evaluation techniques, the use of appropriate sampling procedures and research design, and the analysis of evidence by appropriate statistical and data processing procedures. Of all the functions, this is one of the most highly developed international technologies which can be shared by countries possessing appropriately trained personnel.

4. *The Inservice and Preservice Training of Teachers for Curriculum Changes*

Each nation must find ways of bringing its teachers up-to-date on new subject matter, methods, and ideas finally used in the new curriculum developments. While this is not properly a part of curriculum development, it is clear that new instructional material and methods can not be used in the schools until the teachers have been prepared for the changes. Here again, each nation can profit from the experience of other nations.

With these requirements in mind, it was agreed that the overall aims of the International Seminar would be to review the state of the art in curriculum development and evaluation and to institute dialogue among curriculum workers at different levels and in different subjects in a school system. Furthermore a working relationship should be created between subject matter specialists and evaluators. To this end, it was anticipated that practical work would be undertaken in the Seminar in the creation of small learning units. An important principle to be followed in this practical work would be the creation of a team, a group of persons in each country representing different competencies who would pool abilities such as subject-matter expertise, evaluation and measurement techniques, and skills in planning and implementation of curriculum projects. It was thought that a team so constituted would provide a good nucleus for curriculum work.

A general overview of the complexity of forces determining curriculum was obviously essential and it was agreed that experts in sociology, economics of education, and psychology of learning would be asked to contribute their views.

Three major outcomes of the program were envisaged: learning of general principles in the various areas of curriculum development; practical work in specific areas of curriculum work; and an understanding of the problems, successes and failures of curriculum work in different nations in order that the experience of each nation could provide one basis for a model for others.

It was hoped that all the participants in the seminar would learn:
1. The state of the art in curriculum theory;
2. The many forces (social, political, economic) affecting curriculum development and the ways in which necessary experts can be identified and used in the work;
3. The uses and method of evaluation of curriculum and how evaluation can be built into the curriculum development process;
4. How the software and hardware of educational technology (particularly psychological knowledge) can be used in curriculum development;
5. The ways in which teacher training (both preservice and inservice) must be linked to ongoing curriculum reform.

It was planned that subject-matter groups or specialist groups would be formed to review their own subject matter or speciality in terms of the state of the art. Four subject areas were identified:

Science
Elementary Education
Social Studies
Humanities (either Literature or Second Language).

In terms of the work being undertaken in curriculum centers, it seemed as though these four areas included the subjects where considerable work had been undertaken or planned in the early 1970s. Furthermore, in terms of some of the major difficulties being encountered, it was considered imperative to involve two additional curriculum specialities:

Curriculum Planning and Implementation
Curriculum Evaluation and Research.

The basic team representing each curriculum center was planned to have a person representing each of four areas: Curriculum Planning and Implementation, Evaluation, Science, and Elementary Education. In addition, if they so wished, a specialist in Humanities and/or Social Studies could be included. Each individual in a subject matter field was expected to review (with the rest of his subject matter group) the nature of the subject matter itself in terms of sequencing the subject matter thoughout the school system and then attempt to create a small learning unit together with some sort of evaluation instrument in collaboration with the evaluation specialist from his own team.

The aim of the seminar for specialists in Curriculum Planning and Implementation was to examine the various models which exist in various socio-economic-political contexts for the innovation, reform, evaluation and dissemination of curricula throughout an entire school system. The Evaluation group was to review the state of the art of formative and summative evaluation, the use that can be made of existing survey data for feedback to curriculum planners and the relation of evaluation of curriculum to educational research in general.

The members of each national team were expected to prepare a paper on the implications for future curriculum work in their country in terms of what had been discussed at the Seminar. Teams could also work as a unit to prepare interlocking papers confronting a major national educational problem or as individuals tackling an area of concern within their own fields in consultation with other members of the team to provide different expertise. It was hoped that these two activities — practical work within a subject area and team cooperation — would further the knowledge of each individual and also establish interaction and links between subject-matter experts, evaluators, and curriculum planning and implementation leaders.

Perspectives on Curriculum Work in Other Nations

In each of the endeavors outlined above, it is clear that nations can learn from what is done in other nations and from the successes and failures of particular strategies already undertaken. In addition, the presence of teams from many countries would enable each team to gain perspective on its own work in comparison with work being done elsewhere. Each of the national teams would come from differing cultural contexts and each curriculum has to be appropriate and relevant to the particular cultural context. One of the fascinating problems is the transformation of principles and techniques learned to the particular national context.

Nations vary in their needs to teach values and affect deliberately in their schools systems, and it was expected that the various ways this is undertaken in different nations would prove to be of interest and practical value to all the nations.

Some nations operate on an *ad hoc* basis for the reform of curriculum; a few have models of systematic continuous reform. All wish to institute flexible mechanisms which will allow an ongoing and smooth updating of curriculum. Here again, the various experiences would distill and produce sound and strong models.

The fact that many nations have similar problems of curriculum development and evaluation whatever their state of economic development is of great importance. The recognition of such problems and the will to work together in solving them both regionally and internationally can add much to world understanding and the resolution of major problems in education and other areas. Education exists in every nation. The curriculum is the central component in all schooling. For the first time it would be shown that international cooperation at a detailed operational level is possible. It was hoped that the Seminar would sow the seeds for overall curriculum reform in a series of nations and for international cooperation in solving the many problems which ultimately affect human beings already born as well as those yet to come into this world.

The organizers of the Seminar were extremely conscious of the efforts to be made during the Seminar to discover the most appropriate strategies for following up the work begun by this first international program and also to determine how regional and international cooperation could be fostered for the solutions of curriculum problems.

Selection of Participants

As already mentioned, sponsorship of the Seminar was formally shifted to IEA in December, 1970. Since the program was to be held in the summer of 1971, very little time remained in which to carry out the application and selection procedure to choose the teams to participate. Therefore, instead of inviting a large number of countries to submit applications to send teams and then making the selection of a limited number of countries from a much larger number of applications, a preselection procedure was used. From among all possible country participants, the Steering Committee attempted to identify those countries which would be most likely to be able to assemble teams which would benefit from the program. The following criteria were established to help identify these countries:

1. That the country had already or planned to have a curriculum center of some form on a national or regional basis; and
2. That there appeared to be a sense of commitment to systematic curriculum work within the country and the work now underway showed promise of being continued.

In addition, a few countries were identified which did not meet the first criterion but which, in the opinion of the Committee, would be able to derive a great deal of benefit from the program.

On the basis of personal contacts, background information and published evidence, the following countries were identified as most likely to qualify for admission to this Seminar:

Argentina, Brazil, Ceylon, Chile, Colombia, England, Ethiopia, The Federal Republic of Germany, Finland, Ghana, Hungary, Iceland, India, Iran, Ireland, Israel, Japan, Kenya, Malaysia, The Netherlands, New Zealand, Nigeria, Pakistan, Poland, The Republic of Korea, Rumania, Scotland, The Soviet Union, Spain, Sweden, Tanzania, Thailand, Venezuela, Yugoslavia, and Zambia.

Thus, a total of 35 invitations to apply were sent to countries throughout the world. A formal letter of invitation signed by Torsten Husén, Chairman of IEA, was sent to the Minister of Education in each of the countries listed above. The program was described briefly and the criteria for selection listed. An additional detailed description of the program was also sent.

Initial inquiries and applications were received from 32 nations. This impressive response had not been anticipated, and unfortunately the constraints of both monetary and physical resources, which indicated a participation of about 20 countries as the upper limit, made it necessary to select a more limited number from among these. However, this response did indicate the great interest in and need for further training in this area.

Plans for follow-up measures and the hopes of disseminating the ideas generated by the Seminar led to certain guidelines for the selection of countries being established. It was hoped first to keep a balance between the numbers of "developed" and "developing" countries represented and, second, as far as possible to draw participating countries from all parts of the world. At the very least, the planners envisaged three representative countries from each continent and also representation from different types of political and social systems. Not only would this insure that the work begun at the Seminar would spread, but also a core of trained personnel would be available in each region to help with follow-up programs and future regional seminars.

It was agreed that the financial resources of the country should not be the determining force in selection, but rather the ability to provide a team for the training and the country's need for such participation was to be central in the selection criteria. For those countries identified as "developing," IEA offered to finance the travel and room and board at Gränna, Sweden, for the members of the team. Those countries identified as "developed" were asked to pay these costs themselves though IEA offered to help wherever possible.

In a Seminar of this kind it is necessary to secure as participants people who will have the best background and qualifications possible to make their participation of the greatest value to the countries involved. As preliminary applications and requests for more information began coming in to the IEA center in Stockholm, it became evident that it would be advisable to have personal visits made to a number of countries and personal observations by faculty members while IEA personnel checked others. I visited three countries in South America and five in Africa meeting with Ministry of Education officials to explain the purpose and structure of the Seminar and to interview proposed team members. In addition faculty members reported on the proposed teams from their own countries and on those they visited.

Members of the Steering Committee met in March of 1971 to make the final selection of teams to attend the Seminar. Decisions were made on the basis of formal applications submitted, additional correspondence with people within the country and reports on personal visits and observations. Four criteria for selection had been established in the letters which were sent to Ministers of Education:

1. That the country already had or planned to have a curriculum center or unit;
2. That it could provide a well-qualified team of at least four and preferably six persons for the training;
3. That it planned to use the members of the team in its future curriculum work; and
4. That the proposed members of the team were proficient in English — the language of instruction at the Seminar.

It was obvious from the applications submitted by some countries and from outside reports that all the criteria had been met as nearly as possible. These countries were accepted immediately without conditions. For other countries, the Committee felt that certain changes in the membership of the team would strengthen it greatly. Letters were sent to these countries about such changes and in most cases changes were made or additional information was provided about the special cases.

Although initial plans had limited participation to 20 countries, the Steering Committee finally accepted teams from 25 countries to attend the Seminar. Two of the countries withdrew at the last minute. Teams from the following 23 countries attended the Seminar (the number of team members is shown after the name of the country):

Argentina (6)	India (6)	Poland (5)
Colombia (6)	Iran (4)	Republic of Korea (4)
England (4)	Israel (6)	Spain (4)
Ethiopia (6)	Japan (4)	Sweden (6)
Finland (4)	Kenya (4)	Thailand (6)
Ghana (6)	Malaysia (5)	Venezuela (5)
Hungary (6)	Netherlands (6)	Zambia (4)
Iceland (4)	Nigeria (7)	

A number of countries which were not accepted or were unable to provide the minimum number required to form a team requested the opportunity to send a single observer to the Seminar. Individual observers attended from the following countries: The Federal Republic of Germany, Norway, and Scotland. In addition six curriculum scholars (financed by their own institutions) attended the sessions. These were from Argentina, Sweden, the Federal Republic of Germany, Canada, and The United States. Most of these *have become eminent* in their own field of curriculum scholarship.

Selection of Faculty

The selection of the faculty for the Seminar was a long and arduous task. In the first proposal to UNESCO, I defined the major courses and seminars to be provided and suggested about eighty names for consideration. Following this, the UNESCO staff was asked to provide additional names for the courses and seminars. The IEA Chairman and Executive Director added additional names. Heads of research centers associated with IEA and cooperating education centers supplied about 25 additional names which were also considered. The permanent faculty added additional names to the total list. Altogether, about 250 persons were considered in selecting the final faculty of 33 persons.

The Steering Committee was asked to review the proposed persons for chairing the particular courses and seminars. They finally approved of the following key persons who were considered to be the permanent faculty:

Courses   Ralph W. Tyler — Course A, Curriculum Theory
            Benjamin S. Bloom — Course B, Evaluation Methods
            Philip Foster — Course C, Individual and Social Change
            Robert Glaser — Course D, Educational Technology

Seminars L. C. Comber — Seminar E, Science
            Edwin Fenton — Seminar F, Social Studies
            Alan C. Purves — Seminar G, Humanities (Literature)
            H. H. Stern — Seminar G, Humanities (Second Language)
            John I. Goodlad — Seminar H, Elementary Education
            Benjamin S. Bloom — Seminar I, Evaluation and
              Curriculum Research
            Ravindra Dave — Seminar J, Curriculum Planning and
              Implementation

Following the above selection, each leader was asked to nominate persons whom he would like to have work with him on his course or seminar. These were termed *consultants* and were expected to provide both supplementary types of competence and experience and somewhat different points of view. Each leader proposed up to about a dozen names. Through direct discussions, correspondence and telephone calls, I negotiated with the leaders for a balanced team for each seminar or course. What was sought for each course and seminar was a faculty composed of:

1. Individuals who would be compatible with the seminar or course leader
2. Individuals who came from different countries or who had experience in different countries
3. Individuals who had competence in different aspects of the overall subject
4. Individuals with somewhat different approaches to the subject.

The total faculty finally contained thirty-three persons, of which seven were at Gränna for the full six weeks (5 July–14 August 1971), six attended for two weeks or more and twenty were present for less than two weeks.

In terms of region of origin, the final faculty at Gränna was divided as follows:

North America	12
Europe	14
Asia	5
Africa	2
	33

Structure of the Gränna Program

One-third of the total time at Gränna (60 percent of the scheduled instructional time) was devoted to four courses which all participants were expected to attend. One pair of courses — Curriculum Theory (Course A) followed by Evaluation Methods (Course B) — was offered from 9:00 to 10.30am on each of the working days throughout the Seminar. These two courses were planned in close relation to each other so that they virtually related to different phases of the same subject. While these courses began as lecture courses with opportunity for discussion, after the first two weeks they were converted to workshop sessions in which the participants were grouped by subject matter fields or national teams at tables (seating six persons each) and applied the basic principles and methods of the subjects to specific problems in their own fields of specialization.

It is of interest to note that when grouped as national teams, the participants were able to use their national language and many displayed an energy and enthusiasm not always present when they had to use English as the medium of expression. This was especially noticeable for the sessions on Evaluation Methods. Since each national team included a specialist in evaluation methods, it was possible to use this specialist as a mentor (and secretary) to the members of the team. The progress of each team was particularly good when the evaluation specialist was a highly competent and a respected member of his group. The use of the evaluation specialist as the mentor during the Evaluation Methods course was, in most national groups, one effective way of strengthening the group as a team of specialized workers who could and did work closely together.

Two other course were also offered in the morning. The course on Individual and Social Change (Course C) met from 11:00 to 12:30 each morning for the first four weeks, followed by the Educational Technology course (Course D) during the last two weeks. These two courses were primarily lecture courses offered by a number of short-term faculty members and coordinated by the Chairman of each course. At least one-half of the time of each course session was devoted to questions raised by the participants. Since these two courses were intended to provide a map of the major ideas and methods in each of a series of topics, they were designed to raise major issues, new ways of viewing educational and social phenomena, and to suggest how experts in each country or region might work closely with curriculum groups to help them in attacking some of the most basic problems in the field of education and curriculum. While Courses A and B were intended to be immediately relevant to the curriculum work in each country, Courses C and D were believed to be especially relevant in considering some of the long-term educational problems in each national context.

For each of the courses a set of books and readings was made available to all the participants. Some of these readings were intended to serve as a background for the lectures or workshop sessions and these were assigned for reading just prior to the particular session for which they were needed. Other materials were intended for later reading and reflection since they put the content of the course sessions in a more intensive way or they were to be used for later reference when the participants needed these ideas during the Gränna program or after they returned to their work in their own curriculum centers. In the questionnaires completed by the participants, it was evident that the readings were frequently used to clarify difficult ideas presented in the lectures or workshop sessions.

Since most of the faculty members attended the courses, there was frequent cross-reference from one of the courses to the others and a topic or idea raised in one course session was referred to and elaborated upon by another faculty member at a different session.

As one reflects on the topics, ideas and methods raised in the four different courses, it was evident that somewhere between 50 and 75 percent of the material was new to each participant, no matter what his previous training and experience. When a participant had encountered some of these ideas previously — such as Piaget's ideas, human development phenomena, etc. — they had not previously been considered in the context of curriculum development. A generalization such as this is striking in view of the wide diversity of countries represented, the variation in experience and level of academic training, and the wide variety of academic institutions attended by the participants. Part of the reason for this is that the faculty for these courses emphasized the most recent research findings (especially when they had done the research) and because each faculty member attempted to relate his special area of competence to the problems of curriculum development in very different national contexts.

Another part of the time at Gränna (40 percent of the scheduled instructional time) was devoted to the seminars offered for the different areas of specialization (Science, Social Studies, Humanities, Elementary Education, Curriculum Evaluation and Research, and Curriculum Planning and Implementation). Each of the seminars, which were limited to 25 participants each, was offered from 2:00 to 4:00 in the afternoon of each working day. Each of these seminars was organized by the faculty chairman of the seminar, and they were responsive to the special problems of each of the participants or of subgroups of participants. Each seminar chairman had three to five additional faculty members who spent varying amounts of time with the group. Ideally, these additional faculty members brought different approaches to the area of specialization.

The conduct of these seminars was determined by the faculty and the participants, but it was evident that most of the seminars shifted from presentation of major ideas and methods of the field by both faculty and participants to intensive consideration of the merits of different approaches, to the preparation by individuals (and subgroups) of specific plans and material for use in their own curriculum centers.

Since most of the seminar faculty members attended the morning lectures and workshops, there was frequent cross reference to ideas raised in these sessions to clarify particular points or to provide a common base for the further development of a difficult idea or procedure. It was evident that the morning sessions provided a common language and set of experiences for the more intensive work in most of the seminars.

Each of the participants was expected to prepare a paper in which he

related the work of the courses and the seminar to the special problems
of his own curriculum center and to the particular context provided by
his own national situation. Many of these papers were discussed at the
seminars and almost all were discussed with faculty members of the
seminar at various stages in their preparation. In most cases, each paper
was discussed with the national team who were especially concerned with
how each paper related to the other papers prepared by members of the
team and the extent to which each paper took into consideration the
special circumstances in the national situation.

Almost a third of the time at Gränna was devoted to the activities of
each team. Although this was not scheduled by the faculty, the living
conditions at Gränna were designed to facilitate meetings of each team
for professional as well as social purposes. In the first weeks, it was
apparent that much of the team activity (involving two or more members
of the team) was primarily for the purpose of clarifying the ideas in the
morning courses. As the program developed, most of the team meetings
were concerned with the relevance and application of the ideas
considered at Gränna for the curriculum work in the team's national
situation. In most cases, the team discussed the proposed outline of the
papers to be prepared by team members, and the actual text of the
papers was discussed by members of the team at different stages in the
preparation. Increasingly, the team became a major force at Gränna in
the constant effort to select and relate new ideas to the curriculum
problems in the nation.

The team also played a large role in the social entertainment of groups
from other countries as well as entertainment of faculty members and
groups of faculty members.

It is apparent that the majority of national groups began the process
of forming teams at Gränna. Each national group consisted of a
collection of able individuals who may or may not have known and
worked with each other previously. They began to form a team at
Gränna as they discussed common learning experiences and considered
them in relation to their own national situation. This team formation was
aided by specialized competencies which were developed in the seminars
and could be related to each other. Finally, the common national
language, the need for familiar faces, the difficult new learning tasks,
and the constant need to make meaning out of new learning as it applied
to the national situation — all served to strengthen the group as a team.
The social situation at Gränna also helped to strengthen the team.

The participants — especially in the specialized seminars — did much
to help each other as the need arose. While the team became a stronger
group, it is also clear that the subject or specialist groups also became
groups of colleagues who supported each other in many ways.

Finally, the faculty made themselves available for consultation on individual and team matters. The ease with which one could sign up for a faculty consultation made it possible for most of the participants to have repeated meetings with faculty members.

After Gränna

Of the 23 countries represented at Gränna, 12 (52 percent) already had or created curriculum centers in which the members of the team at Gränna play a leading role in the development of new curricula. Another 4 countries (17 percent) have made effective use of members of the team in curriculum projects or as planners for curriculum change. Two of the countries (10 percent) suffered through major governmental revolutions which quickly destroyed any progress made by the curriculum centers. Finally, 5 of the countries (22 percent) have not been visited by curriculum specialists and little is known about the use they have made of the Gränna teams. In sum, approximately 70 percent of the countries represented at Gränna are known to have made effective use of the curriculum teams trained at Gränna. In the following, we review some of the major educational changes made by these countries.

Evaluation Process

The emphasis on the curriculum evaluation process at Gränna resulted in most of these countries making use of evaluation during the development of new curricula to check on each part of the new course in order to find flaws and correct them at the different stages in the development processes. This resulted in great economies in the process since major flaws were found and corrected before it was too late. In addition, the finished curriculum was evaluated in a sample of the classrooms throughout the country to determine the conditions under which it worked well as well as the circumstances under which it did not yield good results. This use of evaluation was especially necessary to reassure the curriculum team as well as administrators, teachers, and parents that the new curriculum worked well under appropriate conditions.

In-service Training of Teachers for the new Curriculum

In most cases, the new curricula involves new ideas and new methods of teaching. In some of the earlier work on inservice training of teachers (for new curricula), the training program might involve as much as two months of time. When this period of training was given in the capital city or other large centers, it was typically found that most of the teachers trained by these intensive programs had *abandoned* the new curriculum methods and teaching procedures within a six to twelve month period. Inquiries into this suggested that when a teacher encountered major difficulties in the material or the new teaching process, they returned to the more familiar content and methods (that they had successfully used in the past).

Some of the curriculum centers have experimented with different methods of inservice teaching training for the new curricula. What seems to work well is the use of several weeks of intensive teaching training on the *new subject matter* (usually in the large city centers) followed by weekly and bi-weekly one-day training sessions (in the local school situation) on the *teaching methods* as well as to help teachers overcome particular difficulties as they encounter them. When these training methods are used (and especially with local personnel) the teachers become very effective with the new subject matter and the new methods of teaching. And, they continue to use the new curricula successfully over long periods of time. Thus, they have found that the same amount of training time yields far better results when some of the time is devoted to the local teaching situations and is used to help teachers develop teaching methods appropriate to the new curriculum.

Mastery Learning

In some curriculum centers, the evaluation specialists have conducted research on the mastery learning feedback-corrective methods. When these have been found to work very well in a sample of classrooms, the centers have incorporated these features into the new curricula. Introducing these teaching methods as part of the new curricula has met with good acceptance by the teachers as well as the students. When these mastery learning methods have been used with the same group of students over several years, the results have been very positive not only on student achievement, but also on students' attitudes toward school and their own academic self-concept. In some situations, the effect of these methods is to enable most of the students under group instruction to achieve results almost as good as they would have achieved under excellent one-to-one tutoring methods. The point of this is that the curriculum centers have been working with more effective teaching methods as well as with effective new curricula.

Higher Mental Processes

At the Gränna Seminar, all members of each curriculum team were introduced to the *Taxonomy of Educational Objectives* and the distinctions between the lower mental processes (information learning) and the higher mental processes (application of principles, analytical skills, and other reasoning and creative skills). They developed skill in developing learning material, teaching methods, and evaluation techniques appropriate to their curriculum objectives. When they returned to their curriculum centers they experimented further with these methods. One now finds a great deal of emphasis on the higher mental processes in some of the curriculum centers. After much difficulty, they have found excellent ways of incorporating these objectives into the curriculum, the teaching methods, and the evaluation methods. In some ways, this is the great revolution in education — to find ways in which most of the students can learn to use the higher as well as the lower mental processes.

Some Common Problems

In most of the countries, the curriculum centers have become very large organizations which create new curricula, develop new learning material, develop new methods of teaching, make use of radio, television and films, and provide for the inservice training of teachers for the new curricula.

The curriculum centers typically find that it takes 7 to 8 years from the beginning of a new curriculum project until it is adopted and used in the schools. Where the typical tenure of the Minister of Education in a country is only a few years he frequently attempts to use the curriculum center personnel to carry out the short term reforms he wishes to make. Thus, the curriculum projects and the short-term reforms are on different time sequences. This creates friction between Ministers of Education and the personnel of the curriculum center. In any case, it is difficult for new Ministers of Education to accept what must seem a very slow process to improve the curriculum. There is frequent pressure on the curriculum centers to cut out some specific processes such as consultation with experts or steps in the evaluation process.

The need for additional well trained personnel is always present. Some of the centers develop long term plans and provide for the special training of additional personnel either within the country or abroad. Usually, they provide some on-the-job training within the country.

Some of the curriculum centers have developed excellent relations with other curriculum centers — especially those in the same region. These relationships are used to compare notes with each other, to provide some of the training functions, as well as to engage in common projects. In some ways this was the underlying goal of the Gränna Seminar — to bring the national curriculum teams together so they might learn to work with each other.

This was echoed in the major points made by a special committee at Gränna on the *future* of international activities in curriculum construction and curriculum evaluation. This committee stressed the need for an International Center for Curriculum Development which would:

162   *Benjamin Bloom*

1. Organize conferences and seminars*
2. Provide for training of personnel on a regional or world-wide basis
3. Establish an international pool of expert consultants and
4. Establish a communication network for the exchange of information and people.

In closing, the rapid changes in almost every aspect of the modern world make it clear that the role of education must be central in helping people adapt to these changing conditions. Nations with effective curriculum centers will be at an advantage in providing for the needed changes in education. The need for such centers will increase as national governments recognize the social and educational problems that must be solved.

*Some attempts were made to create an International Curriculum Organization. While there was great interest in the organization, it was not possible to secure the necessary funds to maintain it for more than 4 years. In terms of conferences and seminars an African Regional Seminar for Advanced Training in Systematic Curriculum Development and Evaluation was held in Accra, Ghana in 1975. This seminar involved curriculum teams from 15 African nations. There was some overlap with the faculty personnel at Gränna.

The Comparative Education Center at the University of Chicago*

C. ARNOLD ANDERSON

This center was inaugurated in the late 1950s. The Department of Education, which awards a Doctor of Philosophy degree in the Social Science Division of the faculty, already had several members from the Social Sciences. The creation of the Comparative Education Center continued the policy of interdisciplinary cooperation, in this case with a social science emphasis on studies of education and society in diverse countries.

Interdisciplinarity

It was assumed that Comparative Education was not a discipline, but an "approach" that would benefit from the work of the several area centers represented in the social science division. Interests of faculty and students could then shift from one to another set of societies, remaining free of bonds to any particular geographic emphasis. This flexibility provided a fruitful way of enlisting cross-disciplinary research on various topics and issues in studies of education and society.

The Center was opened as a component of the Education and Social Order section of the Department of Education. Under its auspices only a few graduate courses and seminars were added to the curriculum. Congruent with the position of the department as part of the social science division, incorporation of various social science approaches and interests ensued. Active and ramifying collaboration by social science personnel in the work of seminars and on dissertation committees followed. The long established university policy of interdisciplinary linkage was in place as a model that facilitated rich associations with the new program. Virtually automatically, membership of the Center faculty in the Committee on New Nations and the Committee on African States took place from the start.

---

*Two pieces of Husén provide a framework: "Educational research and the making of policy in education," *Minerva* **21** (1): 81–100, 1983; and T. Husén and M. Kogan (Eds.) *Educational Research and Policy*, 1981, Oxford: Pergamon.

From the start, one policy has been to allow students to take their "minor" in another department which was mutually agreed. Although individual cases led to unusual choices, most often students linked up to work in sociology, anthropology, or economics. These required choices of a minor led to competency in a diversity of fields and fostered much interdisciplinary exchange in Center seminars and among the students more informally. Incidentally, this also fostered interdisciplinary exchange among members of the faculty.

A University policy that fostered hospitality to new academic offerings gave generous opportunities to Comparative Education. For example, for several years at the time of annual meetings of professional associations in Chicago the Center offered lectures by colleagues in other departments of the University at a special session on the campus. These vigorous presentations linked Comparative Education to other parts of the University and drew on the latter for presentations to colleagues in Comparative Education from other universities. On two occasions early in our association with the University, students and faculty in Comparative Education took the responsibility for entire issues of the *Review* embodying new work at the Center.

Decisions on Types of Research

In our early days thought was given to opening a special program of research on education in the Soviet Union. There were outstanding programs in other universities that rendered competition superfluous, however, so only a few studies on this topic were included. Nevertheless, there was active collaboration with specialists on Russia elsewhere in the University.

A quick review led to ready acceptance of the University's policy of not engaging in overseas operating projects. Specialized operations of such projects are extraordinarily expensive and entail stateside programs of high cost and relatively limited focus. Avoidance of commitments to such large undertakings permitted us to develop varied research projects and to widen the range of countries from which students were enrolled and to adapt the program to encompass their concerns. Disengagement from operational projects does isolate a teaching program in some ways, but it provides for accommodation of research foci determined by disciplinary interests rather than by operations. This policy fostered a critical point of view on many topics, free of the constraints inherent in commitments to direction of operating programs. It meant also that administrative responsibilities could remain minimal, permitting maximal concentration of members of the faculty on research.

By the same token, resources were available for the less expensive consulting work. Time and thought could be directed to careful planning of conferences around disciplinary foci and the simultaneous examination of an internationally important question in research by students and faculty members drawing on data for several countries. Also, questions relating to programs at UNESCO, by the Peace Corps, or at the World Bank could be taken up for analysis. In such studies undue bounding by questions specific to particular countries could be avoided.

International Educational Achievement Study

In the lecture prepared for my initial visit to the Department I proposed a strong program of inter-societal research on the quality of secondary schools. This quickly led (jointly with Professor Bloom) to talks with Europeans and to an early inauguration (with financing by the US Office of Education) of the still-continuing program of inter-societal research across nations on school performance. Professor Torsten Husén was enlisted virtually from the start in the leadership of this inter-university research.

This comparative research has proved to be surprisingly complex. It has turned out that different countries display various degrees of diversity among schools. In some countries the national tendency for homogeneity in performance of pupils is more conspicuous, while elsewhere pupil variance is more apparent. In some countries the academic performance of boys is a more salient feature than is that by girls. Whatever the capabilities being examined, schools of different countries vary in output, and performance on particular features of a test gives rise to serious discussions about quality. Following upon his earlier work as a student at the Center, Stephen Heyneman (now at the World Bank) has demonstrated that whereas social status backgrounds dominate over measured school differences in the performance of pupils in the developed countries, in the less developed countries differences among the schools has more impact than differences in socio-economic status. The emergence of new data sets on quality and school performance in some of the LDC's (primarily in Asia) has provided a basis for a series of dissertations on this subject in the past few years.

Educational Planning

Work on educational planning moved to a central place from an early day in our program. A considerable part of my writing over the two decades was related to this topic — see especially the series of papers in the *Yearbook of Education*. This was not an emphasis on the teaching of "educational planning" as a technology. Indeed, the position taken consistently by the Center has been that at the heart of educational planning must be understanding of education in society in general and of critical variations among countries in the context of educational planning. Technologies commonly advocated were examined only after students had pursued studies that could provide a background in such understanding.

The fact that I am a sociologist provided a special point of view for writing on educational planning. Tacitly this writing had a dual theme: educational planning is a central social activity in every society, but the institutional structure puts a particular bias on planning in each country. Within the context of organized schooling in contemporary societies "planned schooling" is prominent. The central emphasis on quality of schooling takes a particular focus in each society or type of society. Despite strong national differences with respect to educational planning, this activity becomes marked off in distinct ways in each society. In most societies schools are the preeminent planned sector of public life apart from taxation and military activities, yet analyses of this educational sector lack any clear pattern.

Dissertations

Any program of Comparative Education will confront the diversity of secondary school systems, and interest in American secondary schools leads inevitably to the study of other systems. European systems are of interest for their value in illuminating the deeply historic roots, Latin American and Asian secondary schools illuminate the patterns of cultural borrowing and distinctive interdependencies between development of educational systems amid societal structures. At the same time, within European settings students confront a diversity of options or tracks. The panoply of status distributions reflected in dissertations by students from different backgrounds and countries displays a rich picture of educational systems.

There has been produced also a set of dissertations dealing with higher education in a dozen countries, more in Asia than elsewhere. The specific topics have been diverse, although the social recruitment of students emerged as a common theme — a central theme in the first theses for some countries.

A dozen dissertations have dealt specifically with teachers — mainly teachers in the United States, Europe or Canada. These have included studies of roles of teachers in Appalachian communities, contrasts between England and Germany in the training and status of teachers, contrasts between England and the United States in the structures and functions of teacher organizations, recruitment of teachers for the Congo, and the economics of teacher salary structures and policy in Quebec.

As is true of any graduate department in comparative education, many dissertations have been distinctive in their interests. Examples include dissertations on the training of health personnel, the economics of time in learning, analysis of the flow of personnel to the United States for graduate study and of who returns home and why, vocational training in metropolitan community colleges and by private enterprise, the intents and effects of SENA programs in Latin America, determinants of the spread of literacy and schooling in less developed countries, education and innovative behavior among Japanese farmers, education and innovative behavior among non-farm Japanese enterprisers, contrasts among ethnic groups in perceived educational benefits and school performance in Malaysia, effects and extent of part-time professorships in Argentine universities, and (most recently) a "rational expectations" analysis of the rates of enrollment in secondary and in higher education in Japan since 1950. Masters theses have also been diverse, but relatively few students have written such theses.

A fourth of the doctoral degrees awarded to Center students have been granted to women.

Several years ago I retired. For a brief period Philip Foster and then Douglas Windham were directors of the Center. For the last several years John Craig has been an insightful and committed Center director. His specialty is the history of education, and his book on the history of university education in Alsace-Lorraine has just been published by the University of Chicago Press. He is at the same time an active participant in seminars in the economics department. The basic principles that have governed Center development continue, but with a refreshing influx of new young faculty who contribute to the vitality of interactions among students and staff. Recent dissertations continue to be diverse, reflecting both links with older strands of research and new departures.

Developing Graduate Programs in International Education: The Institute of International Education, Stockholm

INGEMAR FÄGERLIND

When the Institute of International Education (IIE), University of Stockholm, was founded in 1971 with Torsten Husén as its first professor, it satisfied a strong demand in Sweden for an institution which would be responsible for research and training focusing on international problems in education. The main tasks of the Institute have been to carry out research within the field of international education and to run a graduate program for students originating from many different countries.

Considering the input of resources the graduate program has been the most productive one within the Stockholm Faculty of Social Sciences in terms of both quantity and quality of dissertations. There are many reasons for this. The mutual confidence between Torsten and his students resulted in an Institute where everybody tried to do his very best. The number of students was never more than 20 to 25. Most students were actively involved in project research within the Institute. The use of English as a working language, which is very exceptional at Swedish university institutions, was important for the fast transmission of knowledge and experiences from different parts of the world.

The course work that constituted the graduate programs developed within the Institute was usually quite flexible. The core was always a weekly seminar, where research problems within different projects were presented and discussed. Many well-recognized scholars, who visited the Institute for shorter or longer periods of time, were invited to present their research at these seminars where fertile ideas from students and researchers were shared and further developed. Especially within the field of research methodology the competence of the graduate students rapidly developed to reach international standards. When John Keeves (1972) submitted the first thesis of the Institute the rest of the graduate students were brought up to date with the use of regression analysis and path analysis in educational research. Different types of multivariate analyses were developed for educational use during the 1970s and used in several dissertations from the Institute. These included LISREL (Munck, 1979) and PLS (Noonan and Wold, 1983).

The comparative study of educational problems in industrial nations was well catered for in the graduate program. Most of the countries participating in the early IEA surveys were industrialized. However, it was also recognized that more attention should be given to the problems of formal education and its social and economic impact in the Third World. This was an area where most people in the Institute at the beginning had little or no competence. The development of a graduate program in this area can serve as an example of how a new research area developed within the Institute.

During extended visits by two comparative educators, C. Arnold Anderson of Chicago and Roland Paulston of Pittsburgh, it was decided that a graduate program in Education and Development should be prepared and further elaborated as experiences were gained. In order to make it possible for the Institute to prepare a proposal Anderson and Paulston were asked to make an outline of topics to be covered and to list some key references. In the fall of 1974 a proposal was submitted by the Institute to the Swedish International Development Agency (SIDA) for funds to launch an interdisciplinary program at the graduate level under the general heading "Education for Development". After the processing of the proposal in SIDA's Department of Education a grant of Skr 50,000 was given to the Institute to plan and initiate the program. The first step taken after the project had been funded was to gather representatives from the Social Science departments at the University of Stockholm, as well as some experienced practitioners, in order to solicit their advice about the format and content that such a program might have. Professor C. Arnold Anderson, on a return visit to IIE, drew up a guideline of topics for the course and subsequently provided copies of more than one hundred important articles dealing with relevant problem areas for the course program library. Additional articles were also collected from the SIDA library and a reference catalogue to be used by the students was developed.

In the meantime, Dean Nielsen, a Spencer Fellow in the Institute and a former student at the Stanford International Development Education Committee (SIDEC) provided a number of insights into the problems of operating a program of this nature. Three members of the SIDEC staff, Alex Inkeles, Martin Carnoy, and Henry Levin, visited the Institute in the spring semester of 1975, and all made helpful suggestions based on experiences from the Stanford program.

Since Torsten Husén was Chairman of the Board of the International

Institute for Educational Planning (IIEP), UNESCO, Paris, the program used for the IIEP trainees was known to us. In June 1975 I had the opportunity to visit IIEP in order to study their program in operation, and also learn about that Institute's future plans in this field. At the end of the spring semester of 1975 the Social Science Faculty of Stockholm University gave its approval for the program and provided additional funding for the first academic year in order to bring in teachers from other departments for some parts of the course. The program was ready to begin in September 1975.

Objectives of the Program

The goals of the program were by necessity related to the interest of the Institute as a whole, namely the role of education in social systems from a comparative perspective. Thus, the core course on Education for Development did not focus on education only within one specific society, but on the way in which education functions in many societies with different structures. Furthermore, both these perspectives were considered important for the understanding of problems of development, especially in Third World countries. Insofar as the course was policy-oriented, with the focus on applied research, problems related to planning *for* development were also seen as important.

With these factors in mind, the official statement regarding course objectives was as follows:

> "The overall course objectives are to study education as one of several interacting social systems and to consider educational policies and procedures for development in relation to these systems."

> "The emphasis will be laid on the educational situation in the less developed countries. The course will be tied as much as possible to current development research in Sweden and abroad."

It should be noted that during the formulation of the course objectives for the first year a special point of view regarding the relationship between education and development was emphasized, namely education *for* development. The assumption behind this formulation was already questioned by the first students attending the course and later the assumption regarding the nature of the link between education and development changed considerably.

At a very early stage in the planning of the course it was apparent that relevant research in the field of development had been performed within several disciplines. At the same time, the perspective of the Institute of International Education has always had an interdisciplinary focus, including among its staff sociologists, psychologists, economists, political scientists, educationalists, social anthropologists, and statisticians. It was, therefore, natural that the perspective of the course should be deliberately interdisciplinary in character. This orientation is reflected in the following statements found in the first course circular:

> "The course program is intended as a part of doctoral studies not only in Education but to some extent also in Sociology, Economics, Social Anthropology, Political Science, and Human Geography. The course can also as a whole or partly serve as extended training for qualified persons who wish to specialize in this field."

At the time that the course was planned there were no programs in this subject at the graduate level in the Stockholm or Uppsala area. Furthermore, the Institute itself was at that time committed exclusively to the training of doctoral students. Therefore, the core course program, consisting of the Seminar on Education for Development, was designed in such a way that it covered one fourth of the course work required for a doctoral degree.

In order not to exclude persons with a special interest and expertise in this program, the admission requirements covered a wide range of competences. This was stated in the course circular as follows:

> "The course is in the first place intended for doctoral students in the social sciences. Also other persons with qualified academic backgrounds can participate."

A number of pedagogical styles were deliberately included in the course format. The course was conducted on an open-end basis, and participation of the students was sought at each stage. The course included lectures, seminars, group discussions, individual research and extensive reading of relevant literature. Participants, in consultation with the course leaders, were encouraged to plan their own syllabus within the framework of the overall course outline.

The requirements for successfully completing the course included the following specifications regarding examination:

> "Those who study for a doctoral degree must participate actively in course work. Examination will take place in connection with literature reading, a number of papers and presentation of group and individual work. Subjects for group and individual work will be selected in consultation with the professor."

As previously stated, the course program included a variety of topics from a number of disciplines pertaining to the relationship between education and development. The original course outline (Fägerlind and Saha, 1977) included the following topics:

I   INTRODUCTION (2 credits)
    Theories of development and underdevelopment
    Education in the developing countries in a historical
       perspective
    Education seen in the total socio-economic, political and
       cultural context.

II   EDUCATION FOR DEVELOPMENT (8 credits)
 Education as an instrument in national development
 Educational planning in a national perspective
  Education for economic growth and redistribution
  Education for social change
  Education for political awareness
 The politics of education and educational policy
 The economics of education and educational finance
  Education and employment
 Education and rural development
 Types of education
  Education for whom?
  Literacy in the developing countries
 Education and population
  Population movements
  Brain drain
 The organization and administration of education
 Problems of implementation
 The content of education
  Curriculum planning
 Teaching strategies, methods and instructional materials
 Staffing teacher training
 The management of education
 Educational evaluation
 The quality of education

III   METHODOLOGY IN EDUCATIONAL PLANNING AND
 EVALUATION (5 credits) (this course runs parallel with II)
 Research methodology in the Third World
  Needs for research
  Data collection and processing in the developing world
 Methods in educational planning and evaluation
 Labour market analysis
  Cost-benefit and cost-effectiveness analysis
 Other methods for the measurement of educational effects
 Methods in comparative education
  IEA studies

IV   APPLICATION (5 credits)
 Case studies

Visiting Lecturers
One of the main goals of the course was to utilize, for instructional
purposes, professionals and experts with practical experience in the

areas of education and development. To this end, the Institute of International Education was well suited, with a number of world-wide contacts. Thus, visiting lecturers came from many different countries. This visiting lecturer component is considered to be one very important aspect of the whole program.

The Institute of International Education from the mid 1980s

The investment by IIE in a new graduate program in the mid 1970s has been very productive. Hundreds of students originating from all continents have passed the course "Education and Development". Interest in the field generated a demand for more specialized courses, such as Economics of Education and the State and Education with special emphasis on developing nations.

Other universities in Scandinavia were also influenced by the IIE graduate program and included similar courses at their universities. A handbook covering the state of the art, but also presenting models for the systematic study of relationships between education and development, has been published (Fägerlind and Saha, 1983).

The IIE of the mid 1980s has a group specialized in the field of developmental education and the Swedish Agency for Research Co-operation with Developing Countries (SAREC), in its report on research performed through SAREC grants, presented IIE as one of the most active institutions in Sweden and the most productive one (SAREC, 1984). The Swedish International Development Agency (SIDA) has an agreement with IIE whereby the Institute serves as a consultant to the SIDA Department of Education. The Institute is also involved in conducting research for the World Bank, UNESCO and UNDP. Close cooperation with the International Institute of Educational Planning in Paris has been important since the establishment of IIE. A 3-year program of collaboration in the field of research and training with the International Development Educational Committee (SIDEC) at Stanford University began in 1983, and from 1984 an institution to institution cooperation started with the Central Institute of Educational Research in Beijing, the People's Republic of China.

As mentioned at the beginning of this article, the graduate program of IIE has been the most productive within the Stockholm Faculty of Social Sciences. As seen from the list (see Appendix to this article) more than twenty doctoral theses have been published since the establishment of IIE. From 1980 onwards more and more dissertations have dealt with problems in developing countries. Löfstedt (1980) studied Chinese Educational Policy from 1949 to 1979, Gorham (1980) Education and Social Change in Kenya Maasailand, Kann (1981) presented her study on career development in Botswana, Mbamba (1982) studied the prerequisites of primary education for independent Namibia, Duberg

(1982) studied schooling, work experience and earnings in a third world corporate setting, and Chinapah (1983) published a study of equality of educational opportunity in Mauritius. Several dissertations dealing with developmental problems are at present under way.

The Institute of International Education and its graduate program always benefited from the network of the International Association for the Evaluation of Educational Achievement (IEA). As a result of this network scholars from around the world have continued to use IIE as an Institute where they could complete their academic writing at the same time as taking part in university life. More and more developing nations have joined IEA during the 1980s. At the same time, the Institute has been active in helping IEA in its development (Marklund, 1983).

The IIE graduate program has developed well since Torsten Husén founded it. It will surely develop in various new directions over the coming years. And, in the spirit in which it was founded, the Institute will endeavor to contribute to knowledge in the field of comparative and international education and, where possible, help improve the practice of education for the millions of children in the countries in which the Institute's research programs take place.

References

Chinapah, V. 1983 *Participation and Performance in Primary Schooling: A Study of Equality of Educational Opportunity in Mauritius*. Studies in Comparative and International Education, No. 8. Institute of International Education, University of Stockholm.

Fägerlind, I. and Saha, L. 1977 *Education and Development. An Evaluation of an Interdisciplinary Program at the Doctoral Level*. Report No. 24, Institute of International Education, University of Stockholm.

Fägerlind, I. and Saha, L. 1983 *Educational and National Development: A Comparative Perspective*. Oxford: Pergamon Press.

Gorham, A. 1980 *Education and Social Change in a Pastoral Society: Government Initiatives and Local Responses to Primary School Provision in Kenya Maasailand*. Studies in Comparative and International Education, No. 3. Institute of International Education, University of Stockholm.

Kann, U. 1981 *Career Development in a Changing Society: The Case of Botswana*. Studies in Comparative and International Education, No. 4. Institute of International Education, University of Stockholm.

Keeves, J. P. 1972 *Educational Environment and Student Achievement*. Stockholm: Almqvist & Wiksell.

Löfstedt, J-I. 1980 *Chinese Educational Policy: Changes and Contradiction 1949–79*. Stockholm: Almqvist & Wiksell International and N.J., USA: Humanities Press.

Marklund, S. 1983 The IEA Project: An Unfinished Audit. Report No. 64, Institute of International Education, University of Stockholm.

Mbamba, A. M. 1982 *Primary Education for an Independent Namibia: Planning in a Situation of Uncertainty and Instability*. Stockholm: Almqvist & Wiksell International.

Munck, Ingrid M. E. 1979 *Model Building in Comparative Education: Applications of the LISREL Method to Cross-National Survey Data*. IEA Monograph Studies No. 10. Stockholm: Almqvist & Wiksell International.

Noonan, R. and Wold, H. 1983. *Evaluating School Systems Using Partial Least Squares*. Evaluation in Education, Vol. **7**, No. 3. Oxford: Pergamon Press.

SAREC 1984 *SAREC Support to Swedish Developmental Research 1976–1983*. Stockholm Swedish Agency for Research Cooperation with Developing Countries.

Appendix

Doctoral Theses

1972   Keeves, John P. *Educational Environmental and Student Achievement.* Stockholm Studies in Educational Psychology 20. Stockholm: Almqvist & Wiksell.

1973   Dalin, Per. *Case Studies of Educational Innovation.* Paris: OECD.

1974   Bergling, Kurt. *The Development of Hypothetico-Deductive Thinking in Children: A Cross-Cultural Study of the Validity of Piaget's Model of the Development of Logical Thinking.* IEA Monograph Studies No. 3. Stockholm: Almqvist & Wiksell International and New York: John Wiley.

1975   Dunlop, Ian. *The Teaching of English in Swedish Schools: Studies in Methods of Instruction and Outcomes.* Stockholm: Almqvist & Wiksell International.

1975   Fägerlind, Ingemar. *Formal Education and Adult Earnings: A Longitudinal Study on the Economic Benefits of Education.* Stockholm: Almqvist & Wiksell.

1976   Noonan, Richard D. *School Resources, Social Class, and Student Achievement: A Comparative Study of School Resource Allocation and the Social Distribution of Mathematics Achievement in Ten Countries.* IEA Monograph Studies No. 5. Stockholm: Almqvist & Wiksell International and New York: John Wiley.

1977   Nielsen, H. Dean. *Tolerating Political Dissent: The Impact of High School Social Climates in the United States and West Germany.* IEA Monograph Studies No. 6. Stockholm: Almqvist & Wiksell International.

1978   Rosier, Malcolm J. *Early School Leavers in Australia: Family, School and Personal Determinants of the Decision of 16-year-old Australians to Remain at School or to Leave.* IEA Monograph Studies No. 7. Stockholm: Almqvist & Wiksell International and Hawthorn, Victoria: Australian Council for Educational Research.

1978   Clifton, Rodney A. *Socioeconomic Status, Attitudes, and Educational Performance: A Comparison of Students in England and New Zealand.* IEA Monograph Studies No. 8. Stockholm: Almqvist & Wiksell International.

1978   Kelly, Alison. *Girls and Science: An International Study of Sex Differences in School Science Achievement.* IEA Monograph Studies No. 9. Stockholm: Almqvist & Wiksell International.

1978   Nyström, Astrid. *French as a Foreign Language: A Comparative Study on Factors Affecting Student Achievement.* Stockholm: Almqvist & Wiksell International.

1978   Ekstrand, Lars Henric. *Bilingual and Bicultural Adaption: Studies in Assessment of Second Language Learning and of Factors Related to Bicultural Adjustment, with Special Reference to Immigrant Children.* Stockholm: Institute of International Education, University of Stockholm.

1979   Munck, Ingrid M. E. *Model Building in Comparative Education: Applications of the LISREL Method to Cross-National Survey Data.* IEA Monograph Studies No. 10. Stockholm: Almqvist & Wiksell International.

1980   Mählck, Lars. *Choice of Post-Secondary Studies in a Stratified System of Education: A Swedish Follow-Up Study.* IEA Monograph Studies No. 12. Stockholm: Almqvist & Wiksell International.

1980   Isling, Åke. *Kampen för och mot en demokratisk skola, Part 1. Samhällsstruktur och skolorganisation.* (The Struggle for and against a Democratic School, Societal Structure and School organization) Pedagogiska skrifter 262 och Sober-Dokumentation 11. Stockholm: Sober.

1980   Löfstedt, Jan-Ingvar. *Chinese Educational Policy: Changes and Contradiction 1949–79.* Stockholm: Almqvist & Wiksell International and N.J., USA: Humanities Press.

1981   Bergling, Kurt. *Moral Development: The Validity of Kohlberg's Theory.* Stockholm Studies in Educational Psychology 23. Stockholm: Almqvist & Wiksell International.

1981   Kann, Ulla. *Career Development in a Changing Society: The Case of Botswana.* Studies in Comparative and International Education No. 4. Institute of International Education.

1981   Thelin, Bengt. *Exit Eforus. Läroverkens sekularisering och striden om kristendomsundervisning.* (Exit Ephorus: The Secularization of the High Schools and the Dispute Concerning Religious Education) Stockholm: Liber UtbildningsFörlaget.

1982   Mbamba, A. Mauno. *Primary Education for an Independent Namibia: Planning in a Situation of Uncertainty and Instability.* Studies in Comparative and International Education No. 5. Institute of International Education. Stockholm: Almqvist & Wiksell International.

1982   Duberg, Roland. *Schooling, Work Experience and Earnings: A Study of Determinants of Earnings in a Third World Corporate Setting.* Studies in Comparative and International Education No. 6. Institute of International Education.

1982   Fris, Ann-Margaret. *Policies for Minority Education: A Comparative Study of Britain and Sweden.* Studies in Comparative and International Education No. 7. Institute of International Education.

1983   Chinapah, Vinayagum. *Participation and Performance in Primary Schooling. A Study of Equality of Educational Opportunity in Mauritius.* Studies in Comparative and International Education No. 8. Institute of International Education.

Doctoral Theses in France: Can Their Academic Significance be Evaluated and Compared with those of Other Countries?

MICHEL DEBEAUVAIS

The assessment of doctoral theses forms part of the regular duties of a researcher. Reforming the system of doctoral studies and the nature of diplomas is an exercise frequently undertaken in France which is at present tackling its third major reform since 1945. These reforms arise out of a concern to improve the doctoral study programme and, indirectly, to increase the academic value of the theses. But none of these reforms has been preceded by an evaluation of the shortcomings of the present situation or by an examination of theses as academic products. The aim of this article is to suggest a method of evaluation based on the criteria used directly or indirectly by the doctoral examining bodies, drawing on the results of a preliminary investigation carried out in 1983; the method proposed could be used to compare the national output of theses in various countries in a particular discipline.

In every country, doctorates occupy an important place in the university system. They are at the top of the hierarchy of diplomas and determine admission to or promotion within an academic career; the symbolic ritual of defending theses is also a form of academic evaluation depending on the mode of operation of the academic community in a particular country.

Doctorates are also the subject of frequent international comparisons in the international academic community, especially when the creation or reform of doctoral studies in a particular country is under consideration or when young researchers elect to prepare their thesis abroad. But too little research exists to allow verification of the subjective information and national reputations concerning the "academic value" of the national output of theses. Comparative education has devoted more attention to the question of equivalence of secondary school diplomas and first degrees than to masters degrees and doctorates.

On the ladder of success, Sweden occupies first position and France is often placed in the rear cluster of industrialized countries. This is why I am dedicating this article to Torsten Husén, who gives us a detailed account of the vicissitudes of his thesis in his Memoirs and who has made the International Institute of Education of Stockholm University into a center of excellence for doctoral studies of worldwide reputation.

The situation regarding Education in France is not typical of all the disciplines. Its development in French universities has, even more than that of the Social Sciences, been late, slow and controversial. In common with related disciplines, it has had difficulty freeing itself from the "literary" traditions of the classical humanities and this tendency is reinforced by the tradition that the preparation of a thesis should be a solitary task encouraged intermittently by the "thesis superviser".

Since 1945, the North American model has provided the inspiration, more or less directly, for the three consecutive doctoral study reforms of 1950, 1973 and 1985.

Historical review

The "3rd stage thesis" (Thèse de 3 ème cycle) was introduced after the war on the lines of the Ph.D in the USA; this new diploma was intended to give recognition to a first piece of research and was judged a more appropriate form of training in research in the field of natural sciences than the competitive state examination (concours de l'agrégation). It was extended by analogy to other disciplines or rather to other Faculties. The system of the 3rd stage has evolved since then along different paths depending on the discipline and the university concerned.

In the social sciences where there was no competitive examination or competitive system of recruitment in the public sector, the 3rd stage doctorate represented the main criterion for recruitment to higher education, especially for the qualifying lists for assistant lecturer posts (LAFMA).

In the "arts subjects", however, "degrees in education" (licences d'enseignement) and competitive examinations for recruitment to secondary school teaching posts (CAPES — teaching qualification at secondary level — and the competitive state examination) continued to serve as criteria for recruitment to higher education.

The 1973 Reform

The 1973 reform (Decree of 27 February 1973 and Order of 16 April 1974) continued to take as its point of reference training in research in the field of exact and natural sciences. This reform aims at harmonizing the system of the 3rd stage between arts and sciences but more particularly at reducing the number of doctoral students, especially in the arts and social sciences; one of the reasons for this Malthusian approach to reform was fear of possible pressure from 3rd stage doctors to obtain assistant lecturer posts through LAFMA registration. The model (indirect) for selective training in research through a short, full-time period of attachment (1 year for the DEA — Diplome d'etudes approfondies) to a scientific laboratory was not bad in itself; but it was inappropriate to the literary disciplines where full-time students are the exception, apart from foreign students; in the social sciences it would only have applied in cases where there were university research teams in existence, which was rare. In the majority of cases, universities sought somehow or other to shape their requirements in accordance with the principles of reform. But in reality, since this reform contributed nothing to the creation of research teams, the tradition of thesis preparation continued virtually unchanged: a long and solitary pursuit of personal research with "light" supervision consisting of more or less regular attendance at a thesis supervisor's weekly seminar.

Apart from certain notable exceptions, systematic training in research continued to be left to the individual initiative of the candidates. This gave rise to enormous variations in the degree of academic quality of 3rd stage theses and in the implicit criteria employed by the examining bodies. These variations are not controlled by any process of collective evaluation; the chairman of the examining body has of course to prepare a report about the thesis and its defence; but in the absence of written texts or traditions, these reports remain confidential and their content very variable.

It is widely held that the 3rd stage system is less than satisfactory, that the 1973 reform has tended rather to aggravate the situation by imposing additional restraints without offering any positive benefits in return and that doctoral theses are very "unequal".

These subjective impressions should be underpinned by a more systematic evaluation relating to the mode of operation of different 3rd stage groups and to the products, that is, the manuscripts of successfully defended theses and the defence reports.

The 1984 Law on Higher Education provides for the abolition of the three types of doctorate — state, 3rd stage and university — and for their replacement by a single doctorate which will no longer be a national diploma but will be awarded on the sole responsibility of each university (a major innovation in a country traditionally attached to national diplomas). The only national procedure which remains is that of the establishment (created in 1973) of "research bodies authorized to award the diploma of further study (DEA) constituting the first year of doctoral study". It is envisaged that the "level" of the future doctorate should equate to that of the USA Ph.D, that is, higher than the present 3rd stage doctorate.

My aim in this article is not to present a description or a criticism of this reform, but to propose a method for evaluating the output of theses, in order to provide an empirical base for a practical attempt to define precise criteria for common standards of assessment of the "academic value" of the theses, at least in the field of education and social sciences. Any improvement arising from this would be limited, since it could only be applied to the process of final certification, thus avoiding presentation for defence of manuscripts which do not satisfy the qualitative criteria to be defined. This would still not deal with the fundamental problem of improving the conditions for the "production" of theses, that is, the means of training researchers by strengthening or developing research teams where young researchers could be trained in research as envisaged in the 1984 reform (and the 1973 reform before it). But a start could be made with this first step, since it has the advantage of being more short-term and not dependent on the allocation of resources.

The 1974 legal texts were ambiguous, since they defined the 3rd stage doctorate in terms of education and not of the final product: "it recognizes training acquired in the practice of research". The circular of October 1984 is more explicit: "the new DEA" (not the doctorates themselves as in the 1974 law) "should be considered as an essential basis and the first step in a period of training in research and through research leading to the doctorate". But it continues to confuse academic criteria with administrative decisions, by adding: "Coherent doctoral training may be the subject of a specific *recommendation* from the science section of the directorate general of higher education. . . . The use of this designation, as a reference, will simplify matters both for students and for the international community".

It would have been preferable to state that a doctoral thesis is an academic product which should represent an original contribution to knowledge in the relevant discipline and that its approval by a board of examiners should constitute a considered assessment of the academic value of the thesis, involving the academic responsibility of the members of the examining body.

If I insist on the term "academic" it is because this underlines the true nature of a discussion on the operation or reform of the present system of doctorates: it is not only about the fundamental question of the training of researchers, but also the important contribution of doctoral theses to French academic output. The acceptance of this point of view has certain implications, at least for social sciences where theses represent the principal means of recruitment of university teachers and researchers.

The first requirement is for uniformity or at least harmonization of the evaluation criteria employed by the examining bodies and the significance which they attach to the different levels of distinction. Invitations to colleagues from other universities to serve on examining bodies could be issued on a more systematic basis, which would of course involve some expenditure (albeit modest). Candidates could be asked to supply additional copies of theses which would enable them to be made more easily accessible to researchers than at present; this would involve some financial assistance (likewise modest) but would enable the theses to enter into circulation with other academic publications, especially if it was supplemented by the creation of a data bank such as that begun at the central file of theses in Nanterre; this would necessitate ensuring that the recent directive (1981) of the directorate of libraries was put into effect, asking candidates to prepare a summary and a list of keywords. A further improvement could easily be achieved by deciding to annex to each thesis the "reports of defence" (which are drafted by the chairman of the examining body, but which remain confidential) and to make these accessible to the general public, or indeed to publish them (in the annual lists of doctoral dissertations) with the summary and the "submission of thesis". Such publicity would make the examining bodies more conscious of the academic responsibility which they assume in their reports; their asssessments would at the same time be subjected to the criticism of their peers, as all academic judgements should be.

Criteria for evaluating theses

One can go further in seeking to define criteria for the evaluation of doctoral theses.

An analysis — not systematic — of opinions expressed in a series of discussions with university teachers on the criteria they use to evaluate the theses which they have to examine has led me to identify a general principle and to distinguish four groups of criteria:

1. *General Principle*

A thesis should not only demonstrate that the candidate has a detailed knowledge of a chosen subject and the research methods normally employed in his discipline (which is really the role of the DEA): it should also and above all, constitute a "product of research", that is, a contribution to knowledge in the particular discipline.

It should thus be evaluated by the examining body as a piece of research and not (or not only) as a certain amount of work completed by the candidate or as the written record of the candidate's educational progress. In other words, training in research is "judged" by the examining body according to the result as a "final product" and the judgement passed should be based on the same criteria as those used in the discussion of an academic work.

2. *Specific Criteria*

The various criteria referred to in the discussions are grouped around four main axes; apart from the basic qualities of form and presentation, a thesis should satisfy the following requirements:

(i)   it should be clearly placed by reference to the research already undertaken on the chosen subject or on those most closely related;

(ii) it should be based on new "facts" produced by the researcher or resulting from a new formulation of existing data;

(iii) the facts should be analyzed by the best known methods appropriate to the subject chosen;

(iv) the work should display "originality", by making a specific contribution, however modest, to knowledge in the particular discipline.

Given these criteria, it is thus possible to suggest a matrix which could serve as preliminary information for the candidates, as advice for the examining bodies and also as a qualitative analysis of a collection of theses on a particular subject or in a given speciality.

1. *Bibliographical Information*

Does the author demonstrate a detailed knowledge of previous works, particularly the latest, on the given subject, both in France and abroad? Are previous works presented in a synthesis (state of the art) setting out the various views and theories on the particular subject? Is the author's research clearly placed in relation to these different views, and in relation to recent investigations and data on the subject?

2. *Originality of Information or Data Studied*

Does the author present new facts or data or at least a new interpretation of data already published which can be said to constitute a contribution, even modest, to what is already known through previous publications?

Are these new data significant in relation to the subject chosen?

Have the sources used been evaluated by established critical methods?

Has the investigation or collection of data been undertaken in accordance with accepted scientific methods?

Has the population studied — the sample — been precisely defined and placed in context?

Has the significance of the results been evaluated and have the limitations of the study been emphasized?

Have the conclusions been clearly drawn?

3. *Methodology*

Does the author demonstrate a knowledge of the methods of analysis (particularly the latest) used in the chosen speciality?

Has he selected the most appropriate methods in relation to his topic and its problems?

4. *Originality*

This is the most subjective of the general criteria and yet our discussions have shown that faculty appraisal is closely linked to clear appreciation of the originality of a thesis. The points to which they refer most frequently are originality of new data (and their originality in relation to previous work), originality of the questions posed, and mastery of the subject as shown by the thesis as a whole. This criterion seems to be quite separate from the preceding three, since these may be satisfied by a thesis which would not be judged "original" even though it may constitute a contribution to knowledge.

For these four groups of criteria, the comments of the members of the examining bodies could probably be reduced to four scales:

— not up to the standard of a piece of research;
— reasonable average;
— good piece of work, demonstrating ability for research;
— original contribution to knowledge, worthy of publication.

In the recent field of "management sciences", Pierre-Yves Barreyre has drawn up a matrix of 8 criteria for evaluating theses which has been used by the Institute of Business Administration of the University of Grenoble (Barreyre, 1980). These criteria are as follows:

1. Opportunity for and originality of research
2. Qualities of conceptualization
3. Bibliography
4. Research methodology
5. Value of written dissertation
6. Usefulness of thesis, in the short or longer term
7. Qualities of oral defence
8. Examination of the conditions in which the work was accomplished.

Considering theses from the standpoint which we have have chosen, namely their contribution to knowledge, we prefer our own four criteria. Barreyre's criteria 5, 7 and 8 are aimed at evaluating the candidate rather than his academic contribution. Criteria 1 and 6 overlap and correspond to our fourth criterion, the most subjective, that of originality. Barreyre's criteria 3 and 4 coincide with our criteria 1 and 3. As for our second criterion, the "new knowledge" contributed by the thesis, this seems to us fundamental to any evaluation of the academic contribution, even though it is not specifically mentioned as such in Barreyre's framework of criteria.

The proposed matrix could be validated or improved by an investigation among university teachers sitting on thesis examining bodies, particularly in the social sciences to which this article refers. "Educational science" would provide a possible starting point because its creation in France is a recent development and because, owing to its multi-disciplinary nature, the criteria for academic validation are still relatively imprecise.

The discipline of "educational science" has only been recognized in the French university system since 1967. Moreover, departments awarding diplomas in educational science (including doctorates) only exist in some 10 universities (out of more than 60) and by no means represent the total number of academics studying all the different aspects of education.

An inventory of theses on the subject of education should not therefore be limited to the single field of "educational science". Information retrieval undertaken at our request by the Central Thesis Service in Nanterre identified 351 theses on "Educational problems in the Third World" (from 1970 to 1980), of which only 109 (less than one third) were in educational science; 69 of them (19.7 percent) in psychology, 32 (9.1 percent) in linguistics and 14 (4 percent) in economics.

The teacher-researchers who make up the university departments of "educational science" are themselves attached to different disciplines and do not all claim allegiance to "educational psychology". Evidence of this is provided by the list of teacher-researchers registered with the National Centre for Scientific Research (CNRS) for election to the Universities' Consultative Committee: 54 percent appear in Psychology; 28 percent in Sociology; 8 percent in Philosophy; 4 percent in Economics; 3 percent in Linguistics; and 3 percent in History.

The matrix suggested above should thus be applied to a sample of theses whose stratification should take account of these ratios between the different disciplines.

The findings and suggestions outlined above result from a global view of the present situation of social sciences in France and from the direction which any reform should take. The position can be summarized thus: the system of doctoral studies is of crucial importance for future academic output; it is also one of the major components of the academic world. There is no hope of bringing about deep and lasting change in the present situation by administrative measures only (decrees, orders, memoranda), as experience with the 1973 reform has shown.

It would be more worthwhile to attack the essential problem head on: the inadequacies of the French academic world in the sphere of social sciences, of which the deficiencies of the thesis system are only a part and a consequence. The success of an academic community demands that academic products be circulated, discussed and evaluated by peers; its organization demands resources: reviews, publications, symposia, exchanges with international communities and in addition research institutions, means of investigation (surveys, data processing) and means of training young researchers. Nothing strictly new, since this is already the practice in many university systems (particularly in the USA and Europe) and in the natural and life sciences in France.

This is why I am proposing in this article the practical step of assessing the academic value of theses defended during the last few years, beginning with a critical survey in a social science discipline. This would no doubt provoke a lively debate on the concept of "academic value". There is no reason to fear this or to try and avoid it. It would, on the contrary, be the start of an academic debate which would encourage better definition of the evaluation criteria and would restore to the system of doctoral studies its true role in the production of knowledge; similarly, the role of thesis examining bodies would become more like that of an academic authority, presenting properly argued judgements subject to the criticism of peers, rather than decisions of an administrative nature requiring no proper justification.

Of course, assessments such as those proposed in this article would form only a starting point for further debate prior to a gradual modification of the practices of thesis preparation and of their validation.

A reform of the thesis system by continuing evaluation of the departments for training researchers and of the theses which they produce could find its place among the procedures to be fixed by the law on higher education: an inter-university mechanism which would evaluate the training proposed and tested by the universities within the limits of their autonomy and which would frame its advice and recommendations with a view to ensuring harmonization at the national level. (The 1984 law has created a "national evaluation council" which could constitute an inter-university body of this kind.) Paradoxically, this task of evaluation is no more difficult for doctoral studies than for first and second stage university education; training in research can be assessed by its results, given the assumption that a thesis is a product of research and that it is subject to the evaluation criteria used by the academic world, these criteria themselves being likewise subject to continuing critical examination and capable of further refinement.

Reference

Barreyre P-Y. 1980 Les critéres d'évaluation d'une thése de doctorat: le cas de la gestion. In *Enseignement et gestion*, new series No. 15.

International Cooperation for the Development of Education

JAMES A. PERKINS

Cooperation on any subject and on any level is frequently hard to come by. When the subject is education, cooperation runs counter to valuable traditions and instincts of academic freedom, local independence, and institutional autonomy. At the international level, cooperation encounters the additional resistances of national pride and cultural difference.

While these restraints must be recognized, there are strong forces that require cooperation or at least suggest advantages to be gained. Over a million students annually seek to further their education in other countries. For this process to be a constructive one, both the sending and receiving countries must know a great deal about the educational programs and institutions of both countries. Special arrangements have arisen to take care of both leaving and receiving students. Sending countries must cooperate by providing essential information about the educational attainments of leaving students and receiving countries must cooperate with full information on the institutional opportunities that are available, their costs and the probable social climate into which the student will enter. When both parties cooperate in suppling the other with the needed information, students are more likely to have a constructive experience. Without such cooperation they can be lost and the experience can be more damaging than helpful.

The development of education and educational institutions is also a high priority on the agendas of most donor and recipient countries. The role of education in social and economic development is now better understood in most parts of the world. This understanding can only come about through patient examination by scholars and observers. The milestone study of Kenneth Thompson's *Education and Social Change* (1976) was accomplished through the collaboration of regional experts coordinated under Kenneth Thompson's management in the United States. And, of course, research interest on the part of all scholars knows no national boundaries. But accurate information is not just lying on the table waiting to be picked up. It requires patient help from opposite numbers in other countries. Some of the etiquette of this process on the international scene will be mentioned shortly. In all these matters the irresistible force of change through cooperation meets the frequently immovable object of determination to maintain the *status quo.*

Having set the stage on which the drama of cooperation is played, we must ask two questions: cooperation for what? and cooperation by whom? The purposes of cooperation fall into three general categories — the acquisition of needed information, the advancement of understanding, and the formulation and execution of educational policy. The actors in our drama are individuals, their academic institutions, and their governments. Each of these actors and purposes cross-relate to each other and could provide chapters of their own: i.e., governments and policy making, universities and policy execution, individuals and information gathering, etc. A chart of these multiple interconnections would graph like a Jackson Pollack painting.

Cooperation for Gathering Accurate Information

First of all, cooperation requires accurate information. Without such information cooperation is like building sand castles five minutes before high tide. Not much will be seen of it in the immediate future! But to get accurate information requires cooperation so we are in one of those pleasant cycles. It also requires initiatives and instruments. Fortunately, there has been a considerable increase in important information about education in general and a good deal about international education or at least the educational experience and facts of life of other countries. A dangerous gap persists but basic information and understanding is slowing filling this gap — not steadily and systematically but in bits and pieces. For this we have to thank many national and now international agencies. A full treatment of information and its sources available to interested scholars would take a whole volume. Perhaps some high points are not out of order.

Thirty years ago there were only about six books published in the United States having to do with higher education and none of them dealt with anything beyond our borders. Today there would seem to be that many books published every day and, while the attention to the international dimension is by no means adequate, several pioneers in the field of comparative education have arisen like Barbara Burn, Burton Clark, Dietrich Goldschmidt, and Lada Cerych. National institutions, both public and private, now publish volumes of material on their own conditions and systems. These are available to scholars and observers in other countries, unfortunately, not in translation.

And at a somewhat more popular level but still full of careful and precise information and analyses, one would have to mention journals like *Minerva* in England, *The Journal of Higher Education* in the United States, the *Docencia* in Mexico, *the Journal of the University of Hiroshima* in Japan, and the *European Journal of Education.* It must be restated that the business of comparative study to provide full and accurate information about systems in different parts of the world is still in its infancy — really a phenomenon of the last 20 years.

The problem of placing relevant information in the hands of those who need and want it remains. Those who need it have to state clearly what they want. Sometimes they don't know what they want until they see it in print. The provider of information must, therefore, frequently anticipate what the scholar wants even though he has not stated it. So the production and consumption of information are locked together in a symbiotic relationship, requiring each party sensitive to the needs of the other.

The collection of information (or enlightenment) is the first requirement of all levels of cooperation. For the reason just mentioned the process only sounds easy. When information on an international scale is involved this simple process can really be complicated. Language barriers, different statistical methods and standards, and national and institutional pride sometimes might complicate both the selection and the presentation of information. There is no substitute for the presence of professionals in all countries who want their information accurate and objective. They may not succeed because reports, even of prestigious organizations, are frequently edited or even withheld by national authorities.

The eternal tension between professional objectivity and national purpose has led to increased interest in third-party involvement. As a result, collaborative efforts have created private and public institutions whose functions, among others, are to gather, assemble and publish information needed by private and public parties in all parts of the world. Regional and international institutions do not guarantee professional objectivity. Their members and staffs are after all basically citizens of individual countries and they have their own strategies and purposes. But they are, at least, one step removed from internal national pressures and their professional pride requires the approval of their colleagues in other countries. In some very modest degree, standards of universal applicability have become increasingly visible. Such is the case of the statistical work of UNESCO, the OECD, and the World Bank. All three agencies have, in large measure, maintained a high level of reporting. One could wish that the important information in their files were more readily available. But the etiquette of international dealing through public international agencies poses limits; hopefully, they will steadily recede.

Cooperation in Research Projects

The next stage in collaboration involves *research* on topics and problems of interest not only to the researcher but also to his university and his government, and frequently to the object of the research in other countries. This is obviously a more sophisticated process than the collection and presentation of information. But obviously the two go closely hand in hand. We now move from cooperation for enlightenment to cooperation for understanding. Accurate information is essential but it must be used and interpreted to produce understanding. It is not automatically the case that understanding flows from the presentation of information. Information can be presented so as to suggest or obscure understanding, and information honestly presented can be distorted by selecting in a way to prove a point or support a position already determined. Collaboration on the international dimension, as has already been said, requires not only valid information but a determination to seek and present the truth as professionals believe it to be.

But cross-national research that leads to understanding has its own logic and own hazards. It comes in three modes. The first involves collaboration by researchers and their witnesses in other countries. Social scientists who wish to understand another educational system must involve local persons be they students or teachers or public officials, journalists or professional experts. Burton Clark (1977) in preparing his excellent book on Italian higher education had to receive the cooperation of many persons at all levels. Yet the project was his, he would decide what was important to say, and he alone would write the results. It was, and is, imperative that, if a full collaboration is to be achieved, the local social scientists have confidence in the integrity of the research person, that he in turn listens to what they have to say, and that he has a known reputation for objective and professional research. Clark met all of these tests and was, therefore, given full cooperation.

In addition, there is the matter of style, attitude, and the political and social atmosphere in which the research is taking place. Objects of research in any part of the world do not like to feel that they are under some impersonal and possibly unfriendly microscope. They can resent what they suspect may be ulterior motives. Any suspicion that the researcher is really there for his domestic intelligence agency will immediately destroy all rapport. And, finally, when research persons from developed countries come to work in developing countries, a desire to insist on accuracy can all too easily be misinterpreted as intellectual colonialism.

But even if all the sensitive etiquettes are observed, there are two other matters that must be properly handled if collaboration is to succeed. It can be that local deficiencies are well known but native personnel are not too happy to have them advertised. Should the scholar take this sensitivity into account? Will the anticipation of a hostile stance affect the prospects for collaboration, both now and for any future contacts? Finally, there is frequently the awkward question when native collaborators (usually) wish the outside scholar to make critical judgements to support privately-held opinions or to reinforce those already in the public domain but where implementation has not been forthcoming. It is known that a push from the outside can be quoted to advantage. It is, therefore, frequently useful and necessary. But the scholar must tread carefully if he feels that he is being unwisely used.

Faced with these nuances and potential traps in cross-national research, some projects are carried out in partnership. The Halsey-Trow (1971) substantial study and resulting book on the British professoriate is a case in point. Two world-class researchers found that the advantage of a joint collaboration was considerable. The resulting book proves it. Halsey provided both standing and an understanding of the local scene while Trow brought the critical eye of a scholar who had studied not only his own system in the United States but others as well. This, too, was known to his British audience. Halsey was not a parochial scholar either but his reputation in the English academic community surely made local collaboration effective and forthcoming, and Trow's reputation for the highest quality objective scholarship reinforced the desire to cooperate.

Another kind of collaboration may involve a more structured arrangement of two national parties represented on a joint study commission or committee with a comparison of two systems on an equal basis, a staff director, frequently co-chairmen, representing the two countries involved. A good example is the ICED German-USA comparative study of access to higher education policies in the two countries (1978) which was financed by a grant from the Volkswagen Foundation. A Joint Commission was established with equal numbers from both countries. The Commission met several times a year alternately in the United States and Germany over a period of 3 years. Its affairs were essentially managed by the two co-chairmen, Leussing and Perkins and was directed by Professor Barbara Burn in whom the German colleagues had great confidence.

As is frequently the case, the problem that the Commission faced was not with the structure that satisfied both parties, since they were equally represented, and since access to experts in both countries had been assured. The real problem was that the two systems for handling access were so different. All collaborative study is faced with how to deal with collaboration across these institutional differences.

In the US-German case, a complication arose from the fact that German policymaking is firmly in the hands of federal and state governments and now increasingly the courts, while in the US access policymaking is far more in the hands of colleges and universities with, however, an increase in federal government involvement. State universities in the United States have long since come to a working relationship with their state governments. The German system is tightly controlled at the federal and state levels while the US system is highly decentralized. But in spite of these substantial differences, the mutual learning process was considerable. Mostly it took the form of lessons learned to be returned for home consumption. But the final report made important points that were fed into the discussions of the new Rahmengesetz that was being developed in Germany at the same time. There was a special interest in testing, particularly objective testing, as a means of dealing fairly with the fact that many faculties, like medicine and dentistry, were hopelessly oversubscribed. German visits to the Educational Testing Service in the United States became the basis for the serious efforts in North Rhine Westphalia for the introduction of testing programs as a supplement to grades in the Abitur. This interest in testing brought with it the realization that in the United States test scores are only advisory to colleges and universities who have the power to admit while in Germany the universities have no such power. And tests used by public bodies for student admission and allocation are an entirely different matter. To the extent that they became or would become decisive instruments for individual admission decisions they would be immediately projected into the political cauldron. Even in the United States the belief that ETS test scores ultimately determine admission decisions has led to all kinds of complaints and examination of the way in which these tests are constructed and administered. It can be imagined what would be the case if ETS was a government agency!

In spite of the structural differences, and possibly because of the joint nature of the enterprise, the report was approved by all members of the Commission and was supported by five volumes of papers and information, all of which had a rippling effect on subsequent research on student flows conducted by the European Education Institute in Paris and the UNESCO center in Bucharest. There were even reverberations of this discussion in Manila at the annual meeting of the International Association of Universities.

Variants on the joint commission approach to international collaboration were two other ICED projects that based their work on local teams of experts working under a master plan and outline designed in ICED headquarters in New York. The first was a study, already mentioned, of economic and social development and the roles of universities therein in developing countries (Thompson and Fogel, 1976). Local regional teams balanced against central coordination took care of both sensitivities on the one hand and necessary coordination on the other. This gives scant attention to the enormous amount of correspondence that took place between the regional leaders and ICED headquarters, nor does it give appropriate credit to the cosmopolitan views of those who were in charge of the regional studies.

The second project was an international study of the design and management of systems of higher education in twelve countries (Eurich, 1981). Each study was under the control of a selected national authority — in most cases an individual — and others with an associate and still others with a team. Coordination and comparability was promoted by a centrally prepared internationally approve outline, a stream of correspondence between Dr. Nell Eurich, the ICED coordinator and the twelve country leaders, and finally a 13th volume treated key topics that cut through the twelve country studies, and an ultimate volume by Dr. Eurich herself giving her overview and comparisons. The difference in the two studies was the absence of a regional stage in the systems study. It lost some of the advantages of inter-regional comparisons and enlightenment. But for this study regionalism was not as important as the structures of the countries concerned. For example, Australia, Canada, Germany and the United States, all being federal systems, gained more by the comparisons than did any one of them with more unitary systems. Indeed, the interest in this comparison of federal systems led to a subsequent seminar in Aspen on this very topic.

An example of a rather unique arrangement was that conducted by Frank Bowles in the early 1960s under the auspices of a joint commission, the two parties of which were the International Association of Universities and UNESCO. This international study on *Access to Higher Education* (Bowles, 1963), conducted under the auspices of this joint commission, was financed by the Carnegie Corporation of New York, conducted by the president of the College Entrance Examination Board, Dr. Frank Bowles on a leave of absence, and the College Entrance Examination Board acted as the fiscal agent. The advantages of this set of arrangements, which surprisingly did not take very long to work out, were clear at the time and even clearer in retrospect. Since this was an international study, the UNESCO involvement gave access to the excellent statistical office at UNESCO headquarters in Paris as well as providing the legitimacy to the study, particularly for developing countries. The involvement of the International Association of Universities secured the interest of the leading universities of the world in the study. The College Board brought a responsible private institution into the picture that could receive funds from the Carnegie Corporation, work closely with Frank Bowles, their president on leave, and assure the involvement of the experts both on the College Board and the ETS staffs.

But the late Dr. Frank Bowles was the pivot that made it possible and the rapport between the Director General of UNESCO, the president of the IAU, the vice-president of the Carnegie Corporation, and Dr. Frank Bowles ensured the success of the project. Incidentally, other efforts of the same kind did not prove so successful because one or other of the ingredients of the Bowles study was missing. As a result, the access study directed by Frank Bowles is considered, almost a quarter century later, a trail blazer not only on the subject but on the possibility of conducting an international study, on a complicated and volatile subject. It was possibly the first truly international comparative study of a key problem in higher education. Incidentally, it badly needs to be brought up to date.

Associations Further International Cooperation

But all instruments for the gathering of important information and the enlightenment of interested parties is not done solely by *ad hoc*, temporary commissions. In any listing of more or less permanent organizations the various associations that cover the landscape would have to be mentioned. There are geographical associations, both regional and international. They are to be found in Southeast Asia, Latin America, Europe, the Middle East and elsewhere. These are not, strictly speaking, action institutions. In themselves, they rarely make recommendations or sponsor and conduct policy studies and/or research.

They serve the very important purpose of familiarizing the actors with each other, holding annual meetings, and occasionally publishing journals of opinion where individual members of the universities and colleges publish their articles. By listening to and reading each other their understanding and appreciation of the problems of neighboring are forwarded.

But there are also special international organizations like the Association of French Universities, Catholic Universities, and other special interest groups. And finally, there are international associations like the International Association of University Presidents and the International Association of Universities. They both hold annual meetings and they both sponsor round tables and discussions on special topics. The IAU publishes an important journal both with articles and with summary news of activities of the member countries. All of these associations of which there are probably hundreds of one kind or another provide a network of contacts that increases the international perspective of its members.

Some day an important psychological/pathological piece will have to be written on these associations. Their meetings are frequently too large for any real exchange, their individual members are representative of but do not legally represent their institutions and are rarely in a position to speak for them. Their membership is so diverse that rarely can they agree on any important statement, and under no circumstances can they be expected to sponsor serious research without an association with some independent body as in the case of the Bowles study. But to repeat, the contacts, the personal relationships, and the aroma of regional and international interest is an extremely important quality that can be produced by these associations. If research is not their "thing" then research can frequently emerge from such meetings.

There are other institutions, frequently regional in character, that are more important sources of serious study. Organized from the top down rather than from the bottom up, they frequently have an administrative direction and an independence not attainable by the typical regional association. A number of such organizations have emerged in recent decades. One can mention the Institute for Education and Social Studies of the European Cultural Foundation with headquarters in Paris. This institute has members drawn from many European countries but they are not there to represent their countries as such. Nor do they represent the institutions of which they may be members. While the Paris Institute is a creature of the European Cultural Foundation which provides basic institutional support — but by no means all of it — the Cultural Foundation manages its relationship with the Educational Institute with a loose but supportive hand. As a result, the institute has attracted wide support with many contracts for its research projects. It has also taken on the management of the distinguished European-wide educational journal, *The European Journal of Education* and has developed good working relationships with the organs of the European community and with national and international institutions interested in education and rersearch. For example, it has taken on studies for the Carnegie Commission in the United States and the UNESCO Center in Bucharest. It has added immeasurably to the landscape of educational cooperation in Europe but has done so through securing cooperation rather than as a result of it.

By contrast, another European organization, the Institute for Advanced Studies in Florence, has its independence considerably circumscribed by the fact that it is a creature of the nine countries of the European community each of whom has a direct relationship with the Institute and its director. The result can be interminable compromise over appointments and procedures. Cooperation is a function of high political consultation between the member governments that support the Florence Institute. It is to be hoped that some day this institute can be funded directly from the European community budget so as to avoid what seems to be unnecessary complications in the governance arrangement.

Other organizations exist which are neither associations nor free-standing institutes like the one in Paris or the one in Singapore — the Research Institute for Higher Education and Development of the ASEAN countries. There are many examples but one might mention three organizations active in the western hemisphere. The Ajijic Institute for International Education, based at the Autonomous

University of Guadalajara, is run by an advisory board under the genial umbrella of the Autonomous University. Its members are there in their individual capacity, programs are developed by the advisory board and collaboration is secured by inviting experts to participate at the annual meetings. There is a part-time research director but no additonal staff. It is a modest organization with its unique feature that its advisory board is made up of both Latin Americans and persons from Thailand, Spain, France, Sweden, and the United States. Thus collaboration has an international cast through its advisory board and a regional cast through the fact that it centers its attention on priority problems for higher education in Latin America but analyzed through an international perspective.

Two other organizations that are neither associations nor free-standing organizations go by the interesting code name of GULERPE — an organization of individuals concerned with educational innovation — and CAMESA, an organization concerned with the development of collaborative programs between Latin American institutions and those of the United States, particularly in the southern half thereof. These examples are mentioned only to indicate that there are many styles, shapes and forms of institutions established to promote collaboration in education that are outside the public domain.

Finally, we must turn our attention to institutions that have or are indeed anxious to turn understanding of problems into action for their resolution. Sometimes these take the form of direct university relation-ships for the promotion of student exchange and faculty appointment. Sometimes, as in the case of the Cornell-University of Philippines arrangement, the purpose is for the development of Philippine expertise in the field of agricultural research and development. In the more than 20 years of its history the contract and understanding takes Cornell professors to the Philippines to learn something about native agricultural problems and to oversee the preliminary training of future graduate students. These students then come to Cornell for their advanced degree work and eventually return to their university to teach others. The cycle is complete but success is in large part measured, and properly measured, by the extent to which Philippine expertise can, in consider-able measure, replace the American teacher. It may be said without too romantic an interpretation, that the professional relationship between the parties has now developed to the point where the country of origin is less important than the problems they are determined to resolve.

If I can be forgiven another Cornell example, I should mention the rather unique arrangement with the University of Sydney where the two departments of astronomy have in fact been merged so that graduate students can take advantage of the "cross-configuration" in Australia or the "dish-configuration" in Aricibo, Puerto Rico. While nothing works in an ideal fashion, there is, in fact, almost a single department which happens to have two branches, one in Australia and one in the United States. Put together by two brilliant astronomers — Gold and Messel — and given the blessing of the two heads of the universities, the program is probably too unique to be repeated. But as James Conant said in starting his study of the American high school, "I am out to prove the viability of the comprehensive school that provides both terminal and college preparatory work under the same roof. All I need to do is to find at least two or three such comprehensive schools, show that they work, and then my case will be made." At the time he said it was like proving that a person can play the violin left-handed — the thing to do is to find a left-handed violinist.

There remains to mention, in the spectrum of instruments for collaboration, the increasing importance of supportive efforts and collaboration by public agencies. On the first score, regional organizations like the regional banks, the European community in Europe, the Organization of American States in the western hemisphere, and at the international level the family of agencies including UNESCO, the World Bank, UNICEF, FAO, and others, that have their own research staffs, their own programs to secure collaboration efforts both in research and the implementation of research results. Sometimes they mostly just respond to requests for support. But it is surely the case in both UNESCO and the World Bank and in substantial measure in others, too, that collaboration is arranged for by the headquarters staffs working in conjunction with regional and country correspondents and agencies. The Education Department of the World Bank, for example, puts out its sector reports indicating the directions and purposes of World Bank lending for the immediate years to come. In response to these guidelines, countries place their requests, discuss them with World Bank agents generally located in the countries concerned, present proposals that have already received at least a statement of interest from the World Bank representatives, and are then digested, refined, sent back for discussion, and when approved, they become the basis for a Bank program in the country concerned. In the process, the Bank implicates and arranges for consultants from various countries to help with the project. Collaboration requires sensitive handling both on the part of the bank which must not be seen to be directing the educational life of the receiving country and by the receiving country to make sure that the Bank's rules and guidelines are observed in the process.

In the case of UNESCO, it arranged for collaboration as part of the internal process. It has been externalized in the establishment of two centers, one in Bucharest and the other in Caracas, Venezuela, to arrange for examinations of regional problems. It would be interesting to take time, if it were available, to compare the activities of the

European Center of UNESCO in Bucharest and the European Institute of the Cultural Foundation of Paris — one operating under the aegis of an international public agency and the other under a private and independent institution.

No chapter on international cooperation would be complete without a reference to the International Association for the Evaluation of Educational Achievement of Torsten Husén. He is its creator and manager and has established a network of professionals around the world with a solid reputation for the highest level of research and reporting. It is a model for international comparative study.

References

Bowles, Frank 1963 *Access to Higher Education*. IAU and UNESCO, Paris.

Clark, Burton (1977) *Academic Power in Italy*. University of Chicago Press, Chicago.

Docencia. Autonomous University of Guadalajara, Mexico

Eurich, Nell P. 1981 *Systems of Higher Education in Twelve Countries*. Praeger, New York.

European Journal of Education, Carfax/England.

Higher Education. Elsevier/The Netherlands.

Hiroshima Journal. Research Institute of Higher Education, Hiroshima University, Japan.

ICED 1978 *Access to Higher Education*. ICED, New York.

Minerva: A Review of Science, Learning & Policy, London/England.

The Journal of Higher Education. The Ohio State University Press, USA.

Thompson, Kenneth and Fogel, Barbara 1976 *Education and Social Change*. Praeger, New York.

Trow, M. and Halsey, A. H. 1971 *The British Academics*. Harvard University Press, Cambridge/Ma., USA and Faber & Faber, London.

Educational Reform and Learning from Other Nations

Learning from Other Nations for Educational Reform in School and Adult Education: The Case of Germany

HELLMUT BECKER

The Immediate Postwar Period and the Occupation Forces

At the end of the war the Allied Occupying powers, as a consequence of the unconditional surrender, held all powers in the occupied territories including the power over education. The Russians introduced in their part of Germany the Russian system of socialist education and were very successful in creating this system. In the 1980s there are only small differences between the Soviet and East German ideals. Both have the *Einheitsschule*, the unified school, polytechnical education, and a high degree of political indoctrination in schools and in adult education.

The Western Powers, the British, the French and the Americans were not so successful. They tried to introduce their own educational policies in the areas they controlled, but all in all, they were unable to realize their plans and expectations.

The French intended to set up their own highly selective centralized system as an example. The French were successful in at least one point: they introduced the system of centralized examinations which was new for Germans but was adopted with pleasure by the German governments in the French zone despite many warnings from professional educators. In theory, the central examination system appears to be quite fair, but in practice it lowers the level of learning and examinations. If the exams are to cover the very different courses and work undertaken by pupils then the demands of one exam are not so thorough as is possible with several differentiated exams, including taking into account pupils' school work. As a result of this situation, educators were opposed to a centralized examination but administrators loved it.

In adult education, the French introduced many new ideas especially under the influence of the French movement "Peuple et Culture", which had started with the French resistance against the Germans. In the French zone there was a certain dynamism in adult education which had a great impact on the early start of the German *Volkshochschul-*movement in the French occupied territories. Joseph Rovan, a German emigrant to France, and one of the heads of "Peuple et Culture", was a leading figure in the initial creation of adult education in the French zone. Of course, German emigrants played a role given their knowledge of German circumstances but, in principle, they returned to Germany as Frenchmen; this is in contradiction to the Russians who brought back their German emigrants to be new leaders in developing German governmental structure.

The different forms of influence displayed by the occupational powers can be understood only if one realizes the extreme differences in ways of behavior among the different occupational powers. Looking at the Germans today, one could jokingly say that they want to eat and make love like the French and to make money like the Americans. In this connection it would not be untrue to say that through the German occupation of the whole of France and the French occupation of a part of Germany, the French and the Germans have learned more about each other than at any previous time in history. This experience of mutual occupation with all its horrors — perpetrated mainly by the Germans in France — formed the basis of communication between the two countries after the war. Of some significance also was probably the fact that the French, from the very beginning, adhered less to the non-fraternization rule than did the other occupation forces. The difference among the Allies in terms of their Military Government becomes clear when one bears in mind that, in 1946, for every 10,000 Germans in Germany there were 18 French military personnel in the French zone, 10 Britons in the British Zone and 3 Americans in the American zone.

By the mid 1980s, the Federal Republic of Germany was considered to be the most americanized country in Europe. In France there is more anti-American feeling than in any other European country. German tourists travel mostly to the south — to France, Italy, Spain and Portugal. There are more French and Italian restaurants in Germany than ever before.

But even with this strong American influence the Americans did not succeed with their re-education programme and their idea of the introduction of comprehensive schooling. The tripartite school system remained the dominant organizational form from 1945 to 1965 with elite pupils going to the *Gymnasium* (grammar school) a somewhat larger number of pupils supposedly blessed with practical skills in the *Realschule* (technical school) and the broad mass of the population attending the *Volksschule* (modern school). This school system reflected the traditional structure of German society and one prominent foreign observer called these 20 years in education from 1945 to 1965 in Western Germany the "period of non-reform".

Why was the American Military Government not successful with its educational ideas? After national socialism the Germans did not want any further changes (given the bad experiences of the change to national socialism), but only wanted to return to the forms of education which had existed before national socialism began. This going back is typical for a period which Walter Dirks called correctly "The period of restoration" (Dirks, 1950). And the Americans soon gave up their educational plans because they hoped that the Germans would themselves develop some new ideas on schooling.

The British were the most reluctant about introducing educational reform. They attempted to find out what the Germans themselves wanted and then tried to help them achieve this. The result was, that in some parts of their zone of occupation they reintroduced the denominational school and in others they gave their support to a cautious attempt at modernization. The British education officers quite clearly and early saw the clash between the reformists and the conservatives. As an example of how the British acted, the university problem was very characteristic. Robert Birley, later the Headmaster of that famous public school — Eton, was a leading education officer from the British side, and under his influence the British developed a university reform plan and published, together with a few famous German scholars, the so-called "Blue book on university reform". If this plan had been implemented, the student revolt of the late 1960s would probably have never happened because the old-fashioned authoritarian professors in German universities would not have existed and the university would have been an open-minded modern social institution. When this plan — which had received the approval of outstanding German scholars — was rejected by the German university bureaucracy the British accepted this decision because they did not want to use the power they legally had at that time.

The British acted like the Americans who wanted to introduce comprehensive schooling but stopped short of compulsion given the German resistance to the proposed change. A comprehensive review of the educational policy of the occupying powers in the years after the end of the war shows that the chances which existed at the "zero" hour, when the Allies had complete power, were not used by the three Western powers. Such power was not used for very honorable reasons; the Anglo-Saxons did not wish to force any decisions on the Germans for fear of destroying characteristic cultural patterns; but, nevertheless, a chance for educational reform was lost.

The OECD review (OECD, 1971) of German education policy criticizes the Germans for overvaluing career-mindedness; critics point to the bureaucratization of the education system; complaints are heard about the centralization of decision-making procedures in the eleven state (*Land*) capitals, and the lack of freedom and scope for experiment, innovation and modification is censured. There can be no doubt at all that the roots of these problems lie in developments which took place in the very first postwar years. This OECD review of the educational policies of the states (*Länder*) represents perhaps the strongest criticism ever made of the policies of the occupying forces in the years after the war, even though the word "occupation" itself does not appear in the review and not one single measure or action during the immediate period is subject to criticism. But the problems of the centralism of the Länder, the re-institutionalizing of careerism and the absence of concrete and specific reform measures in educational institutions can all be traced back directly to the first postwar years.

The fact that the British occupying forces allowed the re-introduction of the denominational school system is an important point. The denominational school system has since disappeared completely but it took years of unnecessary fighting because the British had been too friendly with those forces in Germany that wished to re-introduce it. The Allies accepted the German wish to replace national socialism values with past values and they failed to create the necessary enlightenment and critical consciousness at the center of the educational system.

In the immediate postwar years the occupying powers were so busy with pragmatic and practical assistance needed for the re-construction of the educational system such as the re-establishment of the necessary buildings and manpower, that they did not risk undertaking any major reform. Again, it must be recognized that all of this was connected with the fundamental problem of the rebuilding of Western Germany: the re-establishment of the German educational system on the basis of a free market economy on the one hand and the re-introduction of the old public service structure, on the other hand; the teachers again became public officials in the formal sense of public officials in the Prussian state without any encouragement of citizens initiative. The Anglo-Saxon powers in particular provided the conditions for the economic miracle and initiatives towards a United Europe, yet they did not immediately provide for the development of a free society. The Allies did no more than clear the way for free elections in a very short space of time and the decisions that were then taken were not their concern. The Allies, especially the British and the Americans, were practical, helpful and tactful, and not hasty in taking decisions on educational policy.

The British Military government in postwar Germany was very successful in all immediate practical actions, but there was not enough far-reaching prognostic thinking. In this sense, the British neglected chances which existed only in the first 2 or 3 years after the war when under the shock of national socialism big changes would have been psychologically possible and the British had the power to take them. But for very understandable reasons, they didn't use the power they had.

The Americans tried more vigorously than the British to introduce their system, the comprehensive school system, but failed because of resistance from the Germans. The British were more cautious but they, too, failed. On the other hand, both were very successful in the field of adult education where the British, in particular, provided many examples for German development. Even in 1986 the only successful university extension experiments take place in the former British zone. The British example, strengthened by many invitations during the immediate postwar years to German adult educators to visit Great Britain, opened the German mind to the fact that university education has to take a place within the framework of adult education. In the 1980s, there is a more general movement in the universities to turn towards adult education, because the predicted decrease in the number of students in the years to come raises the question of how to make better use of the large capacity of the German universities. Therefore, the British influence in terms of the direction and purpose of university extension programmes in the postwar years can be seen in the mid 1980s. Why was it that the Western Allied powers achieved something new in adult education but did not succeed in changing the German school system? It is obvious that in adult education there was no strong existing structure and, thus, it was easier to develop something new. The German school system was so strongly bureaucratized that the resistance against change on the part of German educators and German school administrators was obviously too powerful and difficult to overcome.

Educational Reform — the Late 1950s to Early 1970s

If Western policy in the field of education failed in the years after the war, the influence of English and American educational research on German educational development cannot be overestimated.

The whole idea of the economics of education which was rather alien to the German intellectual tradition was brought into the German discussion mainly through the works of Friedrich Edding and his students. Edding brought the works of Seymour S. Harries, Theodore W. Schultz, Mary Jean Bowman and Edward F. Denison into the German scholarly discussion. It was not accidental that Edding, the leading educational economist in Western Germany after the war, was a historian and not an economist at all. The traditional German economy was not interested in education; the economic value of education was a new concept for them and the concept of human capital, for example, was developed by Edding not in cooperation with his economist colleagues but by learning from the Americans and by cooperating with educators in Western Germany. As early as 1953 he wrote a famous article on the quality of the young as a decisive factor for our future economic achievement. He produced many studies in the economics of education from cost benefit analysis to comparative cost research; in particular, international comparisons were one of the most important aspects of his work. It was the discovery of the economics of education coming from the United States and taken up by Great Britain and by OECD, that German educational development profited enormously in the 1960s. American documents of the late 1950s such as the Rockefeller report *The Pursuit of Excellence* (1958) and the report by James B. Conant about *The American High School Today* (1959) were of great importance for the development of the comprehensive school idea in Germany. John Gardner's famous question: "Can we be equal and excellent too?" also became an internal German question.

The basic question in the 1960s in Western Germany was how to overcome the tripartite school system, which is based on a social class selection mechanism. There was a legend in Germany that there was only a very small number of gifted people living in this country, a much larger number of technically gifted ones but that the mass of the people were just less gifted and should stay the way they were. The social basis of the tripartite school system corresponded to the general idea about the order of society since before the First World War. In the late 1950s and 1960s, English and American research increasingly showed that the number of gifted people was much larger than had ever been anticipated and that the inequality of social chances in the educational system had to be overcome if the talent existing in the German nation was to be discovered and developed. A German emigrant, Reinhold Scheirer, who returned from the United States, won personal influence with Konrad Adenauer. Konrad Adenauer began to wonder if the communists didn't do better work in promoting their talented people than did the West Germans.

When the German National Education Council (*Deutscher Bildungsrat*) started its great reform plan for restructuring the educational system it proposed an orientation cycle and allowed much more transfer between school types. The basic idea of the plan was to change the traditionally vertical structure of the school system to a horizontal one and to replace the authoritarian type of schooling by a more democratic one.

As a basis for these changes, the National Education Council published a thick tome containing many expert opinions under the title *Talent and Learning* (1969). In this book the most important educators, psychologists and sociologists of the Federal Republic of Germany proved that talent was something that can be developed and that the fight against the inequality of educational chances was the most important task for educational politicians. The detailed expert opinions in this book are all based on American and English research. The bibliographical references include all the important American and English names of the social sciences scholarly community of the 1940s to 70s. When the German sociologist Dahrendorf published his book on education as a right of the citizen (*Bildung ist Bürgerrecht*, 1965), his ideas were based on his American experience as a young fellow at the Center for Advanced Studies in the Behavioral Sciences in Palo Alto. When I, myself, initiated the Max-Planck-Institut for Human Development and Education in 1963 my plans were based on experiences I had gained on a study tour through educational institutions in the United States; the study tour was financed by the Ford Foundation.

One of the main topics of the National Planning Commission in the 1960s was the introduction, on an experimental basis, of comprehensive schooling in Germany. This was based on expert written opinion provided by Saul B. Robinsohn and Helga Thomas about differentiation in secondary schooling: the book had the interesting title *Proposals for the structure of secondary schooling in the light of international experience* (Robinsohn und Thomas, 1968).

The international experience is taken from OECD reports, and English reports such as "Early leaving" (1954), and "Half our future" (1963). The Robinsohn-Thomas book is laced with names such as Floud, Halsey, Yates, Pidgeon, Conant, Baron, and Pedley to mention but a few.

However, it was not only English and American authors who played a great role. Beside the Anglo-Saxon influence the most important one was the Swedish one. In particular, there was Torsten Husén, the father of the Swedish School Reform, with his long list of publications. These publications together with his personal appearances in Germany had a decisive influence on the planning of the German educational reform. The recommendations of the National Education Council were based on expert opinions from famous German scholars which, in turn, were mainly based on Anglo-Saxon and Swedish School Reform literature.

The change of the vertical school system with its selective character to the inclusion of an orientation cycle (grades 5 and 6) and thus introducing more flexibility in a more horizontal form of organization was the most important structure of the reform alongside the introduction of a comprehensive school system as an experiment.

At the same time the idea of curriculum reform was taken from the Anglo-Saxon world. Benjamin Bloom through the mediation of Saul Robinsohn became one of the best-known authors in the German educational discussion. It is not an exaggeration to claim that the whole development of curriculum research, including the establishment of such institutions as the Institute for Science Education in Kiel or the

Institute for Mathematics Education in Bielefeld, goes back to the great
influence American research had on increasing interest in teachers and
educational administrators about curriculum questions.

Learning From Each Other

If, on the one hand, after the unconditional surrender of the
Germans, the Allies did not use their powers to change the German
educational system and modernize it, one has to admit, on the other
hand, that educational reform in Germany in the 1960s was based on
American and English research which was transmitted to the German
public by German scholars. The learning process which German
educational administrators underwent in the cooperation of West
Germany with the OECD played a decisive role. But Germany also
followed with interest the failures of educational reform in the United
States. The organizational diversity created by reform, the uncertainty
in curriculum development with the resulting uncertainty in the value
system, created doubts about the possibility of educational reform and
about achieving consensus among teachers, parents, politicians and
administrators. Critical voices ranging from that of Admiral Rickover to
that of Christopher Jencks were repeated in Europe. And, at the same
time, there were conservative forces in Germany which yearned to
return to the old selective system. The formation of elites and
admiration for the French "Grande Ecole" were particularly prevalent
among politicians. In the mid 1980s West Germany has a feeling of
uneasiness about education, and journalists like to quote the Americans,
or the Swedes, the British or the French to show that other nations are
also not entirely happy with their educational reform movements. Since
Lyndon B. Johnson's conference on the "World Educational Crisis", the
feeling of crisis has permeated the world and it has become more and
more difficult to know who really started this feeling of uneasiness or
who followed whom in acquiring this sense of unease. They started it all
together and now they experience some sort of togetherness in facing
the difficult consequences of badly organized educational reforms.

A very special form of international influence on national reforms was
the OECD country reviews. When examining the published country
reviews, it can be seen how helpful it was to member states to have to
explain their own educational system. But the criticisms made by
international commissions were even more helpful. In the case of
Western Germany the OECD review about the German education
system is still in the mid 1980s — years after it occurred — a milestone
for educational thinking in Germany. OECD has had a much stronger
influence in the developed countries than UNESCO — perhaps because
UNESCO's interests have been mainly directed towards the Third
World.

Until the Second World War education seemed to be a national affair. Since the end of the Second World War there has been a growing tendency to see educational policy as something which links nations together. The growing rate of change in social development raises similar questions in all nations and those similar questions very often get similar answers. One can learn from the answers other nations give. Thus, a permanent exchange of problems, expectations and solutions are helpful to all nations, especially the United States and Europe. We *can* learn from each other's failures and successes and we do.

References

Becker, Hellmut. *Auf dem Weg zur lernenden Gesellschaft*. Personen, Analysen, Vorschläge für die Zukunft. Klett-Cotta, Stuttgart, 1980.

Becker, Hellmut. *Quantität und Qualität*. Grundfragen der Bildungs-politik. Rombach, Freiburg i. Br., 1968.

Becker, Hellmut u.a. *Die Bildungsreform eine Bilanz*. Ernst Klett, Stuttgart, 1976.

Becker Hellmut. Retrospective View from the German Side. In: *The British in Germany*. Hamilton, London, 1978.

Becker, Hellmut. *Bildungspolitik. Die Bundesrepublik Deutschland*, Band 2: Gesellschaft. Hrsg. Walter Benz. Fischer Taschenbuch Verlag, Frankfurt, 1983.

Berufliche Bildung, Berufsbildungspolitik, Berufsschullehrerausbildung. Festschrift für Friedrich Edding. Institut für Bildungs- und Gesellschafts-wissenschaften (Berlin TU), 1977.

Bundesminister für Bildung und Wissenschaft, Bildungsbericht '70. *Die bildungs-politische Konzeption der Bundesregierung*, Bonn 1970.

Conant, James, B. *The American High School Today*. A first report to interested citizens. McGraw-Hill, New York, 1959.

Dahrendorf, Ralf. *Bildung ist Bürgerrecht*. Plädoyer für eine aktive Bildungspolitik. Nannen Verlag, Hamburg, 1965.

Deutscher Bildungsrat, *Gutachten und Studien der Bildungskommission*, Bd. 4, Begabung und Lernen, Ernst Klett, Stuttgart, 1969.

Deutscher Bildungsrat, *Empfehlungen der Bildungskommission, Strukturplan für das Bildungswesen*. Bundesdruckerei, Bonn, 1970.

Dirks, Walter. *Der restaurative Charakter der Epoche*. In: *Frankfurter Hefte*, Heft 5, 1950.

"Early Leaving". Report of the Central Advisory Council for Education (England). HMSO, 1954.

"Half our Future". Report of the Central Advisory Council for Education (England), HMSO, 1963.

Hearnden, Arthur. *The British in Germany* — Educational reconstruction after 1945. Hamilton, London 1978.

Husén, Torsten und Boalt, Gunnar. *Bildungsforschung und Schulreform in Schweden*. Ernst Klett, Stuttgart, 1968.

Review of National Policies for Education. Germany. OECD, Paris, 1971.

Robinsohn, S. und Thomas, H. *Differenzierung im Sekundarschulwesen*. Vorschläge zur Struktur der weiterführenden Schulen im Licht internationaler Erfahrungen. Gutachten und Studien der Bildungskommission, Band 3, Klett, Stuttgart, 1968.

Rockefeller Brothers Fund. *The pursuit of excellence; education and the future of America*. Panel report v of the Special Studies Project, Garden City, N.Y. Doubleday, 1958.

Learning from Other Nations for Educational Reform: The Case of Higher Education in the Federal Republic of Germany

DIETRICH GOLDSCHMIDT

1945–1949: Effects of Occupation

Demands for university reform have been repeatedly heard from many quarters ever since the Federal Republic of Germany was founded in 1949. Indeed, immediately after the Second World War, the allied forces, France, Great Britain, and the United States, occupying those regions which were to be consolidated into the Federal Republic began programmes in re-education, and when the German universities reopened in 1945 and 1946, reform was required in three areas:

— institutional reorganization, directed particularly at breaking down the hierarchical faculty structure;

— personnel changes (denazification); and

— revision of curricula in the political and social sciences and related subjects (including projected programmes in general studies).

Despite the great commitment on the part of allied educational staffs and particularly their university officers, above all such men as Robert Birley for the British and E. Y. Hartshorne for the Americans, and despite the many positive conference reports and expert reports written at that time, outside efforts to influence German higher education cannot be said to have had more than a limited effect over the long run. There can, however, be no doubt that great expectations were placed upon these new programmes. In the French-occupied zone, for example, the universities of Mainz and Saarbrücken were established with the idea of making a special contribution to German-French cooperation. The Americans, in their jurisdiction, decidedly furthered the Free University of Berlin as an outpost of liberal thought from its founding in 1949. Shortly afterwards they supported the inauguration of the *Hochschule für Internationale Pädagogische Forschung* (now *Deutsches Institut für Internationale Pädagogische Forschung*) to stimulate research on

211

education by modern empirical methods. Many other scholarly organizations and smaller institutes also enjoyed the support of the occupying
forces and later allies, including their philanthropic organizations (e.g.
the author's own institute, whose establishment was partially promoted
by a grant from the Ford Foundation. Torsten Husén was a member of
the institute's board for many years). Yet on the whole, it is difficult to
speak of a lasting effect of imported conceptions on the institutional
framework of postwar German universities — those at Mainz and
Saarbrücken, and the Free University of Berlin, have long since become
organizationally integrated within the framework of all other
universities. On the other hand, a significant, if imponderable effect, can
be attributed to the many guest lecturers and professors who came to
German universities during the immediate postwar years, as well as to
those German faculty members and students who soon thereafter began
to receive fellowships and travel grants to teach and study abroad.

The programmes in re-education themselves tended to be short-lived;
actually, they foundered even before the Federal Republic came into
being. With the onset of the Cold War, Western policy on Germany
changed in important respects. On the one hand, radical attempts to
alter the socioeconomic and cultural structures of the country were
abandoned in favor of programmes of direct aid, designed to recon-
struct West Germany and make it a strong and reliable ally in the
confrontation with the Soviet Union. On the other hand, the realization
spread that if basic socioeconomic patterns remained unaltered, no
imported ideas would suffice to refashion structures that were deeply
rooted in Germany's cultural tradition, particularly not in the short
term. In any case, outside interference of this kind ran counter to the
ideals of liberal democracy and national self-determination. Moreover,
Germany lacked a sufficient number of suitable university faculty, not to
mention administrators who could have devoted themselves to re-
education efforts. Thus, in practice the universities soon reverted to the
structures and curricula which had been in use prior to 1933, with the
exception of subjects directly affected by recent history.

The Fifties: Reception of Progress in Scholarship and Institutional Restoration

From the founding of the Federal Republic, institutional restoration
lasted until about the early 1960s, despite the growing numbers of
students that had already begun to fill the universities in the mid-1950s
(see Table 1). Though no significant outside influence may have been
felt in institutional terms, continually expanding exchange programmes,
which often brought scholars who had fled from the Nazis back to
Germany as foreign citizens, were certainly effective. About 10 to 15 per
cent of these émigrés returned to stay in the Federal Republic. In

TABLE 1.
Enrollment in Institutions of Higher Education in the Federal Republic of Germany (German and foreign students in 000s)

	1950	1960	1965	1970	1975	1980	1983
Universities and colleges of university type	134	247	320	420	700	840	1,000
Colleges of non-university type	40	70	85	110	145	175	242
Total	174	317	405	530	845	1,015	1,242
Students: Percentage of age cohort 19–25 years	3.4	4.7	7.0	9.9	14.2	15.2	17.3

individual cases the universities and state offices of higher education made great efforts to attract émigrés, though presumably a more concerted attempt — begun earlier and on a larger scale — would have led to a higher returnee quota. Vice-versa, sabbaticals and travel fellowships for German faculty and students became increasingly available (see, for example, the figures on German-American exchange in Table 2). Exchanges of this kind, which have continued to this day, took on special significance during the postwar period because they augmented the reception of those insights and methods which had enriched almost every discipline — outside Germany — since 1933. From that fatal date to 1945 and even for some years thereafter, scholarship in Germany, because of the forced exile, if not murder, of many of its finest representatives, the politicitation of its universities, and the havoc of war, had lost contact with international developments in the arts and sciences. This loss, in many fields, has still not been completely made up to this day.

Hence the German universities profited, and still profit, from multifarious impulses in teaching and research which cannot be classified as educational reform in the strict sense of the word. It is no surprise that historical research in the disciplines has recently and justifiably begun to devote much attention to cross-fertilization through emigration, re-emigration, and exchange, and to the scholarly and scientific progress these entail.

The Sixties: Years of Growth and Institutional Reform

From the mid-1960s to the early 1970s, universities, the federal parliament and government offices concerned, and state parliaments were confronted with the twin task of providing places for rapidly

TABLE 2.
*German-American Exchanges in Education and Science, 1954 and
1978/79 (as Compiled by the Fulbright Commission)*

Category	1954	1978/79
	German nationals in the US	
Students	759[1]	3,200
Professors/research scholars }	48[2]	480
Teachers		30
Medical interns/residents	323	80
High school students	226[3]	880
Trainees	133[4]	330[4]
Total	1,489	4,970
	US nationals in the FRG[5]	
Students	778[6]	3,620[7]
Professors/research scholars	58	500
Teachers[8]	53	55
High school students	(?)[9]	220
Trainees	(20)[10]	320
Total	909	4,550

[1]Including holders of immigrant visa (appr. 30%).
[2]Author has doubts on reliability of information: not included in
1954 statistics were scholars at independent research institutes;
according to US experts, in 1954 probably between 80 and 120
German post-doctoral fellows were working in the US.
[3]"Teenage exchange" included high school students and other
groups (4-H programs, youth leaders).
[4]Mainly short-term.
[5]In some cases including Canadians.
[6]Figure for 1955.
[7]Including 250 students in independent (non-integrated) Study
Abroad Programs.
[8]Including language assistance at German secondary schools.
[9]No reliable data available; the estimates were below 15.
[10]Mainly working for US relief organizations.
Source: Littmann, U.: German-American Exchanges. A Report on
Facts and Developments. Bonn: Fulbright-Kommission
1980, p. 6.

increasing numbers of applicants and, under pressure of this growth
and the student movement, inaugurating long-needed institutional
reforms. International influences made themselves felt during this
period in two respects:

International statistical comparisons revealed that the percentage of students in the 19–25-year age group in higher education had lagged far behind that of other modern industrial nations. Not only did the Federal Republic's programme of equal opportunity in education look meagre by international comparison, but it risked being outdistanced in terms of the so important provision of "human capital". Moreover, a comparison of faculty-to-student ratios indicated that West German universities would have much hiring to do before they reached the British or US ratios.

Criticism from abroad was aimed at the traditional administrative structure of German universities, e.g. their rectorship principle (*Rektoratsverfassung*) by which the head of a university is elected to serve 1 or 2 years on an honorary basis rather than being a full-time administrator; and at the hierarchical composition of the faculty (*Ordinarienherrschaft*). Such criticism, voiced frequently since the universities reopened, was reinforced in the OECD report of 1972, which provided weighty arguments to the reform efforts then beginning in various states. Institutions of higher education were now placed under head administrators — some still known as rectors, others as presidents — whose office, however, still did not entail all of the powers of the American model on which it was based. The old "rule by professors" gave way to a participatory decision-making pattern in which all status groups in the university were represented (*Gruppenuniversität*) — from senior and junior faculty to students and technical and office personnel.

Limits of Institutional Transfer: The Example of German–Swedish Interaction

Under pressure from the student movement, which of course was a supranational phenomenon, many nations began at this time to introduce participatory schemes. Reforms of this type were indeed a topic of international discussion. Yet the question still remains in how far shared general conceptions of institutional reform can be translated into concrete solutions applicable to different systems of higher education. Long before the OECD took leave of its hopes for converging university structures in 1981, work on a commission showed me how futile attempts at institutional transfer can be. I should like to report on this experience here, since fundamentally, it seems to reveal the limitations of international reform effort, and since it was a subject I discussed quite exhaustively with Torsten Husén.

In 1970, the governments of the Federal Republic and Sweden agreed to set up two national commissions to conduct a joint inquiry into the problems of democratization and participation in the educational and research systems of our two countries. Why were German universities in unrest while Swedish universities had experienced far-reaching changes with very much less conflict? With this and other questions in mind, the German Federal Ministry of Education was interested in hearing how status groups were represented in decision-making bodies at Swedish universities. Could they serve as models for their German counterparts? The mandate given to the commissions demanded joint analysis, evaluation, and recommendations from both sides for both countries; it proved to be a political and methodological challenge. Not only those who initiated the project but the commission members themselves proved to have been somewhat naive, underestimating the problems involved in comparing two social sub-systems. The effects of divergent political and social development on these subsystems, and on commission members' thought patterns, were greater than anticipated. Realizing that our backgrounds, attitudes, and social theories differed, we concluded that contrary to the assumptions of our governments, a literal transfer of educational policy measures from Sweden to Germany was not possible.

The members of the German commission were impressed by the achievements of the Swedish government, whose policy was consistently carried out by the central university administration on the basis of a general social consensus. Yet precisely this centralization led the German members to ask time and again how, in an educational structure of this kind, individual members of the university, whether faculty or students, could play an active role in decision-making. Under these conditions, agreement between the two commissions about educational reform as a means of democratizing universities could not help but remain superficial.

The Swedish commission saw democratization primarily as a central government guarantee of equality of opportunity — equalization of social and physical conditions, curricula, examinations, and courses of study. To them, the question of participation thus took on an instrumental and pragmatic character. For the German commission, by contrast, the demand for democratization through participation was a highly political question, linked directly with the political and ideological controversy in their country about aims and tasks of educational reform and with the often contradictory educational policies of the eleven states and the Federal Government. In the German commission members' eyes, participation meant a kind of grass-roots policymaking. We may conclude from this that any subtle treatment of the differences in structure and content between two educational systems must take into account their dependence on the general social context.

The method of investigation occasioned by the decidedly political mandate of our German-Swedish commissions deserves to be stressed. While international comparisons are traditionally limited to formal structures, the German-Swedish commissions were requested to analyze a political problem and derive recommendations from this analysis. The very definition of the subject under investigation — democratization of universities — required each member to reflect upon and articulate his own political interests. This politicization of the commissions' work, being inherent in the task, made the usual "neutral" observation of an educational system impossible. Rather, the subject had to be regarded as a social sub-system, its structure dissected, and its dependence on the larger system elucidated. Thus the commissions' report was not so much an exact description of two systems of higher education as an attempt at political analysis of the conditions within which they operate, their historical development, and the direction in which they are changing.

The Seventies: Further International Stimuli for the University System

During the first half of the 1970s, political resistance gradually quelled the student movement both inside and outside the universities, just as the movement itself was split by increasing radicalization on the one hand and by resignation in the face of political setbacks on the other. Political resignation was further complicated from about 1975 onwards by students' economic difficulties after graduation and during the transition to working life. In some of the German states, reforms were curtailed. The year 1976, with the Federal Framework Law for Higher Education (*Hochschulrahmengesetz*), brought a middle-of-the-road solution to all eleven states and thus a certain quieting effect on the scene. Since 1982, when the conservative coalition under Chancellor Kohl took office, further restrictions of reform measures in certain areas have been planned, particularly in terms of a stronger position of senior faculty in decision-making. They resulted in a new federal law of September 26, 1985. It stresses the pluralistic character of the higher education system, opens avenues for specialization and competition within the system and reestablishes the hierarchical structure of the faculty to a considerable extent.

Since the 1970s, international discussions on structural models and comparisons have influenced the German approach in some problem areas. Traditionally, all young people who have obtained their *Abitur* certificate from a college preparatory school have had the constitutional right to enrol in university — if possible, one of their own choice. Since, despite expansion, the number of applicants rapidly exceeded the available places various measures were taken to lessen the pressure on individual universities. For example, applicants were distributed more evenly among courses and places of study, waiting periods introduced, and the like. In some fields, medicine in particular, standardized tests were adopted as the decisive measure of selection. Tests of this kind have since been subjected to a thorough investigation sponsored by the

International Council for Educational Development, New York. Its results, published in 1978, indicated that in a diversified system of higher education like that of the United States, test scores could serve as only one criterion among many for college admission. Yet despite even this caveat, criticism of the significance of these tests has recently grown stronger in the United States. This was reason enough for us to caution against the use of analogous tests in Germany as the primary screening method, applied by a central office, for admission to a subject like medicine — at whatever university. Here, much could be learned from American experience in designing our reform programmes. Tests remain only one alternative among many screening methods. Since the founding of Herdecke in 1983, the first private university in the Federal Republic, a limited possibility exists for students to be directly admitted to the study of medicine at a single university.

The traditionally quite homogeneous university system in the Federal Republic has expanded rapidly over the past decades (1949: 40 universities and colleges of university type, number of vocational colleges not available; 1983: 66 universities, 54 colleges of university type, 94 colleges of non-university type). This expansion raised the question of whether and to what extent the system might be diversified, not least in view of the demands of the employment market. International discussion of this topic, particularly in the OECD context, gave considerable impetus to plans in Germany. The following lists only the most important of the directions in which our policy was confirmed and stimulated:

— Inauguration of a few comprehensive universities. These offered both short-term studies like those of vocational colleges and courses leading to an academic degree, providing, in a word, educational opportunities of the kind existing in France, Sweden, the United States, and also in Eastern European countries.
— Expansion of continuing education programmes. In recent years, attention has gradually been concentrated on educational models which make the content of university curricula available to wider sectors of the population than before, e.g. evening courses in continuing adult education along Swedish lines, and a correspondence university, Hagen, resembling the Open University in England.
— Encouragement of and grants for talented undergraduates and graduates by a number of foundations.
— Furtherance of coming generations of academic graduates. In its efforts to produce highly qualified graduates the Federal Republic has always looked to systems of higher education abroad, particularly in the Anglo-American countries where a sharp distinction is made between undergraduate training and post-graduate work

leading to an M.A. or Ph.D. degree. Ways of establishing analogous educational structures here are still being sought — in vain except at Bielefeld (cf. below). The traditional German path, which we have succeeded in reforming only step by tiny step these past 20 years, persists in seeming incompatible with Anglo-American models. Nevertheless, scattered programmes in post-doctoral training along American lines have been instituted in recent years, for instance at the Institut für Weltwirtschaft, University of Kiel, which has an international faculty.

— Most recently, a tendency to replace long-term faculty contracts by short-term contracts. This change is certainly primarily a result of the economic recession now obtaining, but foreign example has done much to confirm a policy of this kind.

— Equalization of opportunity in admissions procedures. Numbers of students have greatly increased as a result both of a baby-boom from 1949 to 1964 and higher attendance at Gymnasia and other schools leading to an *Abitur* certificate. The ratio of pupils obtaining the *Abitur* in the appropriate age group rose from 7.5 percent in 1968 to about 20 percent in 1979. However, we have faced greater obstacles than, say, Swedish or American educators in opening the universities to applicants without this certificate. Though certain shortcuts have long been available, these hard ways prevent all but a few applicants from taking them (a possible exception being the Oberstufenkolleg at the University of Bielefeld, a college-preparatory course offering a transition from school to university). In view of the great current demand for university places, complicated by a restorative tendency on the part of institutions to further élites, educational policymakers show little interest in following such leads as those given by the United States, Sweden, and Eastern European countries in opening higher education to applicants without the traditional qualifications.

— Increasing emphasis on teaching subjects of local and regional relevance, and on corresponding research tasks. A special case in point are the technical universities, which have long devoted themselves to projects of this kind. International exchanges of information on similar developments in Scandinavia, the United States, Poland and other countries have led a small but increasing number of institutions in the Federal Republic to intensify systematically their cooperation with municipal administrations, schools, businesses, industries, trade unions, and cultural agencies, thus answering to the needs of their social and natural environments while at the same time facilitating the absorption of graduates by the regional labour market.

— Increasing specification and concentration of certain subjects at a few universities, led primarily by economic considerations. This has been accompanied in recent years by a discussion on the possibility of intensifying competition among the universities in the area of research.

To sum up foreign influences on institutional reform endeavors in the Federal Republic, I can only repeat what I indicated above in connection with the joint Swedish-German commissions on democratization at our countries' universities: international exchanges of information do indeed have a stimulating effect, and developments abroad are closely followed by observers in the Federal Republic. At present the agencies concerned with domestic and educational policy are, for instance, making special efforts to collect ideas on ways to increase the number of highly qualified graduates and augment top-level research — we have still not overcome the trauma of the losses of 1933–1945, and the pressure of United States and Japanese competition in many fields has only exacerbated it. Yet it has proved impossible simply to transfer concrete organizational solutions, even having recognized their necessity, from one nation to another, since such measures must first be tailored to fit a different historical, cultural and social context. Only on a very high level is such transfer feasible. To give an example: in the early 1930s, Abraham Flexner established the Institute of Advanced Studies in Princeton, based on the ideal form of the seminar devoted solely to scholarship found at German universities. The first member of this institute was Albert Einstein. Flexner's example has certainly inspired many others including the Wissenschaftskolleg started in West Berlin in 1981.

The Present: Effects on Teaching and Learning Remain Limited

The complex question remains whether and to what extent the Federal Republic has learned, for its own approach to education, from those of other nations. As I said at the outset, there is probably no academic discipline that has not absorbed a great deal of knowledge and methods from abroad into its curriculum, and reacted to these impulses with independent work of its own. The empirical social sciences, political science, and modern empirically oriented educational science in particular would certainly not have attained the significance they now have without the impulses they absorbed from the United States and other foreign countries. Mutual fructification is especially evident in the natural sciences and technology, at the extreme in those international research institutes which invite scientists from all over the world to perform their experiments — Big Science as it is conducted, for instance, at the European centres of quantum physics, Centre Européen pour la Recherche Nucléaire (CERN) in Geneva and Deutsches Elektronen-Synchrotron (DESY) in Hamburg.

Another field deserves mention because it has profited vitally from foreign research, international exchange, and — unfortunately to a lesser extent — from international comparative studies. This field is extensive research into the universities themselves, whether from the standpoint of political science, history, law, statistics, economics, sociology and psychology, or in terms of such internal fields as organization, faculty, students, etc. Good examples are two reports of a commission of the Deutsche Forschungsgemeinschaft on "The Situation of Didactics in Higher Education" (*Die Lage der Hochschuldidaktik*, 1980) and on "Support for Research in University Didactics" (*Die Forschungsförderung in der Hochschuldidaktik*, 1982). Other key publications in this area are the volume edited by L. Huber, "Education and Socialization at University" (1983) and the trend report compiled by D. Goldschmidt, U. Teichler and W.-D. Webler, "The University as a Subject of Research" (1984). The research in the USA, Great Britain, The Netherlands, Scandinavia, the German Democratic Republic as well as in the Federal Republic of Germany on students' learning techniques is surveyed and compared critically by N. Frank and J. Stary (1980)

Investigations into the conception of the university range from Wilhelm von Humboldt to the Americans Clark Kerr (1964), and Talcott Parsons with G. M. Platt (1973). Manpower research at German universities would be unthinkable without the contributions of many Anglo-American researchers and the OECD reports. Research on students must come to grips with phenomena ranging from K. A. Feldman and Th. Newcomb's report, *The Impact of College on Students* (1969–70) in the United States to the *habitus* theory of P. Bourdieu (1964, 1971, 1977) in Paris. Investigations in Sweden (e.g. L. O. Dahlgren, 1975), and in Great Britain (e.g. L. Elton and N. J. Entwistle, 1971) on individual learning styles and strategies have been digested in German researches employing a related approach.

By far the most strongly represented in this work is the OECD sphere and within it, again, the United States; impulses from Eastern Europe certainly also deserve note. From the Third World, however, hardly any stimulus has come so far, though we are eagerly awaiting critical analyses and suggestions from the so-called developing countries, in such fields related to nature as agriculture, animal husbandry or mining, or subjects like ethnology, philosophy, history and religion. Of specific interest would be these countries' experience in intercultural exchange. There remains the question of the effect of research as a reform stimulus. The *Deutsche Forschungsgemeinschaft* studies mentioned above indicate that considerable progress is being made in the instruction of certain subjects at individual universities. Tertiary "education centres"

(*Didaktische Zentren*) organized along the lines of Anglo-American research and development centres are now involved in transmitting their methodological approaches to the practical sphere of university teaching. In the field of medicine, for example, bedside teaching on the American model has been introduced, though of late the extremely large enrollments in medical schools have sadly led to a considerable curtailment in this programme. Also, multiple-choice tests, another American invention, have been introduced for course examinations, a development not greeted by many of those concerned. Influences from Chicago (George Miller) and from Berne (Hannes G. Pauli) have been felt right down to individual courses, e.g. in the formation of small instruction groups for peer-group learning of anamnesis methods at the University of Marburg (W. Schüffel, 1979), an example that has since been taken up by many other universities. Similarly, a great number of individual examples might be mentioned in other areas and fields of instruction.

Yet on the whole, current practice in West German higher education — except for *ad hoc* surveys conducted for administrative purposes — seems quite rigidly to ignore the results of research on education and instruction that might point to reform. This is particularly true of foreign research, which as a rule finds only belated dissemination after being filtered through German work. By contrast to the broad interest shown by American and probably also Swedish universities in research findings, these remain almost without echo in the Federal Republic. Since the student movement waned, the old approach to institutional design and the organization of instruction has reinstated itself, leaving tradition unaltered wherever this is possible given the conditions of huge modern multiversities. Witness the most recent attempts to water down, by amendment, the Framework Law for Higher Education mentioned above, and the basic fruitlessness of years of efforts to restructure the university curricula. For all the great interest they hold for experts, concrete suggestions for reform made from outside, in national circumstances such as I have described, cannot be expected to have more than a limited effect in practice.

Reference

A variation of this essay, in German, which deals with the international aspects of Hartmut von Hentig's work more in detail has appeared in the Festschrift in honor of H.v. Hentig: G. Becker, H. Becker, L. Huber (eds.) 1985 *Ordnung und Unordnung*. Beltz Verlag, Weinheim.

Bibliography

Bourdieu P. and Passeron J. Cl. 1964 *Les héritiers, les étudiants et la culture*. Minuit, Paris.
Bourdieu P. and Passeron J. Cl. 1971 *Die Illusion der Chancengleichheit*. Ernst Klett Verlag, Stuttgart.

Bourdieu P. and Passeron J. Cl. 1977 *Reproduction in Education, Society and Culture.* SAGE Publ., London/Beverly Hills (Cal.).

Dahlgren L. O. 1975 Qualitative Differences in Learning as a Function of Content-Oriented Guidance. *Göteborg Studies in Educational Sciences*, Vol. 15. Acta Universitatis Gothoburgensis, Göteborg.

Elton L. and Laurillard D. M. 1978 *Trends in Research on Student Learning.* Institute of Educational Technology, University of Surrey, U.K.

Entwistle N. J. 1971 The Academic Performance of Students. In: *British Journal of Educational Psychology*, Vol. 41, pp. 258–276.

Feldman K. A. and Newcomb T. H. 1969/1970 *The Impact of College on Students. Vol. I: An Analysis of Four Decades of Research. Vol. II: Summary Tables.* Jossey-Bass, San Francisco.

Franck N. and Stary J. 1980 Studientechnik — Eine Analyse internationaler Forschung zu ihrer Bedeutung. In: *Hochschuldidaktische Forschungsberichte*, Vol. 15. AHD, Hamburg.

German-US Study Group 1978 *Access to Higher Education: Two Perspectives.* International Council for Educational Development, New York.

Goldschmidt D. (ed) 1973 *Demokratisierung und Mitwirkung in Schule und Hochschule. Bericht der deutschen und der schwedischen Kommission zur Untersuchung von Fragen der Mitwirkung in Schule, Hochschule und Forschung.* G. Westermann Verlag, Braunschweig.

Goldschmidt D. 1976 Participatory Democracy in Schools and Higher Education: Emerging Problems in the Federal Republic of Germany and Sweden. In: *Higher Education*, Vol. 5, pp. 113–133.

Goldschmidt D. and Husén T. 1977 Der Übergang von der elitären zur Massenuniversität Schwedens. In: *Neue Sammlung*, No. 6, pp. 502–537.

Goldschmidt D. Teichler U. and Webler W-D. 1984 *Forschungsgegenstand Hochschule — Überblick und Trendbericht.* Campus Forschung, Vol. 403, Campus Verlag, Frankfurt/M.

Huber L. (ed) 1983 Ausbildung und Sozialisation in der Hochschule. In: *Enzyklopädie Erziehungswissenschaft*, Vol. 10. Klett-Cotta, Stuttgart.

Kerr C. 1964 *The Uses of the University.* Harvard University Press, Cambridge/Mass.

Miller G. E. and Fülöp T. 1974 *Educational Strategies for the Health Professions.* Genf.

OECD (Organization for Economic Cooperation and Development) 1972 *Reviews of National Policies for Education: Germany.* Paris.

OECD 1975 *Education Inequality and Life Courses* (2 vols.). Paris.

OECD 1983 *Policies for Higher Education in the 1980s. Intergovernmental Conference, October 1981.* Paris.

Parsons T. and Platt G. M. 1973 *The American University.* Harvard University Press, Cambridge, Mass.

Pauli H. G. (ed.) 1977 *Das klinische Studium an der Universität Bern seit der Studienreform.* Institut für Ausbildungs und Examensforschung, Medizinische Fakultät der Universität Bern, Bern.

Schüffel W. (ed.) *Sprechen mit Kranken-Erfahrungen studentischer Anamnesegruppen.* Urban & Schwarzenberg, München.

Schüffel W. and Egle. V. 1982 Psychosomatic Education in West Germany. *Journal of Psychosomatic Research* Vol. 27, pp. 9–15.

Schüffel W. et al. 1979 *Does History Taking Affect Learning of Attitudes?* Karger, Bern.

Senatskommission der DFG für Hochschuldidaktik (ed) 1980 *Die Lage der Hochschuldidaktik.* Hochschuldidaktische Materialien, Vol. 74. AHD, Hamburg.

Senatskommission der DFG für Hochschuldidaktik (ed) 1982 *Forschungsförderung in der Hochschuldidaktik.* Hochschuldidaktische Materialien, Vol. 85. AHD, Hamburg.

Learning from Other Nations for Educational Reform: The Case of Poland

JAN SZCZEPAŃSKI

A Sketch of Polish Education Since 1939

The educational system in Poland has changed several times since 1939. After the short war in September 1939 in both of the occupied parts of Poland the occupational powers aimed at far reaching changes in Polish society and consequently also in its educational systems. In the German part the changes were brutal and radical. The institutions of higher education all closed as did the schools of general secondary education. Only vocational education schools remained open as did the primary schools but with a reduced number of years of schooling. In the Soviet part, the educational system was harmonized with the existing Soviet school conditions. In 1944, in all parts of the gradually liberated Polish territories, including the new Western provinces, the first task of the school administration consisted of rebuilding the system according to prewar concepts, but modified according to the revolutionary changes brought about by the new political power.

In 1945 a program for vast reform was adopted by the government which provided for nursery schools for all children aged 3 to 6 years, and 8 years of primary school in which grades 6 to 8 were some kind of junior high school. After that, there were 3 years of liceum (senior high school) providing general or professional education and preparing for entrance to higher education. But the country was in ruins and the proposed reform was never implemented. Nevertheless, in the following years the reconstruction of the school system was undertaken along prewar organizational principles but with major changes in the curriculum. In 1948/49 a new program was adopted this time with 7 years of basic schooling, followed by 4 years of high school accompanied by a vast independent system of vocational schools, according to the needs of the industrialization of the country. The educational system was then conceived of as being closely linked with the planned economy; the manpower planning of education was introduced, curricula were influenced by the idea of polytechnization, and in higher education

3 year courses of study were introduced to provide professional skills. The system of vocational schools consisted of: introductory vocational school, basic vocational schools training skilled manpower, and vocational high schools educating technicians and similar specialists. This system lasted until 1961 when a new law was adopted by Parliament, which reintroduced 8 years of basic schooling thus giving more stress to general education. It must be emphasized that, since 1945, all of these types of schools have been organized at two levels: for youth and, at the same time for adults, thus helping to eradicate illiteracy and allowing for the achievement of a major goal of education: to raise the cultural level of the population.

The economic and political crisis of 1970, accompanied by workers' riots and social unrest in the country, resulted in social and economic reforms, including the preparation of an educational reform. A special national committee was set up to prepare the educational reform. This was the first time in Polish postwar history that an educational reform was to be specially prepared and presented for public discussion. This was also an opportunity to study ideas and programs coming from other nations.

Factors Affecting Educational Reform

Let us begin with some general considerations. Why does a society or a government create a committee to prepare for a school reform? Because the existing state of system is seen as unsatisfactory and in Poland, at that time, the economic crisis was, in part, attributed to the poor qualifications of manpower and management. The slogan of the reform movement was "education for development", and the committee preparing the reform was meant to find better methods of education to achieve that purpose.

The preparation of a reform comprises several factors and components. First, there are the internal needs of the society and the negative evaluation of the existing educational system. The criteria of evaluation may be very different: political, economic, social, cultural, and pedagogical — many of them often used at the same time by various groups. The reform is typically started by political decisions of governments or parliaments acting under the pronounced pressure of powerful social groups, social classes or political parties. The essential element in that process is the stated causal relationship between the state of education and the state of the society and economy. Many reforms are often started without verified knowledge about that relationship; rather they are based on ideological assumptions. Education is always seen as a national value and in Poland, after such a long war and occupation and attempts at cultural extermination, public opinion was, and still is, extremely sensitive to such questions. Thus, education is seen as a factor of national development on the one hand, and, on the other, as a value in itself. This second aspect hampers the process of learning from other nations: first, foreign impact can be seen as a danger to national values, and secondly the opponents of ideas from other nations try to show that such ideas are not applicable to national conditions. Therefore, in any study of the process of learning from other nations, internal factors and conditions of reform must be carefully taken in consideration.

Learning from other nations is in itself also complex and differentiated. Let us distinguish several levels of influence coming from abroad: one level is that of scientific and philosophical ideas taken over by scientists, philosophers, intellectuals, journalists, and the like. They present these ideas in literature, scientific journals, books and from them they penetrate the press and public. Some ideas are accepted and popularized and may become stimulators in discussions about theoretical possibilities for future reforms.

A second level occurs in the official preparation of a report on the state of education and the possibility or necessity of reform. These reports usually contain suggestions for the reform of school organization, changes in curriculum and so on. Here learning from other nations is more controlled, since the reports may become public policy documents. The authors of reports, among whom scientists and educators play important roles, are more or less inclined to borrow from other nations theories and experience. But members of governments and parliaments who accept the report are usually less responsive to new ideas and theories.

A third level occurs in parliament where the report is "translated" into a bill and finally becomes law. Here learning from other nations is more limited. The lawmakers are inclined to look at how other nations achieved acceptable legal solutions to their problems, but parliament is a political body and concerned first of all with political considerations. Therefore, new ideas coming from abroad may more easily be applied in informal education, private schools, and adult education than in the formal school system.

When the reform is finally decreed and a law has established/the shape of school system (years of schooling, relations between school types, levels etc.), important questions then arise as to how the law is applied and implemented, about the day to day activities of school administration, teacher training, methods of teaching, and so on. It is here that ideas can be taken from other nations' theories, practices, experiences; this is the decisive level on which the learning from other nations can penetrate the educational reality.

Preparing for Educational Reform in the 1970s
Let us look at what learning from other nations took place in the case of Poland's preparation for educational reform in the 1970s.

The first stage of the process examined the state of development of educational sciences: pedagogy, psychology, sociology of education, economics of education and others. At this stage the flow of ideas was free and rich. The scientific literature contained many translations of articles from other countries and the scientific journals presented reviews and information about pedagogical innovations, new educational theories, and foreign school systems. In universities, education colleges and research institutions, contacts with pedagogical science abroad were fairly well developed, not only with neighboring countries in Central and Eastern Europe but also with Western Europe and America. In the late 1940s and 1950s the ideas of polytechnization, the educational methods of Makarenko, the early studies of Strumilin (published in the 1920s) on economics of education, and ideas about education for the new type of socialist personality, were vividly discussed. In the late 1950s and 1960s contacts with Western science expanded. New theories and concepts, methods of teaching, ideas about the organization of school systems and internal organization of schools, and methods of classwork found a broad reception in Polish universities, teacher training colleges and teacher unions. It is important to distinguish clearly between the state of pedagogical sciences, their concepts, methods of research, theories as expressed in writings, conferences and congresses on the one hand, and the educational policy of the government, pedagogical practice of school work, the curricula and everyday school reality, on the other. This is because the immediate impact of pedagogical sciences on teacher behavior, methods of teaching, and the content of teaching does not determine the quality of schools, since a sole teacher can not change the conditions in the schools resulting from organization principles, the quality and content of curricula, and other factors important for the quality of teaching.

But we have to stress that all the theories which were *à la mode* from the late 1950s to the early 1970s received great attention in Poland. The idea of lifelong or permanent education in all its various shades and shapes, was popularized and discussed, and found broad acceptance. Many new concepts and methods of teaching, such as problem-oriented teaching, programmed learning, micro-teaching, game-teaching, collective teaching, and the like found their devotees in Poland. New theories and results from the US in the economics of education profoundly influenced Polish thinking about the links between education, society and economic growth. Theories about open schools, informal education, and the educative society found their followers. In Poland in 1928/30 Florian Znaniecki published two volumes entitled *Sociology of Education*, expounding the idea of an educative society, a theory of education as a social process in which the educant is prepared for participation in adult life. He stressed the importance of the family, peer groups and the social environment which together might have more impact on the personality of youth than schools do. This theory was resurrected and brought into contemporary discussions. Works containing a severe criticism of schools as published by Coombs (1968), Illich (1971) and others were also translated and published.

So, the discontent with the Polish school system also received important input from foreign influences on pedagogical thinking. On that level, learning from other nations is relatively simple because the diffusion of ideas, concepts and theories does not involve any immediate practical consequences. The resistance comes from the followers of other theories and the fight goes on in the sphere of intellectual activity. Of course, that type of resistance also has an ideological aspect and is of some political importance. From the Marxist point of view, social and educational theories are also the manifestation of certain class interests, and must have practical political consequences. But the real fights begin in the next phase of preparation for reform.

The Political Reality of Preparing a Reform

Writing a report presenting the existing state of education and designing a new model for education is not only an intellectual exercise but also a political action. Thus, in this report writing phase many social and political forces become involved. Not only is educational theory at stake but also educational policy.

In the early 1970s, the Polish government formed a national committee with the task of writing an evaluation of the Polish educational system and preparing a design for its reorganization according to national needs. The report was prepared and published in 1973. To examine this report from the point of view of what was taken from theories and experiences in other nations let us first briefly review its content. It is in six parts. The first part presents the basic theoretical and ideological assumptions of the whole report, the methods of analysis, the tasks of education in society, the conditions for its effectiveness and the conditions for the effectiveness of an educational policy. The second part gives a sociological and economic analysis of the Polish society, its development trends and a forecast for the last decades of the century, as a basis for establishing the principles of the functioning of education in that society. The report presents the predicted growth of the population changes in the economy, the development of science and technology and its impact on the economy, the foreseen changes in social structure, changes in national culture, evolution of educational ideals, and the needs for modernization. It also includes a theory of education as a factor which can cope with these problems. In the third part, an evaluation of the existing school system and adult education is presented. It describes the postwar conditions in which the reconstruction of schools took place, the functions of that system, its effects on the economy and culture and human beings, its costs and organization, shortcomings, failures and the need for change. This part also laid the foundations for solutions proposed for the future. These solutions were presented in part four, where the committee put forward four general models for the reformed school systems. But the general aims of the reform had already been fixed by the government, namely, a secondary education for all citizens. The committee had to propose ways and means to achieve that aim. The proposed solutions were:

(a) Keeping the existing organization of schools; the committee proposed the admission of all able and motivated students to high schools, accompanied, at the same time, by an enlargement of preschool education, a reform of teacher training, and changed curricula. A system of permanent education was to be introduced slowly.

(b) Making some changes in vocational education, having 12 years of education for everybody with about 50 percent of an age group in high schools of general education, and again improving teacher training, developing better curricula, and having a bigger investment in schools, etc. There were some fragments of public opinion supporting this variant, but the committee did not recommend it too strongly, considering the high cost of such a school system which would amount to 8 percent of the national income.

(c) Having a 3:5:3 school system for everybody. This is the model the committee emphasized. Beginning with 3 years of elementary education, the next 5 years would be comprehensive with a unified curriculum for all students, and the last 3 years would be differentiated in several tracks e.g. mathematical-physical and technical, chemical-biological-agricultural, social-economic; humanistic, and so on. During these last 3 years, students would be prepared for: (1) work after a stage in an enterprise; (2) specialized professional schools; or (3) higher education. A whole series of changes in curricula, in teaching methods, in teacher training, and in the orientation of school work were foreseen.

(d) The fourth variant proposed a unified school of 10 years for all children except those who were disabled or unwilling to learn. For the disabled a system of specialized schools was envisaged and for drop-outs some other forms of training. But the 10 year comprehensive school system could only be started after careful preparation, namely: investment in buildings and equipment, better education of teachers, better curricula and programs, and better teaching methods. After the fulfilment of these conditions and after the creation of the necessary infrastructure, the committee thought, that a 10 years school could be introduced starting in the mid 1990s.

The fifth part of the report gave an overview and picture of all other out of school institutions and organizations, social groups and circles, all important for the development of the individual and leading to certain types of formal instruction. This was a picture of an educative society and a "total educational societal system". The report analyzed the educational impact of the family, medical care, welfare institutions, peer groups and youth organizations, employment and work institutions, trade unions, military service, adult and postschool education, cultural institutions, mass media, press, libraries, theatres, cinema, museums, music, sport, legal system, and the church — and, the relation between the school and all of these other educational influences. Taking into consideration the theories of lifelong education and the rapidly growing scope of scientific knowledge which the school should transfer to the pupil, the report foresaw some kind of division of tasks between schools and these other institutions, some kind of coordination and some cooperation. This idea, however, received very little support. Neither schools nor other institutions felt inclined to participate in the required cooperation. The sixth part of the report gave an analysis of the economic costs for each of the four reform models, a suggested timetable for implementation, and a prediction of the effects and impact of the reformed schools on society.

In writing its report, the committee profited a great deal from the experiences of other nations and international organizations. The Faure report *Learning to be*, published in 1972 by UNESCO was well known to its members, and its ideas were considered and used in discussions. The committee also studied all educational reforms undertaken in socialist countries since the 1940s. The Japanese report *Basic Guidelines for the Development of an Integrated Educational System Suited for Contemporary Society*, published by the Central Council for Education in 1971, and other reports on the reform of Japanese schools were also known. The German *Bericht der Bundesregierung zur Bildungspolitik* presented by Chancellor Willy Brandt in 1970 was also considered. And, of course, most committee members were acquainted with Swedish publications, both research and reform proposals. The works of Torsten Husén are very respected in Poland and he was made a foreign member of the Polish Academy of Sciences. American reports such as *To Improve Learning. An Evaluation of Instructional Technology* (1970) were also studied.

All of these reports had a great impact on academic thinking about education in Poland. But in writing a report and proposing a reform of the school system, the committee had to take into account the social, economic, and political reality in the country. To propose an American school system for a socialist country would be as difficult as to propose a Soviet educational system in United States. So the report took, as a starting point, the traditional values of Polish culture, the requirements

of a socialist political and economic system, the state of the economy and
the need for development. The last idea, education for development was
accepted as a major theme. All ideas put forward in foreign reports were
studied and analyzed in terms of their use or modification for use in
conditions existing in Poland.

Thus, learning from other nations for educational reform is a very
complicated process, an exercise in comparative analysis, in foreseeing
the possible effects of the application of ideas developed in other
countries, confronting the underlying values in various systems with
national values, considering the "maturity" of one's own society as
compared with others, and so on.

The Final Stage

The next stage of reform, namely the work on the legislation to be
presented to parliament, is much closer to politics than to academic
work. Writing a report is still a task for academicians, but enacting laws is
a task for members of parliament who, usually, do not care very much
for scientific correctness, but consider first and foremost all the political
conditions and requirements. In Poland the report was presented to the
government, and it stayed there. This was because at the same time as
the national committee was working on the report, the Ministry of
Education created its own commission which prepared its own proposals
for school reform, suggesting the immediate introduction of 10 years of
compulsory schooling. The government presented this to the
parliament, and in the autumn of 1973, to celebrate the two hundredth
anniversary of the first Polish National Commission of Education
(created in 1773) a resolution (but not a law) was adopted calling for
school reform along the lines proposed by the Ministry of Education.
The Ministry was also obliged to prepare — within a 2-year period — a
bill stating the legal foundations for the integrated reform of education.
That bill was never prepared but in the ensuing years the Ministry
started some reform activities for introducing the 10 years school to start
in 1980. However, with the advent of an economic and political crisis,
these activities were stopped and the school system returned to its
previous shape. Thus, at the level of preparing bills and laws for
educational reform very little can be said about the Polish experience in
learning from other nations. But even from these beginnings for the
legal preparation of a reform of education it can be seen that the
acceptance of foreign ideas is made difficult by the requirements of
parliamentary work, by the necessity of the logic of the legal system —
the new law must be within the framework of the constitution, must fit
into the legal system, and must also be within the logic of the political
system. This is the case in every country. And so it usually happens that
only some general organizational forms of education such as years of

schooling, numbers of pupils in a class, and the like are accepted, but seldom the essential ideas concerning the content and methods of teaching.

Although I have little to say about what was taken over in the everyday work of teachers from the experiences of other nations, I should say, that that is the most important aspect of learning from other nations, where new ideas and approaches into everyday life of teachers, into the experience of pupils and graduates, and find their expression in the vocational activities and value systems of citizens. This aspect of the problem was scarcely touched upon by the scholars. They usually concentrate on the academic aspects of the diffusion of educational innovation. Because, after all, that is rather easy to study!

References

Coombs, P. H. 1968 *The World Educational Crisis: A Systems Analysis.* Oxford University Press, Oxford.
Illich, I. D. 1971 *Deschooling Society.* Harper and Row, New York.

Reform and Policy Analysis

Efficiency and Quality of Higher Education*

ALAIN BIENAYMÉ

The Two Crises for the University

At the beginning of the 1980s, in a period of economic recession, higher education faces two challenges: financial austerity and its ability to give the ever increasing number of young people a better preparation for working life at a time when the rate of increase in jobs available has declined. In countries with a traditional policy of centralization, such as France, there is a great temptation to entrust political leaders with the task of initiating changes in the field of higher education. If intervention by central government is to be an asset rather than a handicap, however, the basic nature of the institution should not be misinterpreted; no attempt should be made to impose, under cover of a noble and ambiguous objective like democratization, the yoke of an ideology which may be completely at variance with the university's own dynamics of self-reform.

In most Western countries, higher education is expected not only to accommodate an ever increasing proportion of secondary school leavers or adults requiring continuing education, but also to achieve higher productivity by reducing the number of drop-outs and repeaters. It must therefore perform every miracle: accommodate, retain and grant diplomas to the maximum number of students within the statutory time scale. (See for example the Law of the 9th Plan 1984–1988: Priority implementation programme no. 2) For higher education (which has, in the space of a few years, become a mass institution) to regain its credibility in this new situation, society requires an improvement in the quality of its services, effectiveness of its actions and efficiency in the use of its resources.

Such requirements, which are formulated in vague and general terms, may, like some unifying myth, serve to justify the effort which the nation

---

*This article is the English translation of *Efficience et qualité de l'enseignement supérieur*, published in Chroniques d'Actualités de la SÉDEIS. June 15th, 1984. Paris.

has agreed to devote to its university. To rely simply on notions of quality and efficiency without being more precise will however allow some people to invite or precipitate change while others will fight such change with all the sincerity of the Crusaders.

These notions are neither a scientific statement nor a precept for action. Indeed, there are fears that the dual crises mentioned above may result in automatic pressure for a reduction in the quality of services. On the other hand, the definition of aims intended to avert this risk and to encourage a more effective development of higher education is based primarily on a correct diagnosis of the realities. And a good diagnosis depends less on a constant refrain from on high concerning the deficiencies of both universities and academics — and these deficiencies do exist — than on a better understanding of their operational logic.

To arrive at this diagnosis, two paths can be followed. The first consists in putting higher education systems in a historical perspective by considering the origin of the problems and the accumulation of successive solutions which are a novelty for a time but which eventually become obsolete without disappearing completely (Bourricaud, 1977; Husén and Kogan, 1983). The second path — the only one to be examined in this chapter — deals with higher education as a system, giving precedence to its overall architecture and the interdependence of its key elements (Perkins *et al.* 1973 and Perkins, 1978; Clark, 1983; de Romilly, 1984), having first identified these. This "systems" approach lends itself more readily than the historical approach to comparison with other countries. Such comparisons are all the more essential in that the university, working with and on knowledge, is linked to the academic community worldwide.

The Spider's Web

Borrowing Trow's image of the spider's web to describe this system (Trow, 1981) it is clearly impossible to touch the web at a given point without shaking the whole web; furthermore, the impact of this either remains this side of breaking point, causing no change, or goes beyond this threshold, causing the destruction of the whole web.

Thus, while it is legitimate to seek a better quality university system and consequently greater efficiency for a given cost, intellectual exactitude demands that this policy respect the fundamental logic of the institution.

Figure 1 attempts a depiction of the network of those variables which seem to exert an influence, either predominantly or significantly, directly or indirectly, on the quality, cost and efficiency of higher education systems. These variables, which have been clustered into separate blocks, have three characteristics:

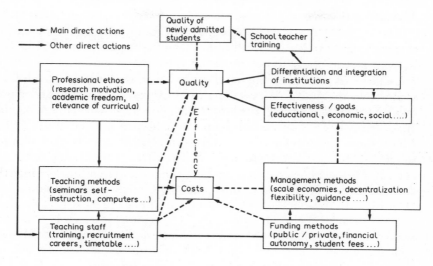

Fig. 1. Main Variables Affecting the Efficiency of Higher Education

(a) being of a more operational nature than quality, efficiency or even cost, they lend themselves better to analysis and measurement;

(b) because of their very number, they indicate the complexity and difficulty of judging the progress or decline of a system;

(c) in a period of great debate concerning the distribution of resources and time, these families of variables call for different kinds of action which are often complementary but inevitably competing.

The political debate and the departmental and union strife throw only partial light on the system. Each country has its own gray areas and taboos. France devotes less time and thought than the United States, Sweden, the Federal Republic of Germany and the United Kingdom to studying its university system. However, the research by OECD (CERI) in which French university teams participated (1972–75), the work of IREDU researchers under the guidance of J. C. Eicher, B. Millot and J. Orivel and the CRSU study by Girod de l'Ain (Paris-Dauphine) should not be forgotten. In the following remarks, the intention is not to assess the strength of the system's interdependent links, but rather to underline their plausibility and durability as well as the absolute necessity of taking such links into account in determining the direction of higher education in France as well as in any other country.

The spider's web is in the shape of an ellipse whose two foci represent the two notions of quality and cost which are often set against each other on the assumption that improved quality inevitably leads to higher costs. What, then, is the exact situation?

Measuring Quality

The quality of a country's higher education system is not easy to measure directly. Indirect indicators which are generally used include job and career opportunities available, the time needed to find a job and the salaries of graduates. Such indicators are indispensable provided one is aware of their bias. They reflect the progress of a utilitarian or even materialist view of society, the long-term benefits of which are debatable. It is also necessary to consider more qualitative indices (Trow, 1984) which show the development of a culture, the progress of "qualities of mind", such as an improvement in the capacity of human beings to communicate with each other, an increasing understanding by society of the problems of freedom and equality, a spirit of initiative and enterprise and the vitality of artistic and aesthetic creation. Clearly, there are differences between countries concerning the actual scope of contributions to higher education in these areas. Perception of these contributions is a sensitive matter. Furthermore, any attempt to measure them raises doubts about the relative weight of related causes such as state policy on matters of youth employment, freedom of enterprise, salary scales, artistic creation and the like. There is no agreement, for example, even in the United States, on the meaning of the relationship between the level of exposure of the population to higher education and the quality of management (cf Peters and Waterman, 1982). In France, on the other hand, a CERC study seems to demonstrate that the main variable explaining disparities noted in profit returns is the school-leaving age of the head of the firm (CERC Document no. 24, 1974).

Despite these difficulties, some consideration can be given to those variables which are most likely to be associated with the quality of results achieved by higher education.

The Effectiveness of Higher Education

As academics are aware, it is not right to begin with this topic (Clark, 1983). This involves starting from the top of the system "while the best starting point is located at the base", that is, with the intangible substance which forms the focus of higher education work, namely, knowledge. There are, of course, those academics who like to remind us of Kepler's joke about the university being the "guardian of ignorance" but who can, through their own work, falsify this notion.

The only excuse for starting with the theme of effectiveness is that, in a country as centralized as France, with universities whose resources are so dependent on the political decisions of central government, it is necessary to begin by using the language most familiar to people in government as well as to their electorate. For it is in the name of this language that institutional decisions are made.

In the first place, the quality to be valued and promoted depends on the effectiveness with which the higher education system as a whole performs the duties as defined in the 1968 education law and revised by the law of 26 January 1984. The latter includes a double listing in Articles 2 and 4: the first listing defines the three contributions expected from higher education as a public service to knowledge, economic growth and the reduction of social and cultural inequalities. The second contains a more precise definition of its tasks, including basic and continuing education, research, dissemination and evaluation of its results, both academic and technological and cultural, and international cooperation. The law of 1984 thus provides written confirmation of the extension of the scope of higher education initiated in 1968. This development, which is found in many countries, deserves comment.

In the first place, by their very nature, higher education institutions are labour-intensive units of activity. (For example, in France in 1984 staff costs accounted for 88 percent of the total expenditure budget of the universities and related institutions.) This labour-intensity is further accentuated by the budgetary accounting method which, in France, takes no account of the cost of fixed assets. Consequently, this activity is not the focus of significant increases in internal productivity, even though it may contribute to an improvement in the productivity of other sectors (Benveniste, 1984). Furthermore, the educational objective must be viewed in relation to other neighboring objectives which are clearly complementary but nonetheless competing, owing to the lack of time available. It has been accepted for a long time that true higher education can only be conceived of in partnership with research at the individual level, either by the teacher or the advanced student although Ernest Renan expressed the opposite point of view in the last century (Rétat, 1984). It can thus be put at risk by the increasing volume of related tasks imposed upon teachers, by the decline in the recruitment of bright young teacher–researchers with outstanding doctorates, by the diminishing significance attached to the quality of publications when assessing academics, and by the *de facto* division between full-time professional research bodies such as CNRS and the university. In this respect, the 1982 legislation (planning of scientific research and technological development) and the 1984 legislation seem to have widened the gap separating the university community from the rest of the scientific community by placing the CNRS under the authority of a Ministry overloaded with industrial change and redeployment problems (the Ministry of Industry) and by reducing academic representation on the bodies concerned with assessing CNRS staff. Since July 1984, however, the Ministry of Research has become a completely separate entity.

The establishment, under the 1984 legislation, of a national authority designed to evaluate the results obtained in performing the tasks allocated to higher education could be considered a step in the right direction, provided three conditions were to be met. The committee should consist of members chosen for their own academic qualifications, regardless of their political or trade union affiliations. (They should be either elected by their peers under a system of uninominal voting — which is not easy with several thousand voters covering some fifty academic disciplines — or appointed by bodies able to exercise total objectivity, such as the Academies, Collége de France, and so on.) The inevitably political judgement regarding the contribution of a given university to economic growth, employment policy and the reduction of social and cultural inequalities (Article 2 of the 1984 legislation) should not interfere with the evaluation of the tasks assigned to higher education (training and research) under Article 4. And thirdly, the multiplicity of aims and tasks assigned to higher education in general should not be automatically translated into aims and tasks for each individual institution. Differences in size, age, location and other constraints are such that it would in reality be both contrived and injust to attempt to apply national objectives at the level of each institution. This seems to be stating the obvious. The danger remains, however, that in the pursuit of social and cultural equality and an implicit desire for democratization of knowledge, university teaching might be made available to the masses in uniform institutions as alike as grains of sand. At a time of scarce resources, leveling down is bound to win. The opposite of uniformity lies in the clearly accepted differentiation of institutional infrastructure, even if this means achieving all the co-operation possible.

Organizational Differentiation

Within a given country, higher education systems differ in four complementary though separate aspects which are too often confused. These are:

— the division of the institutional infrastructure into sectors;
— the combination of disciplines offered;
— the tier arrangement or progression of studies in stages; and
— the hierarchy based on the presumed value of the institutions.

Only the first aspect will be discussed here because of its high degree of dependency on state preference. At the same time, however, the connotations associated with it and the repercussions of such preferences for the other aspects must not be ignored.

Until 1968, the system was completely binary: on one side, a diverse set of institutions preparing students for careers in engineering and commerce, and on the other, a monolithic group of universities cast in the same mould for each academic region. The creation of the IUT (University Institutes of Technology) in 1965 introduced a new measure of variety into the system without disturbing its logic. Between 1968 and 1981, universities entered upon the path of differentiation with some reticence but not without effect. A measure of competition was introduced as a result not of the autonomy conferred on the universities by law but rather of the sub-division of the major universities and the development of master's degrees in sciences and the professions. Some institutions even had to select candidates on the basis of their school performance. But throughout this period and more so since 1981, the universities have only exercised their right to be different within these very narrow confines. Central government thus continues to control the distribution of teaching posts, to identify the national diplomas of equivalent value in law, and to submit projects presented to it for funding to national committees for consideration. As a matter of principle, the 1984 legislation prohibits selection even on entrance to the second stage. Since selection is limited to post-secondary non university higher education ("Ecoles"), medical schools and IUTs, the superficial equality of the candidates is consequently preserved, regardless of their aptitude and motivation, thus undermining the adaptability of the system as a whole.

On the other hand, some advocate, unsuccessfully at present, a generalized selection process (that is the recognition of the right of all institutions to select their own candidates) in order to allow each institution a large measure of autonomy in the definition of its programmes (Ellrodt, 1977, Bienaymé, 1981 and Schwartz, 1983). Two substantial arguments support this thesis. The extraordinary development in the amount of knowledge has led to a fragmentation of disciplines and this, in turn, has multiplied the combinations of courses offered to students. Furthermore, the cultural and economic development of society brings with it an increase in the variety of demands made on post-secondary education. Two apparently sound objections to this can be dismissed. The first is that the generalized selection process is founded on a Malthusian approach: nothing could be further from the truth. It was in fact during the period of most pronounced increase in student enrollment that Harvard, Princeton, Yale and other institutions became more selective (Clark, *op. cit.* p. 100). The second objection is that generalized selection would favor an elitism inconsistent with democratic equality. This is quite wrong. Nothing will prevent newspapers from responding quite skillfully to the demands of pupils, parents and employers for a classification of the numerous higher education institutions in order of excellence, even when the latter are all ruled by the principle of uniformity. Despite the progress achieved in the variety of distinguishing elements, it is a sad fact that the various

league tables currently published in France continue to sanction the old
simplistic practice of measuring the quality of the graduates of any
institution according to their accomplishments in mathematics, the
degree of selectivity for entrance and the duration of the studies. These
criteria ignore the quality of activities specific to each institution; in
other words, those very areas where differentiation could have the
greatest impact.

For all these reasons, only a system of differentiation combined with
the principle of generalized selection can justify the creation of options
offered to students, strengthen the internal coherence of curricula, offer
a second chance to those disappointed by their first experience and
stimulate innovation.

In the French context, where corporate and ideological trade
unionism assumes an importance unknown in other countries, the
superficial uniformity imposed upon the university tends to foster
internecine conflict rather than stimulate progress by mobilizing
teachers in the direction of better quality educational programs.

As a result of the sector differentiation accepted in France, the
training of future teachers at other levels of education is assigned to
various teacher training colleges with syllabuses and methods different
from those of the old Faculties or Departments of Arts and Science as
they are now known. The quality of students admitted to higher
education will depend, in the long run, upon the quality of graduates
from these colleges.

Quality of New Students

Teachers and employers regularly complain about the decline in the
level of knowledge and the standard of behavior of their new recruits.
This complaint overlooks the fact that the progress of knowledge has, in
part, made obsolete that knowledge on which teachers and employers
were themselves assessed and selected in the past. Furthermore, it is
important to recognize the great leap forward achieved in the education
of women over the last two generations.

But given these reservations, the complaint has become too widespread and too specific to be rejected out of hand. The same words
describe "The rising tide of mediocrity" (Boyer, 1983, Trow, 1982,
Ravitch, 1983) in the United States and "Le flot montant de l'ignorance"
(the rising tide of ignorance) (de Romilly, *op. cit.*) in France. Various
instruments are beginning to measure this phenomenon, such as the
Scholastic Achievement Tests which decide university entrance for
young Americans; in France, the tests taken by young army recruits as
well as reports from juries or academic inspectorates could be systematically used. The information already collected suggests that while the
deterioration theory is not yet proved, it should at least not be rejected.

But academics would be wrong to think themselves relieved of any responsibility with regard to the quality of the "bacheliers" (secondary school leavers) whom they accept. Their responsibility is threefold.

First of all, the university has probably been premature in attempting to introduce into schools the methods and results of new trends in scientific research. These methods and results are fascinating to specialists and the international academic community but too esoteric to be usefully translated into the classroom teaching of mathematics, French language, history and geography. More fundamentally, there appear to be two skills missing from the education provided in schools: the ability to keep to the facts and to communicate. The excessive and premature degree of specialization demanded by the baccalauréats (secondary school leaving certificates) should certainly be reconsidered, as should the order of priorities among disciplines and, last but not least, the very meaning of education in school.

Secondly, the training of future primary and, in particular, secondary school teachers is open to debate in terms of the balance between mastery of a developing discipline and the acquisition of teaching skills of which at least one — without doubt the most important — is not much in evidence nowadays: dedication. It was once stated: "The strength of teachers lies in their knowledge; that of educators in their dedication". And this raises the problem of school teaching as a vocation.

Finally, the universities and their teachers both pursue a policy of splendid isolation with regard to their neighbors and participate only too rarely in the launching of common initiatives such as intensive training of future students, refresher courses, information for future secondary school leavers on what the university expects from its students etc. The centralization of university registrations — which is desirable in many respects — should not however discourage university faculties from establishing special links with the neighboring schools.

The previous findings, combined with the increase in admissions both in absolute numbers and as a proportion of an age group, point to a significant change in the demands placed upon the first stages of higher education. In the United States, where education is traditionally of a more heterogeneous and less intellectual nature than in France, the higher education system provides, through the Community Colleges (which account for 50 percent of the higher education intake, 30 percent of the total student population) and/or during the first years at university, a very wide general education which can be considered as an extension of incomplete school studies. At the other end of the spectrum, only 20 percent of American students and teachers follow the German or British model of universities devoted to research and to the teaching of courses based on in-depth study of a central discipline (Clark, *op. cit.* pages 49–50, 61 and 79).

As a result, the quality of higher education depends to a large extent on the professional attitude of its own teachers; it would be difficult to ignore their extreme unease at the emergence of these new demands in France and at the way in which central government is responding to them.

Professional Ethics of the Academic

Academics' professional ethics are critical to quality. The answers to the questions raised by this topic determine the content and the value of the knowledge imparted to the majority as well as the spirit in which it is taught. In assessing the productivity of the universities, there is usually too great a readiness to rely solely on the number of graduates as the determining factor. This convenient criterion ignores the main issue which is the quality of the young people educated. The importance of the motivation of the executive for the vitality of the firm is well recognized nowadays, but how much more important is the motivation of teachers whose influence can have a lasting effect on an individual's development.

Merton identifies four norms in the academics creed: universalism, unselfishness in the advancement of knowledge, controlled scepticism and the availability of scientific results and methods (Clark *op. cit.* page 93). These norms, which are common to both teacher and scientific researcher, do not however take account of the dilemmas and doubts which beset academics nowadays. Every academic has two professional native lands and belongs to four cultures. He is or should be acknowledged firstly by his peers in a given academic discipline with its own traditions, history, language and world-wide tribe. He performs his activity in an institution to which he is assigned and cooperates in an educational program with representatives of other disciplines. As a member of an academic or intellectual profession other than journalism, school teaching or the literary profession, and a citizen of a nation with its own particular academic and historical preferences (Janetti-Diaz, 1980), he must reconcile and synthesize various differing requirements. In addition, the academic community has been unable, in France at least, to protect itself against the invasion of simplistic theories of class or generation conflict promulgated by a certain trade unionism (Bienaymé, 1984, *op. cit.*).

More fundamentally, the academic finds himself torn by the sudden development of demands directed at him to which he is unable to respond owing to the uniformity of his situation. The dilemma consists in finding an ideal compromise between the requirements of research and academic freedom and the need to ensure relevance of curricula and a professional attitude to teaching.

The term "teacher–researcher" which has been widely used since 1968 underlines the idea — a relatively new one in France — that any academic should devote part of his time to activities leading to publications. This trend which is characteristic of the better known American universities and of the British and German systems, appears however to be queried by supporters of the 1984 Savary legislation on higher education. According to them, too much weight is given by academics to publications and research. Secondly, the reduction in the number of appointments lessens the attraction of research for young people. And finally, they take the view that priority should be given to accepting large numbers of new students more concerned with employment prospects at the end of their course than with pursuing an academic discipline for its own sake. This view is further reinforced by the emergence of a new category of teachers no longer with the term "researchers" attached. The functional presentation of the state budget demonstrates a similar approach by confirming the distinction between the main body of research on the one hand and higher education on the other. The 1984 university research budget amounts to 500 million francs, excluding salaries (since no method permits a satisfactory breakdown of salary in relation to each item of activity in the timetable of an academic.) At the same time, the budgets for CNRS, agronomic research and health amount respectively to 7.4, 2 and 1.6 billion francs, including salaries. Academic research, which seems relegated to a fringe activity by this type of presentation might, in the eyes of the layman, appear as the self-indulgent pastime of mandarins anxious to escape from students. Discredited by this and other statutory provisions (such as, for instance, the draft ordinance under which teachers must obtain prior authorization of the Minister to publish and receive royalties), academic research, in spite of allowing CNRS to recruit its researchers and operate part of its laboratories, is threatened with extinction. The disappearance of French academic publications would only increase an already considerable scientific and cultural debt to other countries in a number of disciplines.

This state of affairs could be remedied by giving some universities the opportunity to set themselves up as research and teaching institutions in which the first activity would not be sacrificed to the second.

Another potential conflict divides academics aware of the need for academic freedom but at the same time under pressure to develop curricula more relevant to the needs of society. Napoleon's France was the first to launch a model of higher education aimed at preparing students for a wide range of higher professions. Universities nowadays are without exception required to perform the same task for a much greater range of lower-level professions. The way in which the Ministry intervenes in the detail of curriculum at the first stage of higher education in order to introduce vocational relevance (a political decision which is both enforced and capable of amendment) can only endanger the survival of the centres of excellence which have up to now prepared students for key professions through the teaching of a basic discipline, the acquisition of advanced techniques and an introduction to research.

If the first term is to be devoted to information, for the purposes of "probationary training and the learning of scientific methods", there is unlikely to be any opportunity to begin basic teaching *from the start* of a university course. For this first term must end, by agreement with each student, in a "training run" which will direct him either towards a short period of training in preparation for working life 1 year after leaving secondary school, towards a 2-year vocational training (inevitably of a lower standard than that of the university institutes of technology which select their students) or towards the second stage of higher education. It is indeed debatable why the 9th Plan, which is so vague on the subject of innovation at secondary school level and so dependent on a controversial Legrand report, should entrust the first stages of higher education with the task of "motivating and advising students". Would it not have been possible to avoid this 2-year delay by extending the role of the advisers concerned with information and guidance?

In many professions, intellectual drive (in terms of active participation in the revision of professional practices) generally occurs to an outstanding degree among approximately 10 percent of the relevant population. (This figure is based on the percentage of voluntary attendance at training centres and membership of professional bodies concerned with research and retraining.) Let us suppose that, in the case of young people, a proportion of one third or one quarter must be retained to take account of the crucial period needed to reach intellectual maturity. Let us also accept as a fact that France's objective is to increase the higher education intake as quickly as possible to 35–40 percent of the age group, as opposed to 28 percent in 1984. Is it reasonable to impose on *all* students, at the start of their course, a period of "pre-vocationalization" taken out of the lecture time, which is devoted to "explaining the administrative structure of the institutions", to seminar discussions "on the work place", to "introductory workshops" 15 percent of the time), to the learning of "basic languages" assimilation of which has not been achieved across the board by the secondary school (20 percent of the time)? In other words, would it not be advisable, on the basis of school results, to pick out a third or a quarter of the young students admitted (that is, according to the total admission rate observed between 9 and 13 percent of the total population) and allow them to embark *without delay* on the study of basic disciplines without which the in-depth professional training provided by the second and third stages will be wasted? As an illustration we may quote an American report (The Gourman Report: "A rating of graduate and professional programs in American and International Universities."

Edit. National Educational Standards 617 West-South 7th Street, suite 300, Los Angeles.) This document, which is available in all American universities, raises doubts about the soundness of some of the ratings established in France. According to the one published by *L'Express* on 6 April 1984, for instance, Paris II-Assas would be in 49th position in France. This is scarcely compatible with the findings of the Gourman Report which rates the Paris universities as first in the world for the study of law with a score of 4.97 out of 5; they precede Harvard, Michigan (Ann Arbor), Yale, Oxford, Chicago and Berkeley in that order. In its general introduction, the same document states that, on the basis of a certain set of criteria, "higher education in France and the USSR was found to be clearly superior in several professional fields to that of the United States, the United Kingdom, Canada and other countries."

Thus, while it is perfectly appropriate to draw the attention of academics to the students' preoccupation with finding a job, this must not be at the expense of high ability streams. Since these streams are mainly — though not exclusively — based on the in-depth study of an academic discipline of universal significance, they represent not only a means of participating in international competition and academic progress but also of replenishing the "reservoir" of higher grade professionals which cannot be provided by the *Grandes Ecoles* (non-university higher education) alone. Therefore, if legislation rejects differentiation between universities, this differentiation will have to be accepted within each university. This will not be achieved without some — largely unnecessary — conflict, which may often be aggravated by ideological considerations used to disguise arguments of a constitutional or personal nature.

Teaching Methods

The sets of variables analyzed above have a significant and lasting influence on the results of higher education. Costs, however, are not directly affected except in one respect: the number of students admitted to the university. Conversely, teaching methods influence both quality and costs. Their selection depends partly on professional ethics but also partly on the influence of interested parties. Fundamental to the method/cost relationship is the sequential organization of syllabuses by stage and year, according to a progression agreed among the staff. If no one teaching method emerges as preferable to all the others, they should be combined. In order to promote optimum and genuine achievement of educational objectives, the choice of combinations should take into account the various disciplines, their degree of difficulty and the potential audiences and their level of maturity. Unfortunately, cost considerations may exert an undue influence over this choice. Because of this, French universities have for too long been satisfied with *ex-cathedra* teaching for audiences which are too large and too heterogeneous to derive all the benefits from it. But experiments with active teaching methods in small seminars have on the other hand often deteriorated into pale reproductions of *ex-cathedra* teaching. The universities should overcome their reluctance with regard to methods lectures where the student is actively trained to organize his own documentation and arguments and the expression of his views and findings.

Modern methods of transmitting knowledge (computer assisted teaching, remote learning, television) are still rarely used, with the exception of some disciplines such as information science and foreign languages. Tutorials and small seminars, which can be very successful with a good teacher and a homogeneous group of students, do not lend themselves readily to mass introduction.

There is a regrettable inertia which arises from two complementary sources: the conservatism of the teaching profession and the cost of introducing new systems. The preparation of an administrative or management case study requires many more hours than the preparation of an equivalent lecture. For a given discipline and stage, the cost of the student-hour varies with the method of grouping selected and the number of teaching aids used. A teaching period — the visible tip of the iceberg — is the result of a combination of activities of which the audience is barely aware — documentation, thought and knowledge management (which brings out the particular character of higher education activities: curriculum organization, supervision of theses and papers, examinations, assessment of abilities and so on.) This same audience on the other hand is fully aware — and rightly so — that this or that famous television presenter in fact works for a much longer time than his or her two or three hour screen appearances each week. A teaching period given during the first stage, which may be repeated three or four times from class to class usually requires less preparation than a postgraduate level lecture. Nevertheless, the fact remains that an experienced teacher can deliver in one period a synthesis which is only arrived at through innumerable hours of study. A methods lecture focused on "knowing how to think" and know-how generally involves considerable effort on the part of the student and demands other qualities of the teacher than the mere ability to transmit knowledge.

Internal differentiation of universities, provided it does not reflect the results of unresolved conflict, enables the universities to find solutions most appropriate to the spread of ability and motivation of the students. It is advisable sometimes to compare the best students with the others: the "year group" system; at other times it is more appropriate, through the system of cumulative credits, for the teachers to be in contact only with the most demanding and advanced students. The best students contribute to the reputation of the university, while the other students require equally appropriate care and attention. The productivity of a university is often assessed by reference to the proportion of registered students who succeed in graduating. In order to improve this score, however, without introducing excessively strict entrance requirements, efforts would have to be made to reduce the number of failures, repeaters and drop-outs. This would involve an additional cost in the shape of diversification of teaching matter and modification of teaching methods.

Teaching Staff

The efficiency of higher education systems is determined by the teachers, since their competence is reflected in the services they provide and their number and seniority determine a large proportion of the cost of the system.

Methods of recruitment and promotion vary from one country to another and in France from one discipline to another. But one general tendency remains: that of ascertaining the teacher's academic qualifications in a given discipline. The weight of research, the quality of publications, the assessment by peers on as wide a geographical basis as possible to avoid intellectual nepotism — all these factors confirm the importance of academic ability as a criterion. But higher education is organized on the basis of a matrix: the teacher's personal and professional qualities are judged primarily within the framework of each institution. Therefore universities must be able to select their future teachers themselves while of course securing the necessary academic safeguards.

Costs are determined by salaries and salary scales and by the relative extent of promotion and recruitment. But from 1968 to 1974 recruitment at the base of the pyramid was such that France was not able to finance a policy of promotion similar to that of previous years (Bienaymé, 1984, *art. cit.*) The resulting delays and bottlenecks in career development have fueled a dissatisfaction which has encouraged younger teachers to become more trade-union minded and made disagreements more extreme. The French university has indeed already made its contribution to the sacrifices which state withdrawal will impose upon most of the protected professions. This withdrawal is already implicit in the debate on the reduction in the rate of taxation.

Teaching costs are also influenced by the sometimes excessive rate of teacher specialization. When circumstances necessitate a redeployment of activities, the specializations in decline will always find arguments in their own defence, some of which are perfectly sound. The fact that teachers in France are civil servants — unlike the United Kingdom and the United States — does not seem to be a particular asset or handicap for the university. The really important thing is to encourage teachers to accept some flexibility of teaching matter when the disciplines they study have become somewhat static and to participate in a system of dual subjects, one corresponding to their basic discipline and the other of a multi-disciplinary nature associated with the study of a given problem.

The involvement of experts is indispensable to the diversification of teaching matter. The 1984 legislation provides for the creation of a body of non-research "teachers", recruited probably from secondary education, to share in the life of the university by assuming a heavier load of teaching in the strict sense of the word. This development is understandable in view of the increasing importance of school-type teaching. It should not however be regarded as an 'easy way out; nor should the research centers and associated teaching be drowned by a tidal wave of first stage institutions.

Funding Higher Education

The French higher education system is for the most part a state asset and as such depends on the submission of financial proposals to Parliament for approval. Discounting the importance of individual benefits which the graduate himself enjoys, this state of affairs, dating back to Napoleon, subjects most institutions to the rules of public accounting. It is not challenged by the limited flexibility promised by the 1984 legislation in the distribution of operating resources within the universities.

Thus, higher education follows rules which are different from those governing expenditure on health, since the latter depends on the needs of patients covered by the National Health Service, medical prescriptions and the cost of treatment. H. Wilenski (1975) recently pointed out that Western countries devote more resources to health the less they spend on education, and conversely.

The distribution of public funds and total resources among institutions of all kinds and its comparison with the corresponding student populations is not uniformly presented. Hence, the information available (such as the functional presentation of the state budget: the statistics from the Ministry of Education (SEIS) and information collected from the appropriate departments of this Ministry and the Ministry of Economy and Finance) does not fully satisfy our curiosity.

Tables 1 and 2 present per student enrollment and per student funding in different types of higher education institutions in France.

The complexity of the funding process does not enable too much importance to be attached to expenditure per student per type of institution. But there are considerable differences in the order of magnitude. These differences underline the extreme poverty of

TABLE 1.
Distribution of Student Enrollments (Multiple registrations not yet identified slightly affect the value of these assessments. The public and private sectors are combined.)
(1982–1983)

Preparatory grades for entrance to non-university higher education	41 907)		
Higher technician Streams (STS)	76 620)	in the public sector	82 500
Universities	913 973	in IUTs	55 314
Non-university higher education ("Ecoles") (all Ministries)	110 698	in { engineering commercial	39 000 23 317

TABLE 2.
Distribution of Higher Education Budgets[1] for 1984

Student Enrollments 1982–83

	Billion French francs		per student
Preparatory grades + public sector STS	1.5	for 82,500 students	18, 180 FF
Universities	11.5	for approx. 850,000 students	13,530[2]
IUT	1.7	for 55,314 students	30,733
State colleges of engineering dependent on all ministries	1.7	for 21,388 students	79,483
Higher technological education dependent on the Ministry of Education alone (IUT + colleges of engineering dependent on this Ministry + Compiegne)	2.6	for 77, 009 students	37,766
Total	16.4[3]		15,250[4]

[1]Personnel, operating and capital expenditure appearing in the proposed budgets for 1984 for the public sector (in round figures)
[2]i.e. much less if medicine is excluded
[3]1.8 billion dollars at a rate of exchange of 1 $ = 9 FF
[4]Roughly 1700 dollars per head.

non-medical universities, which in many cases does not allow them to perform even the minimum number of educational tasks regarded as important, like the preparation of case files, for instance. These differences reflect, on the one hand, the cost specific to each discipline, and on the other, disparities in the strictness of selection procedures and study programs. It is to be hoped that future budget presentations will allow better understanding in an area which is of such importance in comparing the quality and efficiency of the various institutions.

Some people pin their faith on the possible diversification of funds collected by the universities. This deserves comment. The 1968 and 1984 reforms have opened up membership of university boards and committees to people from outside. But since these external members are not entitled to collect or bring in financial contributions, the implicit rule of the US trustee ("Get, give or get off") does not apply (Clark, *op. cit.* pages 117 and 172, 173). The relationship created inside the committees is ill-balanced since these external members appointed in part by outside bodies have no feeling of personal responsibility towards the university they serve. They have mainly their own interests in mind.

Greater autonomy would give the university the right to diversify its resources — more realistic registration fees, grants from organizations, associations and firms etc. The university could then pay more attention to the needs of its users and the users would show more concern for the livelihood of their institution. The state would still have to protect those disciplines whose existence is threatened by their apparent lack of practical value but which are nevertheless indispensable to the academic and cultural reputation of the country.

It might also be possible to consider a return to a formula of fixed term contracts to allow the university to take advantage of young talent without committing itself for life. So many assistant professors in the 1970s were made civil servants that it is impossible for higher education now to recruit the brightest students of recent years: this is both injust and inefficient and will have serious consequences for the future.

Flexibility and partial privatization of resources however have their price. In a period of lean years, competent teams run the risk of breaking up (although the program of teacher redundancies which the UK universities had to carry out recently was apparently conducted with efficiency and fairness.) But bearing in mind the relatively low level of resources allocated to higher education by France (approximately 20 billion francs or 0.5 per cent of GDP* as compared with other major industrial nations) this scope for manoeuvre would be worth exploring.

---

*The difference between this figure and the 16.4 in Table 2 is partly due to the inclusion of the budgets of the major institutions (Paris Observatory, Natural History Museum etc.)

Administration and Direction of the System

The higher education system is subject to threefold control. The first level of authority is represented by the teacher–researchers whose main focus of interest is a recognized discipline. The 1968 reforms have moderated the individualism typical of the profession by increasing the number of collegiate structures (UER, specialist committees, research departments) instead of professorships. The university has shown itself to be a very important intermediate tier: without achieving full autonomy, it has become a specific center of life and power. Whether acting as holding company or conglomerate, or whether concentrating on a circumscribed task, the university stands at the intersection of the offers (disciplines) and the demands placed upon it by the students. At the top, the administrative management has had its power consolidated and transformed by the mere fact that the number of students and the variety of their requirements have in the last 20 years become a political problem which no government can afford to ignore.

The power at the top is often regarded as meddlesome, bureaucratic, "politically apolitical" (Benveniste, 1977) and, for the past few years, over-influenced by certain trade unions with dominant political affiliations. It is moderated by the profession's own internal pressure groups (non-university higher education institutions, and associations) and by the esoteric nature of a system which cannot be properly directed without recourse to the expertise at the base.

In this context, questions are often asked about how change takes place, whether the innovations are sound and what additional expenditure they entail. No overall answer can be given. Indeed, the system cannot be properly directed without an understanding of the nature of the two primary forces for change. The first of these springs from the development and explosion of disciplines under the thrust of research and academic discovery. The second, which is also powerful, lies in the variety of expectations on the part of both young and adult students concerned for their future careers and anxious for the sort of advice, guidance and tips which teacher–researchers often have difficulty in providing.

These two currents both combine and collide at the same time. The weight of teaching received today by many students is the result of a slow assimilation and integration of yesterday's research. The more the teacher attempts to give a precise answer to the student's questions, the more he stumbles against the uncertainty of present knowledge and the more he catches sight of the avenues to be explored in the future. This change is demonstrated by the appearance of new diplomas and teaching matter. It is often said that while these modifications improve quality, the new does not replace the old and costs therefore increase proportionately. Indeed, progress is achieved more by addition than by redeployment and subtraction. Such a finding requires two comments. In the first place, there are disciplines (particularly in the arts) where new knowledge does not of itself make existing knowledge obsolete.[4] On the relative situation of sciences and arts see: J. De Romilly, *op. cit.* chap. VII. I. Prigogyne and I. Stengers: "La nouvelle alliance" NFR 1979 and I. Ekland: "Le calcul, l'imprévu" Seuil, 1984 Chap. 2. As for Economics and Management, to insist as Guillaume does (*Le Monde* 22–23 April 1984) on the limitations of these disciplines which he terms impersonal does not justify abandoning them. This attitude would be as naive as the pan-economics of the New Economists. This existing knowledge remains of interest not just for purely historical reasons. Keynes does not discredit Ricardo and neither do Hayek or Debreu replace Marx, Walras or Keynes. Tocqueville or Durkheim can still be read to advantage, even though the opinion survey techniques or the modern analyses of Cofremca still retain their interest.

Secondly, the judgement of peers must outweigh that of the student in deciding on the cancellation of obsolete courses, even though the student's judgement may serve as an indicator when it is accurate, coherent and determined. Comparison with foreign universities is also beneficial.

Parallel with these basic considerations, the quality of direction could be improved upon in France by some transfer of management responsibility from central government to the universities themselves, by improving information techniques and by introducing greater flexibility in the use of resources. It would, for instance, be possible, without reducing the "vacation time" which teacher–researchers should normally devote largely to research, to organize activities over twelve months of the year on a rotational basis. Capital would be put to better use in this way.

Is French higher education too costly? The answer must be no. With 0.5 per cent of the GDP, the present government has still not improved upon the situation criticized in 1980 (Bienaymé, 1980). A student today costs the state an average of 16,000 francs a year, which is less than a secondary school pupil (20,400 FF) and slightly more than a primary school pupil (7,000 FF). This scale of expenditure is extremely modest compared with other developed countries (not to mention the unhealthy situation in certain developing countries where a student costs up to 100 times more than a child in primary school). Figures estimated by Philip Coombs in his new edition of *World Education Crisis* (1985).

In this article, an attempt has been made to reveal the workings of a refined and frequently enigmatic system on which apparent manifestations of student unrest or teacher strikes throw a spotlight which is a little too one-sided to be of help in undertstanding the system in general.

"The stated purposes of reform are like all formal goals: they are to be assumed guilty of hiding the truth until proven innocent by congruence with operational patterns." (Clark, *op. cit.* page 227). The 1984 legislation is in no way proven innocent by the proposed statutory provisions or by the priority programme of the 9th Plan. The university will not in fact achieve the transition to mass education unless the following principles are implemented:

1. Differentiation between post-secondary institutions, particularly universities in the strict sense of the word.
2. Generalization of selection based upon a wide variety of criteria appropriate to the aims of the institutions.
3. Diversification of both public and private sources of funding.
4. Improvement of career prospects for teachers with recognized academic and teaching skills.
5. Reliance on fixed term contracts for the first few years of teaching and research.
6. Development of a European policy for the promotion of student and teacher exchanges as well as the exchange of information on degrees and diplomas.

As Boissonnat (1984) states: "Without the European Monetary System, the leftist experiment in France would have collapsed in financial ruins; for it would have lived longer under the poetic delusion of the state of grace". The French university also lives within a kind of invisible international currency system embracing all the industrialized countries. Even though adjustments occur more slowly than in the financial field, they nevertheless place the French university on a comparative scale which may well become less favorable to it. It is a pity that French legal documents continue to adhere to a strictly national and isolationist view of post-secondary educational problems. Europe must be revitalized through the commitment of the younger generation. The French university must be stimulated by giving it a more European look. Europe must be freed from inappropriate and untimely state intervention. The university must not be made the refuge of an outdated ideology of class struggle, where both the protagonists and the stakes are too vaguely defined to achieve any positive contribution whatsoever.

The 1984 legislation and its regulatory content do not come to grips with the real questions raised by the future of the French university. The present state of the university ought at least to have been exposed.

References

Benveniste, G. 1984 *Technocracy, Politics and Public Universities.* School of Education, University of Berkeley.
Benveniste, G. 1977 *The Politics of Expertise.* Boyd & Fraser, San Francisco.
Bienaymé, A. 1980 *L'Attribution des Ressources á l'Enseignement Supérieur.* Chroniques d'Actualité de la SEDEIS, Paris (Sept. 15th, 1980).

Bienaymé, A. 1981 L'Autonomie Financiére des Universités en Période de Récession Economique. *Administration et Education* No. 1, Paris.

Bienaymé, A. 1983 Higher Education: The Case of France. In: Husén T. and Kogan M. *Educational Research and Policy: How Do They Relate?* Pergamon Press, Oxford.

Bienaymé, A. 1984 Higher Education Reforms in France. In: *European Journal of Education*, Vol. **19** No. 2, July 1984.

Boissonnat, P. 1984 L'Expansion. *Editorial*, 16th March, 1984.

Bourricaud, F. 1977 *La Réforme Universitaire en France et ses Déboires*. Institut Européenne de l'Education, Paris.

Boyer, E. 1983 *Report on Secondary Education*. Carnegie Foundation, New York.

Clark, B. 1983 *The Higher Education System: Academic Organization in Cross-National Perspective*. University of California Press, Los Angeles.

S. Coombs. "The World Crisis in Education, The View from the Eighties", pp. 157–161. Oxford University Press, 1985, Oxford.

De Romilly, J. 1984 *L'Enseignement en Détresse*. Fayard, Paris.

Economic and Social Council, 1978 *Opinion and Report*. L'Organisation et le Développement de la Recherche dans les Etablissements d'Enseignement Supérieur. Journal Officiel, 4th of April 1978, Paris.

Ellrodt, R. *et al.* 1977 *Pour que l'Université ne meure . . .* Le Centurion, Paris.

Janetti-Diaz, E. 1980 *La Sélection des Etudiants á l'Université*. Third stage doctoral thesis. Université de Paris-Dauphine, Paris.

Merton, R. K. 1957 *Social Theory and Social Structure*. Glencoe, Illinois Free Press.

Perkins J. *et al.* 1973 *Higher Education: From Autonomy to Systems*. ICED, New York.

Perkins, J. 1978 *Higher Education Systems: A Twelve-Country Study*. ICED, New York.

Peters T. and Waterman, R. 1982 *In Search Excellence*. Harper & Row, Chicago.

Ravitch, D. 1983 *The Troubled Crusade*. Basic Books, New York.

Rétat, L. 1984 *Renan et l'Université*. Commentaire, Paris (No. 27, Fall, 1984).

Schwartz, L. 1983 *Sauver l'Université*. Seuil, Paris.

Trow, M. 1982 *Confronting the Challenge of Underprepared Students*. University of California, Berkeley.

Trow, M. 1984 Relation of Higher Education to Society — Non-Measured Effects. In: *Colloquy of the Association of Latin American Universities*. Gulerpe, Mexico.

Trow, M. 1981 "Comparative Perspectives on Access" in O. Fulton (ed.) *Access to Higher Education*. Society for Res. into Higher Ed., Guildford, UK.

United States, The National Commission on Excellence in Education 1983 *Nation at Risk: The imperative for Educational Reform*. U.S. Government Printing Office, Washington, D.C.

Wilenski, H. 1975 *The Welfare State and Equality, Structural and Ideological Roots of Public Expenditures*. University of California Press, Berkeley, pp. 3–7.

Researchers, Policy Analysts, and Policy Intellectuals*

MARTIN TROW

Models of the Relation of Research to Policy

In a recent paper (Husén, 1982), Torsten Husén argues that the relation of research to policy is far more complex, far more indirect than it formerly appeared. Drawing on the informed writings of Carol Weiss and Maurice Kogan, among others, and from his own rich experience, he dismisses as irrelevant, at least to the field of education, two classical models of the application of research to policy that Weiss lists among seven different models or concepts of research utilization: the "linear" model, which leads neatly from basic knowledge to applied research to development to application, and the "problem-solving" model, in which research is done to fill in certain bodies of knowledge needed to make a decision among policy alternatives. These are dismissed on the grounds that they simply do not even roughly describe what happens in the real world. The remaining models he merges into two. One is an "enlighten-ment" or "percolation" model, in which research somehow (and just how is of greatest interest) influences policy indirectly, by entering into the consciousness of the actors and shaping the terms of their discussion about policy alternatives. The second, the "political model," refers to the intentional use of research by political decision-makers to strengthen an argument, to justify positions already taken, or to avoid making or having to make unpopular decisions by burying the controversial problem in research.

Of these two models, the first or "percolation" model is the more interesting, since it is the way through which research actually has an influence on policy, rather than merely used to justify or avoid making decisions. Moreover, the percolation model and its mechanisms and processes are so subtle that they challenge study and reflection.

The bulk of Husén's paper is devoted to an exploration from various perspectives of the complexities in the relation of researcher to policy,

---

*Originally published in *Educational Research & Policy: How Do They Relate?* T. Husén and M. Kogan, editors, Oxford: Pergamon Press, 1984.

with special attention to the variety of forces and conditions that come
between the researcher and the policymaker. These help explain why it
is that research, when it does have a bearing on policy, does so in
complicated indirect ways rather than through the simpler more direct
ways of the classical, but now discredited models.

In Husén's words:

> The "percolation" process is a very subtle, and in many respects, intangible
> one. The direct contact, either face-to-face or through the reading of
> scholarly reports with all the paraphernalia of technical jargon, seems to play
> little role. The role of "middle-men" should be carefully studied, because this
> appears to be a key one. One can identify entire "informal networks" of
> intermediate linking mechanisms. Newspapers, journals with popularized
> versions of research findings, friends of the politicians, and their staff
> members play important roles ... Certain research-promoting, private
> bodies can also play an important role in spreading the information that
> relates to the idea of fiscal neutrality and equality of finance ... The
> "percolation" is of particular importance to the staffs of legislators and top
> administrations in a ministry of education or state board of education
> (Husén, 1982, p. 5).

In a recent unpublished paper by Ulrich Teichler describing some of his
preliminary thoughts about a study on "research in higher education
and its impact," he notes that:

> The underlying hypothesis [of the study] is that the way that research on
> higher education develops and has impact on decisionmaking is highly
> influenced by the general climate of interaction between researchers and
> decisionmakers. In the Federal Republic of Germany, the conditions are not
> very favorable for research on higher education: Administrators tend to
> prefer very controlled ways of major data collection, believe in the strengths
> of administrators to solve almost all problems without relying on research
> and mistrust the political inclinations of researchers. There are, however,
> exceptions as regard to the administrators, the researchers accepted as well as
> the topics of the research desired. On the other hand, researchers are heavily
> inclined to take over political roles themselves (Teichler, 1982).

Similarly, Runé Premfors, drawing on the writings of Lindblom and
Wildavsky, argues that analysis, a category broader than research,
including "intellectual cogitation" with or without the data base that we
associate with research,

> ... is generally accorded an exaggerated role in studies of ... public policy
> making. Social scientists tend to underestimate the importance of various
> forms of social interaction as problem-solving mechanisms, even in contexts
> where analysis seemingly provides the basic criteria for policy choices. Social
> interaction — which has two basic forms in problem solving contexts: politics
> and markets — is more often than not the major determinant of outcomes.
> When analysis of intellectual cogitation appears in various guises it is
> normally as "partisan analysis," i.e., analysis tailored to policy positions
> already adopted (Premfors, March 1982, p. 1).

But Premfors, like Husén, does not wholly agree that research and analysis are merely devices for legitimating policies whose sources and determinants lie elsewhere. He continues:

> However, we are dealing with a complex relationship. The literature on knowledge utilization in social problem-solving has in recent years taken pains to illustrate the many ways in which policy analysis and social research may enter such processes . . . . A lack of impact in the short run does not preclude considerable effects in the long run. The fact that analysis does not provide the "objective" criteria often sought by policymakers and analysts, does not preclude that such activities slowly permeate the definition of problems and the formulation of choices (Premfors, *ibid*).

Premfors here is suggesting that analysis and research, on the one hand, and social interaction on the other are not alternative forms of reaching decisions, but are complementary. Both market behavior and political behavior are affected by analysis and research, but as all these commentators appear to agree, more commonly through a process of percolation whereby knowledge and ideas "slowly permeate the definition of problems and the formulation of choices." How market behavior is affected by research is an interesting but separate problem. It seems likely that some actors in markets, for example, students choosing a college or career, use the findings of educational research as these are publicized and interpreted by commentators, popularizers, and school and vocational counselors. A useful line of research is one pioneered many years ago by Coleman and others, who studied the role of personal influence in decisionmaking (Coleman, *et al*, 1957; Katz, 1957).

In exploring this complex topic, it is desirable to avoid premature cross-national generalizations. Even if we confine ourselves to the field of education, countries differ enormously in where and how educational decisions are made, how centralized or dispersed those decision points are, and what kinds of decisions are made at what levels. They differ also in the development and organization of research and analysis about education, where that work is done, at whose initiative, and under what constraints. And countries differ also in what Teichler calls "the general climate of interaction between researchers and decisionmakers." Indeed Teichler warns that "one has to compare the 'interaction climate' in different countries in order to explain the potentials and the shortcomings of the impact of higher education research in a given country" (Teichler, p. 4).

Researchers and Policy Analysts

In his paper Husén speaks throughout of "researchers," by which he clearly means social scientists employed in universities. In part his discussion of the gulf between researchers and policymakers arises out of the quite different training, time constraints, and work situations that characterize the university social scientist as compared with the decision-maker, the politician, or civil servant.

I want to contribute to this discussion of the influence of research on policy in education by talking about a different kind of actor in the process — an actor who is sometimes very much like a researcher, defining a problem, doing analysis, and gathering and interpreting new data; sometimes like a "middle-man," bringing together and inter-preting for decisionmakers the findings of research by others; and sometimes himself a decisionmaker. This actor has come to be called a "policy analyst" in the United States, but he may have his analogues and counterparts with different names in other countries.

The past decade has seen in the United States, and to some extent elsewhere, the emergence of a profession, that of the policy analyst, whose training, habits of mind, and conditions of work are expressly designed to narrow the gap between the researcher and the policymaker and to bring systematic knowledge to bear more directly, more quickly, and more relevantly on the issues of public policy. Let me try to compare and contrast the researcher and the policy analyst to see how this breed of staff analyst/researcher, inside as well as outside government, may affect the ways in which research comes to bear on policy. My comparison is not intended to be invidious, that is, I am not implying that the invention of policy analysis has in any way solved the problems of the relation of research to policy that Husén, Weiss, and others have identified. But it may be of interest to see how this emerging profession affects that process, and how it generates new problems — intellectual, political, and moral — as it solves some of the old.

Policy analysis developed as a formal discipline about 10 years ago through the coming together of a number of strands of work and thought in the social sciences. These included operations research developed during World War II on a strongly mathematical basis for improving the efficiency of military operations — the deployment of submarines, bombing raids, and convoy management. Added to this were new forms of micro-economics developed in the 1950s and 1960s; the long-standing tradition of work in public administration; the newer and increasingly strong strain of behaviorism in the political sciences; organizational theory; certain lines of applied sociology and social psychology; and the emerging interest in the role of law in public policy. Graduate schools of public policy were established in a number of leading American universities about 1970 — for example, the Kennedy School at Harvard, the Woodrow Wilson School at Princeton, the LBJ School at Texas, schools of public policy at Michigan and Minnesota, and the Graduate School of Public Policy at Berkeley. Twelve leading universities now have genuine graduate schools of public policy; there are literally hundreds of others which offer programs which include some measure of policy analysis in their schools of management, public administration, or business administration. To the mix of social science and law, some schools have added scientists, engineers, and others interested in public policy problems. These graduate schools for the most part offer a 2-year postgraduate professional degree, ordinarily the Master of Public Policy. Their graduates go directly into public service at national, state, or local levels, or get jobs in think-tanks or private agencies concerned with public issues — for example, organizations concerned with the preservation of the environment, with education, overseas trade and so forth. These latter "private" organizations, however, are directly involved for the most part in public policy — indeed, much of what they do is to try to influence public policy, so the conditions of work for public policy analysts in them resemble those of analysts who enter governmental service itself.

There are several aspects of the training of policy analysts that need to be emphasized. As must already be clear, the training of the policy is intensely interdisciplinary. This is required first because of the diverse nature of its intellectual antecedents; the field itself reflects the coming together, the mutual links among diverse currents of what Harold Lasswell called the "policy sciences" (Lerner and Lasswell, 1951). But more important, the training has to be interdisciplinary because that is the way the problems present themselves to decisionmakers. Real decisions, as we all know, do not respect the boundaries of the academic disciplines: they always have political, economic, and organizational components; they may well have also legal, educational, biological, or other technical implications as well.

Perhaps the most important distinguishing characteristic of the policy analyst as contrasted with the academic research social scientist is that he or she is trained, indeed required, to see and to formulate problems from the perspectives not of the academic disciplines, but of the decisionmaker. In his work, he accepts the constraints and values of the decisionmaker — the political pressures on him, the political feasibility of a proposal, its financial costs, the legal context within which it will operate, the difficulties of implementing it, of shaping organizations, and of recruiting, training, and motivating people to work in the service of its purposes. He is, if effectively trained, sensitive to the costs and benefits of programs, to the trade-offs in any decision, and to the alternative advantages of government and the market in achieving social purposes. In a word, he tries to see problems from the perspective of the decisionmaker, but with a set of intellectual, analytical, and research tools that the politician or senior civil servant may not possess. He is, and is trained to be, the researcher in government at the elbow of the decisionmaker, or if not in government, then serving the "government in opposition" or some think-tank or interest group which hopes to staff the next administration or agency on the next swing of the political pendulum. Of course, not all policy analysts are "researchers," as the university conceives of research. But what they do, bringing ideas and information to bear on social "problems" in a search for "solutions," is the kind of "research" that has the most direct influence on public policy.

By contrast, the faculty members of schools of public policy are not, for the most part, like the students that they train: the former are almost without exception academics with Ph.D.s, trained in and drawn from the social science disciplines, specialists originally who have a particular interest in public policy, and who do research on policy issues, but not on the whole like the research that their students will be doing in their government or quasi-government jobs. The faculty members of these schools are for the most part what James Q. Wilson has called "policy intellectuals," while their students are policy analysts — the staff people and bureaucrats serving their policy-oriented clients in and out of governments. The relationship of the policy intellectual in the university to the policy analyst in government bears on the issue of "knowledge creep" and "research percolation" that Husén and Weiss speak of, and to which I want to return.

Let us look at some of the characteristics of "researchers" as Husén describes them, and at some of the "disjunctions" between research and policy that the nature of the researcher in the university gives rise to. The field of policy analysis and the new profession of policy analyst were, one might say, invented precisely to meet the need of policymakers for analysis and research carried out within the same constraints that the policymaker experiences. Policy analysis thus aims to narrow those "disjunctions" between research and policy of which Husén speaks. He describes three conditions under which researchers work that are different for policy analysts:

1. "Researchers are usually performing their tasks at . . . universities. . . . They tend to conduct their research according to the paradigms to which they have become socialized by their graduate studies. Their achievements are subjected to peer reviews which they regard as more important than assessments made by the customers in a public agency." (Husén, 1982, pp. 4–5) Analysts, by contrast, work for the most part in government or in shadow governmental agencies, like Brookings and Rand, or in large private business organizations. The paradigms of research that they acquire in graduate school emphasize the importance of serving the client, of defining or clarifying the nature of his problem, or identifying the policy options available to him, of evaluating those alternatives in terms of their cost, probable effectiveness, political feasibility, ease of implementation, and the like — the same criteria which the decisionmaker himself would use in planning and choosing a

course of action. The analyst is trained then to make recommendations among the action alternatives that he has identified, supporting his recommendations with appropriate agruments and evidence.

Much, perhaps most, of what such analysts do is not published, is not reviewed by peers, and will almost certainly appear, if at all, in greatly modified form, either anonymously or under someone else's name. The analyst's reputation will be made *not* in an academic setting, but in his agency, and more importantly among the small but active community of analysts in government agencies, on legislative staffs, in think-tanks, and special interest organizations who know of his work and its quality. Incidentally, it is in that arena of discussion and assessment — the analyst's analogue to the scholar's "invisible college" — that we need to look for the mechanisms of information "drift" and "creep," and for the processes of percolation through which research and evidence come to influence policy.

2. "Researchers operate at a high level of training and specialization, which means that they tend to isolate a 'slice' of a problem area that can be more readily handled than more complicated global problems" (*Ibid.*, p. 5).

By contrast, analysts are trained to be as interdisciplinary as possible, to follow the requirements of a problem in their choice of ideas, theories, and research methods, rather than to allow the theories and methods of their discipline to select and shape their problems. This is not wholly successful, in part because their teachers in these schools are not themselves equally familiar with the variety of research methods and perspectives across disciplinary lines, and because their students, the fledgling analysts, inevitably come to be more familiar and comfortable with some kinds of analysis rather than others. Nevertheless the requirement that they see problems as the policymaker would were he an analyst requires analysts to transcend the constraints of a single discipline and to tackle problems as wholes rather than by "slices."

3. "Researchers are much less constrained than policymakers in terms of what problems they can tackle, what kind of critical language they can employ and how much time they have . . . at their disposal to complete a study" (*Ibid.*, p. 5).

Analysts, by contrast, ordinarily are assigned their studies, or do them within circumscribed policy areas. That does not wholly preclude their exercise of discretion; and indeed, they may exercise very important amounts of initiative in how they formulate their problems, and in the range of responses to the problems they consider (Meltsner, 1976 pp. 81–114). From the researcher's perspective, the captive analyst is merely "a hired gun" doing what he is told by his political or bureaucratic superiors. But from the perspective of the analyst, discretion, even within the constraints of a given policy problem or area, may be very considerable. How to control air pollution in a given area, for example, allows a variety of regulatory solutions, from setting standards for allowable emissions for different kinds of plants and industries to setting charges on pollutants, requiring polluters to pay for each unit of pollutant emitted. The issues are political, technical, economic, legal, and normative — and they are not always decided *a priori* by political or administrative decisionmakers.

It is true that analysts are ordinarily held to a closer time frame than are academic researchers; in my own school, students become accustomed to doing analyses of various policy problems, drawing upon the best available data, research, and advice, within 48 or 72 hours, exercises designed to prepare them for the fierce time pressures of legislative hearings or the negotiations that accompany the writing and revision of legislation. Other exercises allow them a week, and a major piece of research equivalent to a master's essay will take up to six months. Time constraints on the job also vary; analysts become skillful in knowing who has been working on a given problem area, and where published or unpublished research or data on the issue can be found. For the analyst, knowledgeable people are a central research resource, and the telephone is part of the student's equipment alongside calculators, computers, and the library.

But as he develops the skill of rapidly bringing ideas to bear on data, and data on ideas, the analyst becomes heavily dependent upon existing statistics and on research done by others. He is often skillful, and even bold, in drawing analogies between findings in different areas of social life, allowing him thus to use the findings of research in one area for informing decisions in another. The analyst cannot often meet the scholar's standards of depth and thoroughness in his research — for example, in his review of the research literature, or in his critical evaluation of the findings of relevant research. Yet working under time and other pressures in the political milieu, the analyst knows that the alternative to what he is doing is not a major university-based research project, but more commonly the impressions, anecdotes, and general wisdom of a staff conference. His own report, which includes a discussion of alternative lines of action based on data regarding their comparative costs and benefits, must, he believes, be better than an unsystematic discussion among friends and advisers.

Policy analysts in government as we have described them have some of the characteristics of researchers, but are more narrowly constrained by their bureaucratic roles. They also have some of the characteristics of Maurice Kogan's middle-men, professionals who serve a liaison function (Kogan, Korman, and Henkel, 1980, pp. 36–38), though they are more active and ready to take research initiatives than the term "middle-man" implies. But they also are not infrequently the decisionmakers themselves.

One almost always talks about research *influencing* decisionmakers — and if the researcher is a university social scientist then the decisionmaker is almost certainly someone a distance away with his own concerns, political commitments, interests, and prejudices. But the policy analyst has the advantage of acting within the bureaucracy to make or directly affect a myriad of administrative decisions that rarely get into the newspapers, are not debated by politicians or on floors of legislatures, but nevertheless have very large consequences. Sweden can surely supply a myriad of illustrations of administrative decisionmaking, some of which may even have been informed by research done inside or outside the bureaucracy.

One illustration comes from the University of California, half of whose budget — the half which pays the operating costs of the University, faculty salaries, and the like — comes from the State of California. The preparation of the University's budget and its incorporation into the Governor's budget is a complicated procedure. Very substantial parts of the University's budget are governed by formulas, for example, relating support levels to enrollment levels, that have been negotiated over the years between the budget analysts in the central administration of the University and their counterparts in the State Department of Finance. These formulas, essentially bureaucratic treaties, are mutual understandings which give the university a greater degree of fiscal security and predictability than one would ever guess from reading the newspapers, which almost never report these matters, but only the visible debates in the legislature and speeches by the Governor.

The formulas, of course, do not cover all contingencies, especially in an institution as fluid and diverse as the University with so many different sources of energy and initiative, creating new programs, facilities, and claims on public funds all the time. Claims for resources, old and new, are argued out or negotiated annually between the University analysts and the State Department of Finance analysts; they speak each other's language, and often have been trained in the same graduate schools and departments, not infrequently in Berkeley's School of Public Policy. In these negotiations, "good arguments" by the University are rewarded; that is, requests for additional support funds that are supported by a good bureaucratic argument are often accepted, and new activities are built into the Governor's budget. The arguments made for these programs are the arguments of analysts, often based on analogies with existing state-funded activities, and backed by data showing the actual nature of the activity and its costs. For example, the University wants the State to revise the formula allocating funds for the replacement of scientific equipment used in teaching; it wants more generous provision for teaching assistants; it wants the State to assume the costs of certain athletic facilities; it wants the State to support

remedial courses for underprepared students; and so on. In support of
these claims the University analysts do research on the actual useful life
of laboratory instruments in different scientific departments and on how
that record compares with the life of instruments in other universities
and in commercial labs; it studies the use and distribution of teaching
assistants in University and how their work contributes to the instructional program; it studies who uses the athletic facilities and for what
purposes; and so on. These are not matters of high principle; there
exists a broad area of value consensus between the negotiators, but the
quality of the research backing those claims is crucial to whether they are
accepted, and indeed whether they ought to be accepted. The sums of
money that are allocated in these ways are in the aggregate very large.
There are many areas of public life in which civil servants exercise wide
decisionmaking discretion, though they are often wise enough to deny
that they are in fact making policy or decisions, but merely "implementing" them. Nevertheless, when we reflect on the influence of research on
policy, we should not neglect the realm of bureaucratic and technocratic
decisionmaking in the public sector where researcher and decisionmaker
come together in the person of the policy analyst. University-based
researchers need to be reminded that not all research has to percolate
down through a complex network of relationships to enter another
complex process of "decision accretion"; some research has access to
decisionmakers quickly and directly, and is done for and by them.

The newly emergent field of policy analysis seems to be thriving in the
United States, at least in a modest way, even in the face of budget cuts
and hiring freezes in the federal and in many state and local
governments. Policy analysts are in demand whether public expenditures are rising or falling; the problems posed to government by
budgetary constraints are even more severe than those posed by
expansion and the proliferation of public programs and services. And
with all the cuts, most governments are not reducing the absolute level of
public expenditures on social services, but merely reducing their rates of
growth. In any event, public life is becoming increasingly more complex
and there is no shortage of work for policy analysts.

Four Problems Facing the Policy Analyst

But it should not be thought that the emergence of policy analysis, and
of the infrastructure of graduate schools, journals, professional associations and meetings which give it definition and self-consciousness, solves
all the problems of the relation of research to policy. For if policy
analysts solve some of those problems, they also create new ones. I would
like to discuss four such problems in the realm of policy analysis as
currently practiced, though I do not mean to imply there are only four.
These are all problems which in significant ways affect the quality of the

analyst's work and his influence on policy and decisionmaking.

First, and this is a problem that the analyst shares with academic research in education, policy analysis makes relatively little use of ethnographic field methods, the method of direct observation of customary behavior and informal conversation. One consequence of this is that the policy analyst, as I have suggested, is a captive of existing and usually official statistics; where those statistics are wrong or misleading or inadequate, the analyst's work is flawed, misleading, and inadequate also. By contrast, university researchers are more likely to question the quality of research data, though my sense is that they rarely question the quality of official statistics.

Second, the outcome of public policy analysis, its reports and recommendations, is affected not only by the analyst's own preferences and biases and those of his client, but also by how the analyst bounds his problem, the phenomena and variables that he will take into account. These boundaries are sharply constrained by his position within the bureaucratic work setting, more so than for the university-based researcher.

Third, for every policy analyst outside the university there is tension between the needs and requirements of his client, on one hand, and his own professional commitments to intellectual honesty, to the searching out of negative evidence, to his freedom to speak and publish what he knows or has learned, on the other. Bureaucratic research settings put severe strains on those scholarly and professional values. Indeed, the moral issue of how a given analyst deals with his dual loyalty to his professional identity as a policy analyst and to his political masters and clients is at the heart of policy analysis and not, as moral issues often are, at the margins.

Finally, I would like to speak of the relation between policy analysts and policy intellectuals as that relation bears on the nature of communication and persuasion in the political arena, and more broadly on the processes of "decision accretion" through enlightenment and the percolation of research findings, ideas, and assumptions in the decision-making process.

The Absence of Ethnography and its Consequences

The near absence of ethnography from the research armamentarium of the policy analyst places a major limitation on the policy analyst's contribution to public policy. Ethnography, the direct observation of customary behavior and the reporting and evaluation of the significance of that behavior, is extremely expensive of time. It involves the primary collection of data rather than the analysis of data, for example, statistics gathered by agencies of government. Policy analysts often work under

severe time constraints, and it is almost impossible to reduce the real
time required to come to know and be accepted by people whom one is
living among and observing closely. Those who use other methods of
research can substitute money and assistants for time, but on the whole
that is not possible for ethnographers.

One source of resistance to ethnography by policy analysts lies in the
canons of verification held in the various disciplines which have
contributed to the faculty of public policy schools. Ethnographic
methods are, for the most part, non-quantitative, and it is hard to use
them to "prove" hypotheses. Part of the resistance to ethnography lies in
the difficulty that its users have in demonstrating control over
researcher bias. This control is built into the training and systematic
though qualitative methods of the professional ethnographer, but that is
hard to demonstrate to laymen. Unlike anthropology, which is written
for other anthropologists, a good deal of policy analysis is addressed
to laymen, including politicians, and it has to persuade laymen. Field
methods are not sufficiently esoteric to be persuasive to laymen, and that
is an important weakness of that kind of data for policy analysts. The
persuasiveness of research, based in good part on its methodology, is
absolutely central to policy studies. This surely accounts for the high and
often inappropriate degree of formalization of policy analysis, its
esoteric forms of modeling and statistical manipulation. By contrast,
ethnography simply is not enough like the esoteric hard sciences to
borrow their persuasive authority.

Another reason that ethnography does not appeal to policy analysts is
that it tends to force a degree of disaggregation of phenomena that is
incompatible with the generalizing tendencies of public policies. Public
policy analysis is not really interested in the fine structures of social life,
partly because it is generally impossible to develop legislation, rules and
policies appropriate to the variability of the specific circumstances in
which policies are actually implemented. Policy analysis for the most part
rests on certain brutal simplifications, the chief one being that the
activities, people, or phenomena that are grouped within a category are
in fact sufficiently alike so that they can be dealt with under a common
set of assumptions and by a common set of rules and regulations.
Ethnographic studies continually reveal the inadequacy of the categories
which underpin policy and policy analysis, and thus are, in a way,
subversive of broad and uniform laws and rules. At the same time,
ethnographic studies provide another perspective, that of the objects of
policy, one that could strengthen the capacity of policy analysis to be
responsive to the rich variability of social and economic life.

Ethnography is also suspect to analysts because it tends to uncover
politically inconvenient facts. When ethnographers study organizations
or communities, they often learn quite a lot about how rules and laws are

bent or broken and by whom. But analysts and their bureaucratic superiors are not interested in or rewarded for muckraking, which ethnography often makes possible and even unavoidable.

Finally, ethnography does not seem to be a really serious and hard-to-acquire skill. Analysts can imagine themselves spending time in the library or even better in front of a computer console or at their desks with calculating machines and recorder. They find it hard to imagine themselves "hanging around" a streetcorner, or in a classroom, or in the other ordinary places where the objects of social policy spend their time. That simply does not seem like dignified work appropriate to people with the high skills and rare abilities to analyse public policies. And not least, very few policy analysts have been trained to use themselves as an instrument for recording, describing, and understanding social life. They are, in short, not anthropologists, and they find it much more difficult to acquire the skills of ethnographic field work than, say, to acquire new skills in the use of computers or the ability to do survey research.

These are only some of the reasons that policy analysts so rarely employ ethnographic methods, and some of these reasons apply to university-based researchers as well. But the failure to employ ethnographic methods is a serious handicap to making research useful and relevant to public policy. And that is because without field methods we are severely handicapped in learning why it is that some of our public policies are successful, while so many others fail.

One example: in all advanced industrial societies, I think without exception, the national statistics on the labor force show a rise in unemployment rates among youth in recent years, even larger than one would expect as a consequence of economic recession. These figures are much discussed, many explanations are given for them, and large and expensive public projects are developed to do something about this grave and growing social problem. Yet almost no one goes behind the published statistics to ask what they mean, whether there are in fact growing numbers of young people who are anxiously seeking gainful employment and are unable to find any. What we ought to do, and most policy analysts do not do, is to question the quality and meaning of the published statistics on this issue. What statistics on youth unemployment do not reflect, for example, are certain developments in modern industrial society in recent years, reflecting a liberalization of welfare policies that make it easier for young people to get public assistance, but only if they are "unemployed." The statistics also do not reflect the rapid growth of the gray or "subterranean" economies which employ young people in casual, but uncontrolled, unreported, and untaxed occupations (Trow, 1979). Moreover, they do not reflect the development of youth cultures and attitudes towards work and leisure which make young unmarried people far more discriminating about the kinds of jobs they will accept and for how long (Roberts, Noble, and Duggan, 1982). Field studies of youth cultures are, I believe, necessary to get a better understanding of the varied and changing attitudes toward work among different kinds of youth; they would help to give us a better sense of the extent of the unrecorded subterranean economy and the role of youth in it; and would even be of some help in seeing the extent to which liberalized welfare provisions encourage young people to be "out of work" for periods of time after leaving school and before they marry or "settle down."

I hasten to add that I am not saying that there is no real problem of youth unemployment in western societies, but only that the official statistics tell us very little of its character and extent. The statistics on youth unemployment on which policy analysts are so dependent do not provide a good data base for the creation of effective public policies aimed at ameliorating the problem. If in fact youth unemployment as a national phenomenon is not accurately reflected in the official statistics, if, for example, it is really two or three quite different problems, then our public policies and programs ought to be responsive to its true character and not to the common sense notions so crudely measured by the central statistical offices.

But in this policy area, like others, the constraints on the policy analyst's time, on the nature of the problems he pursues, and how he attacks them may make it impossible for him to go behind the published figures. Moreover, it is hard to imagine an analyst in one branch of government making a fundamental critique of the work of the central statistical office of the same government. It remains for the relatively free university researcher to question the quality and meaning of published statistics about youth unemployment, and about many other aspects of life on which government agencies gather statistics. Policy analysts are dependent on published figures, and that I fear is a serious limitation on their contribution to good public policies, at least in some policy areas.

What I have been saying may be less true for Sweden than for many other countries, by virtue both of the quality and extent of its public record-keeping and of the relative homogeneity of its population. When a culture is widely shared, its participants may not have to do research into its character; they live it, and to know how people feel they need only observe life around them and reflect on their own experience. And this applies to researchers as well as to civil servants and policy analysts. Ethnography becomes more important as one's national culture becomes more diverse, and as more of it becomes foreign to one's own experience and understanding. In order to understand our own complex world we have to study the society that we live in. This is, of course, true to an extreme degree in the United States with its extraordinarily varied population and ethnic subcultures. For example, the few ethnographic studies of the life of American blacks in northern cities reveal patterns of life and values at variance with the assumptions of social welfare programs designed to help them (see Liebow, 1967, and Stack, 1974). But I suspect it is becoming true for Sweden as more of its population come to have its recent origins in other countries, and especially in Mediterranean countries. Moreover, it is those groups that are disproportionately liable to be the objects of public policy.

My second illustration is drawn from that important and influential study published in 1966 known as "Coleman I" (Coleman, 1966). The major findings of the first Coleman report were that differences in a number of readily measured characteristics of schools — per pupil expenditures, pupil/teacher ratios, teacher education, building quality, and the like — have little or no effect on academic achievement once you control for aspects of family background. Moreover, this was true for both whites and blacks. The study also seemed to show that there were some gains in achievement for blacks enrolled in integrated schools without any evident loss for the whites in the same schools. But these findings, showing very slight effects of school characteristics compared with the much larger effects of home environment, were seized upon as evidence of the desirability, indeed the necessity, of integrating the schools forcefully, and by busing if necessary.

Subsequent analysis and discussion led many to believe that the Coleman report's measures of "school effects" were simply not powerful enough to capture the subtle aspects of schools and schooling that do indeed make a difference to whether and how much children learn in them. These include such aspects of the school as how teachers conduct their classes, how principals manage their schools, the degree of order and discipline in them, and much of what might be called the school "ethos," its institutional values and culture. These characteristics of a school are all difficult to capture through large scale survey instruments, and the processes through which they have their effects are even more elusive. But ethnographic studies of schools as institutions and communities help us to learn more about the subtle but powerful forces that make some schools and teachers much more effective than others with the same kinds of pupils. Policy analysts, and indeed many other educational researchers, tend to focus on the inputs and outputs of schools. Ethnographic studies allow us to get inside the black boxes that schools are to researchers to see what goes on inside them, not only the specifics of pedagogic techniques and teaching, but the life of the school as a community. James Coleman wrote about many of those matters years ago in his book on the adolescent society in the school (Coleman, 1961).

We need to go back to some of those ideas and insights and see to what extent the social pressures that he saw at work in high schools 20 years ago can be found at work today.

The study of school effects through close observation may give us a research base for developing better public policies for schools (Wax, Wax, and Dumont, 1964). But I think this work will have to be done by university-based researchers rather than by policy analysts in public agencies.

The Bounding of Problems

Another major limitation on the policy analyst is the effect of his work setting on the way he bounds his problem in time, space, and relevant variables. One illustration of the effects of the bounding of research on its implications for policy can be drawn from how policymakers used the Coleman report, which addressed the effects of school and home characteristics on student achievement. It was, of course, a central referent in the heated debate over school integration during the next decade and a half. The racial integration of urban schools, and especially their forced integration through busing, as Coleman and others subsequently pointed out, accelerated the flight of white families from the cities where busing was imposed, and thus helped both to defeat efforts at school integration, and also profoundly affected the character and viability of many American cities. If these unintended and unanticipated effects of busing were known, it is likely the debate over busing would have been conducted quite differently, and perhaps with different outcomes. The bounding of the problem, as Coleman saw and studied it, was constrained both by the legislative charge to his study group, and by his (and our) ignorance at that time of the effects on residential patterns and mobility of forced integration within the political boundaries of the big cities. My point is that no one saw then that the quality and character of American public education would be affected not only by the characteristics of the schools themselves, but also by the characteristics of the cities in which they were located, and that in turn might be substantially affected by policies directed rather narrowly at changing the racial ratios of urban public schools. We are all continually being thwarted and defeated by the unintended and unanticipated consequences of our purposeful social action. I drew my example from policy-oriented university-based research, but I suspect that policy analysts, constrained as they are by their bureaucratic work settings, are even more likely to bound their research inappropriately narrowly, and are more likely than other social scientists to be unpleasantly surprised by the inextinguishable inventiveness of society's responses to political intervention into its life and institutions.

Another illustration of the effects of the bounding of problems is drawn from a bit of counter-factual history. Some years ago I reflected on the significance of the historical fact that the United States did not establish a national university supported by federal funds, as was warmly recommended by George Washington during his presidency and by the five presidents who succeeded him (Trow, 1979). While exploring that event, or non-event, I asked myself what I or any of my colleagues concerned with higher education might have advised President Washington if we had been alive then and he had called on us to offer him advice about the wisdom of creating a University of the United States. If we can imagine policy analysts before 1800, then I am sure that we would at that time have strongly urged President Washington, and anyone else who would listen, to carry through his proposal to create a national university, one that would immediately have become the strongest institution of higher education in the young country, and would undoubtedly have exerted a powerful, and, to our minds, positive influence on all the other colleges and universities in the country, public and private, and on its secondary schools as well. Our recommendations would have met all the requirements of good policy analysis. But we would have been wrong. I believe the University of the United States, however attractive it seemed to Washington and would have seemed to policy analysts at the time, would in fact have had bad effects on the evolution of American higher education.

But the hypothetical advice of policy analysts to that President would only come to be seen to be bad advice in the perspective of nearly 200 years, from the point of view of the whole system of higher education and, even more broadly, of the welfare of society as a whole. The problem, as we analysts would have surely bounded it, would have addressed itself narrowly to the viability and character of one specific federal university and its relatively short-term effect on other existing institutions of higher education. Moreover, and this would be taken as an absolute assumption beyond question by any analyst, our aim, like Washington's, would have been to assess the possibilities of creating in this country at that time a university of strength and high quality, firmly funded, with a distinguished faculty, a progressive curriculum, and the highest academic standards. A University of the United States, if it had been established as Washington wished and urged and as we policy analysts would have encouraged, would have been that kind of institution. But that capstone university, however excellent it might have been, would almost certainly have thwarted and inhibited the rapid and uncontrolled growth of colleges and universities of every shape and description all over the United States over the next 150 years, and perhaps effectively prevented the emergence of that diversity, arising out of almost uncontrolled growth, that has made the American system of higher education appropriate to the society in which it has developed.

Now no policy analyst can reasonably be expected to make a recommendation about a problem at hand while taking into account all of the ramified consequences of a decision on other institutions of the society across a time span of two centuries. He can only do that in this case retrospectively and speculatively; I cannot really know what other third and fourth order effects might have occurred if the University of the United States had been created as Washington urged. And yet without trying to play God, and to see all the possible futures that might have occurred had that event been different, there is a principle that emerges from our reflections on the case of the University of the United States that may have more general significance. And that is that the kind of advice we offer to decisionmakers is almost always focussed rather narrowly on the quality of the program under consideration, and on its very short-term effects on narrow target populations. This, I think, is inherent in the policy analyst's training and in his work situation. It is not to the same degree a constraint on the researcher in the university, who has the time and freedom to take into account a much wider range of factors and forces over a longer period of time. Here we see one of the central limitations on the work of the policy analyst as compared with that of the university-based social scientist. It is simply that they do not have the same freedom to define their problems and to bound them broadly. That is the great strength, at least potentially, of the free intellectual — that he can raise any question, question any assumption, and seek connections among causes and consequences as broadly as he can stretch his imagination and find empirical chains of linkage.

This is not to say that the analyst, even the government analyst, has no discretion in his choice of problems or in the way he formulates them. Analysts have and exercise considerable discretion in their research, but the extent and nature of that discretion will vary in the agencies of different societies, and in the same country under different governments, in different ministries, and indeed in different sections of the same ministry. A research problem worthy of our attention would be to explore the scope of discretion that is available to analysts under different working situations, whether and how they take advantage of the discretion available to them, and what difference that makes to their work and to their influence on public policy.

Tensions Between Professional and Bureaucratic Roles

A third major problem that faces the policy analyst in government is the continuing tension between his professional role and his role as an employee in a government department, and thus indirectly a servant of the government currently in office and of its program and purposes (Trow, 1980).

One set of moral issues for policy analysts arises out of the fact that they are employees and professionals, often civil servants, and some-times political appointees. For each of those social groups there are reasonably clear norms and expectations. But the analyst is not exclusively an employee, professional, civil servant, or politician, but something of them all. And this is the source of great uncertainty as he confronts the questions of what his guiding principles are and where his primary loyalties lie, questions that arise constantly in his daily work.

Related to this is the issue of who is the analyst's "client." Toward whose interests is he oriented? To his immediate superior, or the divisional chief, or the secretary of the department, or the agency's external clients or constituency, or "the public interest?" And to what extent is he responsible to his profession and its norms of truth-seeking and truth-saying, a set of expectations quite different from those of the various other constituencies who claim his loyalty? The multiplicity of the policy analyst's "clients" contributes to the difficulties analysts face in their professional lives, and introduces moral complexities that university-based researchers do not face, or can choose to ignore.

Policy Intellectuals and Policy Analysts

In his paper identifying several models of connections between research and policy, Torsten Husén is drawn, as I am, to the enlightenment or "percolation" model. He quotes Carol Weiss to describe research as permeating the policymaking process, entering the policy arena not through specific findings or recommendations, but by its "generalizations and orientations percolating through informed publics in coming to shape the way in which people think about social issues" (Weiss, 1979).

There is, I think, broad agreement that much of the impact of research on policy (I would not say all) occurs in this subtle, difficult-to-measure way. But is this not at variance with the image of the policy analyst directly at the policymaker's elbow, preparing papers and reports at his request, speaking to issues and problems that the policymaker will be facing even if he does not yet recognize their character or his options? This image of the policy analyst is in fact compatible with the metaphor of the "percolation" of research, and of the notion of research entering into the general debate and discussion about an issue going on among interested publics, an ongoing debate that crystallizes into policy at a moment when a political actor chooses to place it on the agenda for action and not merely discussion. The analyst in government cannot often do basic research; he cannot do long-range studies; he is to a large extent a consumer and adapter of research, part of the attentive audience for research, and among the most active participants in the critical discussion about the issue and the literature that grows up around it. In the United States the analyst who is educated at a school of public policy is especially trained to take part in that discussion because his former teachers and his teachers' peers in other policy schools and professional and academic departments do the research and comment on the research of others in such journals as *The Public Interest, Policy Analysis, Public Choice, Policy Studies Journal, The Journal of Policy Analysis and Management,* among others. These university-based writers and researchers, some of whom teach in the schools of public policy, are what James Q. Wilson calls "policy intellectuals." And his view of their influence on policy is not far from that of Weiss and Husén's notion of the percolation model. Reviewing the role of policy intellectuals over the past decade, Wilson observes that

> If the influence of intellectuals was not to be found in the details of policy, it was nonetheless real, albeit indirect. Intellectuals provided the conceptual language, the ruling paradigms, the empirical examples . . . that became the accepted assumptions for those in charge of making policy. Intellectuals framed, and to a large degree conducted, the debates about whether this language and these paradigms were correct. The most influential intellectuals were those who managed to link a concept or a theory to the practical needs and ideological dispositions of political activists and governmental officials (Wilson, 1981).

Wilson goes further than most of us in downplaying the role of research *per se* as over against the power of the arguments of skillful intellectuals.

> At any given moment in history, an influential idea — and thus an influential intellectual — is one that provides a persuasive simplification of some policy question that is consistent with a particular mix of core values then held by the political elite . . . Clarifying and making persuasive those ideas is largely a matter of argument and the careful use of analogies; rarely . . . does this process involve matters of proof and evidence of the sort that is, in their scholarly, as opposed to their public lives, supposed to be the particular skill and obligation of the intellectual in the university (Ibid., p. 36).

But Wilson would agree that there are some — James Coleman is one and Torsten Husén another — who are both researchers and policy intellectuals, and whose contributions to the ongoing policy discussion is an odd mixture of their research work and their policy analysis in a more qualitative and rhetorical sense. One might almost suggest that their research work and findings get into the policy discussion chiefly by way of giving greater weight and authority to their writing as policy intellectuals; indeed, in both cases their research findings have been seized upon by others after publication, and put to uses rather different from their own interpretations and preference.

The role of the policy intellectual in policy debates, independent of his research, is of great importance and deserves to be studied more closely.

The influence of such informed discussion and argument will, I think, vary in different policy fields. But of special interest is the combined effect of policy intellectuals based in the universities and the policy analysts whom they have trained, or who were trained to read them, to understand them and to use their arguments in the preparation of their reports for decisionmakers in government. These staff papers, reports, and memoranda give the policy intellectuals' ideas and work access, in ways that the intellectuals themselves do not always have, to the committee rooms and governmental conversations where decisions are made.

Policy Analysts Versus Interest Groups

The structure of government in the United States, both in Washington and in the state capitols, is changing, becoming even more open and responsive than it has been to vocal, well-organized special interest groups, less and less managed by traditional elites. In the field of education, says Jerome Murphy,

> State policy systems, no longer the captive of state education establishments, are now far more accessible to interest groups and open to public view. The adoption of a large number of policy reforms reflects a new responsiveness on the part of state government to these groups.
> Within government, the most important change is the heavy involvement of legislators and governors in educational matters. Spurred on by worries about money, school quality, and social issues (e.g., integration), general state government has used its new staff and expertise to challenge education professionals and to remove education from its privileged perch "above politics."
> There's a different cast of participants outside government as well . . . Some of the new lobbies promote equality, representing such interests as urban areas, the poor, blacks, Hispanics, the disadvantaged, the handicapped, girls. Reform of state school finance laws has been promoted for the past decade by a network of scholars, foundation executives, lawyers, government officials, community organizers, and citizen groups. Other groups work for efficiency and effectiveness, lobbying for comprehensive planning, improved budgeting, accountability laws, standards for graduation, competency tests for students and teachers. More recently, some of these groups have been promoting tax limitation measures and controls on expenditures. Still other lobbies promote "the public interest" (Murphy, 1981, p. 128).

All this energy and activity (in part a consequence of mass higher education) generates an extraordinary level of noise, demands, charges and counter-charges, court actions, and so forth. Pressures of every kind are felt by legislators, elected officials, and their staffs. Policy analysts inside government provide some counterweight, some degree of stability, predictability, and rationality through their professional patterns of response to these pressures and demands. This is not to say that the political activists and their pressure groups are not often successful. But how a government agency responds to organized political pressure may well be shaped by the anonymous analysts in the executive and legislative staffs and agencies. And it is through them that a larger, or at least a different, set of ideas comes into play in these discussions, and these ideas at their best are less narrow and parochial, more likely to be illuminated by historical and comparative perspectives and by the ongoing discussion that policy intellectuals carry on among themselves in the professional journals.

The structure of politics, the character of the policy areas in which discussions and debate about policies are carried on, are quite different in Sweden than in the United States. Careful studies of actual policy formulation and implementation in specific areas must illuminate the patterns of "social interaction" that more often than not are the major determinants of outcomes in the policy arena (Premfors, 1982, p. 2). In these increasingly complex networks of social interaction, the relations between policy analysts in government and policy intellectuals in the university are of large and growing importance in the United States, with close analogues in Sweden and other western societies.

Conclusion: Research and the Rhetoric of Politics

It is natural that we members of the research community be concerned that the research we do be true and illuminating accounts of the institutions and processes that we study. Some of us also are interested in whether our research has any influence on the shaping of policy and the making of decisions, and if it does, how it enters the decision process and affects the outcomes of those decisions.

But it may be useful, and not wholly subversive of the research itself, to reflect that policy research has value independent of its truth or quality or its influence on policy. That is because social research is one of the ways in which political discussions are carried on in democratic societies, a way that is supportive of liberal democratic politics. Political argument is increasingly conducted in the language of research and analysis; concepts like "cost-benefit" and "trade-off" have found their way into the daily language of politicians and bureaucrats. Moreover, social research and democratic politics have some close affinities. For one thing, like democratic politics, social research is a process not of assertion or demonstration, but of persuasion. Moreover, it is a form of persuasion that appeals to reason and evidence rather than to supernatural authority, or tradition, or the charisma of an individual, or the authority of a legal order. The appeal to research findings is very far from the coercive domination of others by force or threat, and equally far from political manipulations which depend on the exploitation of a differential of knowledge and awareness between manipulator and the manipulated. The appeal to "research findings" is the appeal to the authority of reason, to a rationality that connects means and ends in ways that are consistent with strongly held social values. Max Weber has said that the contribution of sociology to politics is not to affirm ultimate ends, but to help clarify, if possible to "make transparent," the connections between means and ends so that choices can be made in greater awareness of the consistency of the means chosen with the ends intended. Insofar as social science attempts to do that, it becomes part of the persuasive mechanism of politics, rooting politics, at least in part, in persuasion based on an appeal to reason and knowledge. It need not weaken our professional concern for the quality and truth of our research to suggest that social research makes its largest contribution to liberal society not through its findings, but by its steady affirmation of the relevance of reason and knowledge to the politics of democracy.

REFERENCES

Coleman, James S., Katz, E., and Menzel, H., "The Diffusion of an Innovation Among Physicians," *Sociometry, 1957,* **20,** pp. 253–270.

Coleman, James, *et al., Equality of Educational Opportunity,* Washington D.C.: U.S. Government Printing Office, 1966.

Coleman, James, *The Adolescent Society: The Social Life of the Teenager and Its Impact on Education,* New York: The Free Press of Glencoe, 1961.

Husén, Torsten, "Two Partners With Communication Problems: Researchers and Policy-Makers in Education," paper presented at the Symposium "Researchers and Policy-Makers in Education: How Do They Relate?" held at Wijk, Lidingo-Stockholm, June 1982.

Katz, E., "The Two-Step Flow of Communication: An Up-to-Date Report on An Hypothesis," *Public Opinion Quarterly,* 1957, **21,** pp. 61–78.

Kogan, Maurice, Korman, Nancy, and Henkel, Mary. *Government's Commissioning of Research: A Case Study,* Department of Government, Brunel University, 1980.

Lerner, Daniel and Lasswell, Harold, Editors, *The Policy Sciences,* Stanford, California: Stanford University Press, 1951.

Liebow, E., *Tally's Corner,* Boston: Little, Brown, 1967.

Meltsner, Arnold, J., *Policy Analysts in the Bureaucracy,* Berkeley: University of California Press, 1976.

Murphy, Jerome T., "The Paradox of State Government Reform," *The Public Interest,* **64,** Summer 1981, pp. 124–139.

Premfors, Runé, "Analysis in Politics: The Regionalization of Swedish Higher Education," paper presented at a conference on "The Functions and Problems of the Urban University: A Comparative Perspective," City University of New York, New York, March 1982.

Premfors, Runé, "Research and Policy-Making in Swedish Higher Education," paper presented to the Symposium "Researchers and Policy-Making in Education: How Do They Relate?" held at Wijk, Lidingo-Stockholm, June 1982.

Roberts, Kenneth, Noble, Maria, and Duggan, Jill, "Out-of-School and Out-of-Work . . . Is It An Unemployment Problem?" *Leisure Studies,* Volume **I,** No. 1, January 1982.

Stack, C. B., *All Our Kin,* New York: Harper and Row, 1974.

Teichler, Ulrich, "Some Remarks Regarding a Project Proposal 'Research on Higher Education and Its Impact,'" April 1982, mimeo.

Trow, Martin, "Aspects of Diversity in American Higher Education," in Herbert Gans, Editor, *On the Making of Americans: Essays in Honor of David Riesman,* Philadelphia: University of Pennsylvania Press, 1979.

Trow, Martin, "Moral Dilemmas of Policy Analysis and the Policy Analyst," Graduate School of Public Policy Working Paper #104, University of California, Berkeley, April 1980.

Trow, Martin, "Reflections on Youth Problems and Policies in the United States," in Margaret Gordon, Editor, *Youth Education and Unemployment Problems*, Washington D.C.: Carnegie Foundation for the Advancement of Teaching, 1979, pp. 127–164.

Wax, M. L., Wax, R. H., and Dumont, R. V., Jr., *Formal Education in an American Indian Community*. An SSSP Monograph. Supplement to *Social Problems*, 1964, **11**, No. 4.

Weiss, Carol H., "The Many Meanings of Research Utilization," *Public Administration Review*, September 1979, pp. 426–431.

Wilson, James Q., "Policy Intellectuals and 'Public Policy,' " *The Public Interest*, Summer 1981, pp. 31–46.

Index